Corporate Social Responsibility, Private Law
and Global Supply Chains

CORPORATIONS, GLOBALISATION AND THE LAW

Series Editor: Janet Dine, *Director, Centre for Commercial Law Studies, Queen Mary, University of London, UK*

This uniquely positioned monograph series aims to draw together high quality research work from established and younger scholars on what is an intriguing and under-researched area of the law. The books will offer insights into a variety of legal issues that concern corporations operating on the global stage, including interaction with the World Trade Organization (WTO), international financial institutions and nation states, in both developing and developed countries. While the underlying foundation of the series will be that of company law, broadly-defined, authors are encouraged to take an approach that draws on the work of other social sciences, such as politics, economics and development studies and to offer an international or comparative perspective where appropriate. Specific topics to be considered will include corporate governance, corporate responsibility, taxation and criminal liability, among others. The series will undoubtedly offer an important contribution to legal thinking and to the wider globalisation debate.

Titles in the series include:

Corporate Social Responsibility, Private Law and Global Supply Chains

Andreas Rühmkorf

Lecturer in Commercial Law, University of Sheffield, UK

CORPORATIONS, GLOBALISATION AND THE LAW

Edward Elgar
PUBLISHING

Cheltenham, UK • Northampton, MA, USA

Published by
Edward Elgar Publishing Limited
The Lypiatts
15 Lansdown Road
Cheltenham
Glos GL50 2JA
UK

Edward Elgar Publishing, Inc.
William Pratt House
9 Dewey Court
Northampton
Massachusetts 01060
USA

A catalogue record for this book
is available from the British Library

Library of Congress Control Number: 2015933453

This book is available electronically in the **Elgar**online
Law subject collection
DOI 10.4337/9781783477500

ISBN 978 1 78347 749 4 (cased)
ISBN 978 1 78347 750 0 (eBook)

Typeset by Columns Design XML Ltd, Reading
Printed and bound in Great Britain by T.J. International Ltd, Padstow

Contents

Preface

I first became interested in the role of business in society when I studied for a Masters in law at the University of Sheffield in 2004–5. Coming from a German legal background, I was particularly intrigued by the differences in the regulation of companies in English law and German law, compounded by discussions I had with Andrew Johnston during that year. Following the LLM, I qualified as a German lawyer and looked at companies from a rather practical legal perspective, until 2008, when I was given the opportunity to run the LLB Law with German degree course at Sheffield.

In the meantime, the new Companies Act 2006 had been enacted. Its underlying enlightened shareholder value theory caught my interest; moreover, the concept of Corporate Social Responsibility (CSR) had gained prominence in the public debate. When I returned to the issue of the regulation of companies and the relationship of the company with its various stakeholders, I noticed that there was a substantive body of literature on CSR in international law and in socio-legal studies. Upon reflection, I wondered what the contribution of private law could be to the promotion of CSR. I felt that the literature on CSR and the law had, so far, largely neglected the role of private law in relation to CSR and as a consequence became particularly interested in the role of law for the promotion of CSR in global supply chains. Recent disasters such as the collapse of the Rana Plaza Building demonstrate the significance of responsible corporate conduct in global supply chains. This book reflects this interest as it moves the perspective from CSR more generally to its particular application in the context of global supply chains.

The writing of this book would not have been possible without the help of many people. Duncan French, Tammy Hervey and Veronica Ruiz have been exemplary throughout the whole process and I would like to thank them all for their support, guidance and hard work. Duncan French encouraged me to develop my ideas from the beginning and his comments have been very helpful. I benefitted immensely from discussions I had with Tammy Hervey as well as from her incredibly prompt feedback on chapters. Additionally, Veronica Ruiz, was a great support and she has been extremely helpful and responsive throughout. I am also grateful to

Charlotte Villiers and David Millon for making very valuable comments that helped me to further develop my ideas.

I must also thank several colleagues, former colleagues and friends for their support and encouragement during the work on this book. In particular, I would like to thank John Birds, Kate Bracegirdle, Paul Cardwell, Vicky Chico, Richard Collins, Liz Hall, Simon Holdaway, Andrew Johnston, Sorcha MacLeod, Zoe Ollerenshaw and Joanna Shapland for help and advice. I have been fortunate to work alongside excellent colleagues, many of whom have become friends. They have been very supportive during the whole process. I am also very grateful to Thomas Lundmark who raised my interest in Common Law during my undergraduate law studies in Germany and who supported my application for the position at the University of Sheffield in 2008.

I would like to express my gratitude to the staff at Edward Elgar and in particular to my Commissioning Editor, Ben Booth, for encouraging me to write the monograph and for being supportive throughout the process.

On a personal level, I would like to thank my parents Ingrid and Uwe Rühmkorf for their love, encouragement and support throughout my studies and for always being there in times of need. My biggest thanks go to my wife, Dagmar Rühmkorf. Words cannot express how grateful I am for her love and support. I would have never been able to complete the book without her constant encouragement, patience, reassurance and understanding.

Abbreviations

BIS	Department for Business Innovation & Skills
CA	Companies Act 2006
CBI	Confederation of British Industry
CMCHA	Corporate Manslaughter and Corporate Homicide Act 2007
COP	Communication on Progress
CPRs	Consumer Protection from Unfair Trading Regulations 2008
CSR	Corporate Social Responsibility
ETI	Ethical Trading Initiative
FRC	Financial Reporting Council
GLO	Group Litigation Order
ILO	International Labour Organization
NGO	Non-governmental Organisation
OECD	Organisation for Economic Co-operation and Development
OFR	Operating and Financial Review
OFT	Office of Fair Trading
RBS	Royal Bank of Scotland
SRSG	Special Representative of the Secretary-General on Human Rights and Transnational Corporations and other Business Enterprises
UKFI	UK Financial Investments Ltd
UN	United Nations

Table of cases

EUROPEAN CASES

UK CASES

US CASES

Table of legislation

United Nations

1. Corporate social responsibility and private law

I. INTRODUCTION

The global economic and financial crisis has strengthened the interest in the concept of Corporate Social Responsibility (CSR). The public concern about irresponsible corporate behaviour and the impact of businesses on, for instance, the environment or their employees has increased. This interest has now expanded to the supply chain of companies and the working conditions of suppliers. As a consequence of these developments, many corporations have adopted CSR standards in which they pledge to conduct business in a responsible manner.[1] These CSR standards are often passed on to the suppliers. The engagement of companies with CSR is partly due to the negative reputational effects of reports about irresponsible conduct of companies. For example, human rights violations committed by the subsidiaries and suppliers of Western companies in the developing world such as the use of child labour or excessive working hours have particularly harmed the reputation of brands.[2]

CSR has become an important issue on the political agenda. The United Nations (UN) has given prominence to CSR through the work of Professor John Ruggie from Harvard University who worked as Special Representative on the issue of human rights and business (SRSG) until 2011.[3] Upon completion of his mandate, he published the UN Guiding Principles on Business and Human Rights which were called 'a landmark

---

[1] A study published in 2010 shows that 77 out of the 100 constituent FTSE 100 firms had adopted codes of conduct which contain the CSR commitments of the companies. See: L Preuss, 'Codes of conduct in organisational context: From cascade to lattice-work of codes' (2010) 94 *Journal of Business Ethics* 471, 475.

[2] C Soosay, A Fearne and B Dent, 'Sustainable value chain analysis – a case study of Oxford Landing from "vine to dine"' (2012) 17 *Supply Chain Management: An International Journal* 68.

[3] The website of the Special Representative of the Secretary-General on human rights and transnational corporations and other business enterprises gives

in the CSR debate'.[4] Moreover, in 2011, the EU Commission published a communication on CSR which contains an action agenda for the period 2011–14.[5] The European Parliament and the Council adopted a Directive on the disclosure of non-financial and diversity information by certain large companies in 2014.[6] The Directive aims to enhance the reporting on CSR issues among European companies with more than 500 employees. The UK government, too, continues to engage with CSR and published a response to call for views on corporate responsibility in April 2014.[7] Notably, the discussions in the consultation also covered the regulation of global supply chains which are, increasingly, seen as a key issue in the context of CSR. In 2013, the UK government also published its Action Plan on the implementation of the UN Guiding Principles.[8] These

---

a useful overview about the work done within the mandate, available at http://business-humanrights.org/ (accessed 9 November 2014).

[4]   J Ames, 'Taking responsibility' (2011) *European Lawyer* 15. For the Guiding Principles see: Report of the Special Representative of the Secretary-General on the issue of human rights and transnational corporations and other business enterprises, John Ruggie, *Guiding Principles on Business and Human Rights: Implementing the United Nations 'Protect, Respect and Remedy' Framework*, 21 March 2011, available at http://www.ohchr.org/Documents/Publications/GuidingPrinciples BusinessHR_EN.pdf (accessed 11 November 2014).

[5]   European Commission, 'Communication from the Commission to the European Parliament, the Council, the European Economic and Social Committee and the Committee of the Regions: A renewed EU strategy 2011–14 for Corporate Social Responsibility' COM (2011) 681 final, available at http://ec. europa.eu/enterprise/policies/sustainable-business/corporate-social-responsibility/ index_en.htm (accessed 11 November 2014).

[6]   European Commission, 'Statement: Disclosure of non-financial information: Europe's largest companies to be more transparent on social and environmental issues' (Brussels, 29 September 2014), available at http://europa. eu/rapid/press-release_STATEMENT-14-291_en.htm (accessed 14 November 2014).

[7]   Department for Business Innovation & Skills, *Corporate Responsibility: Good for Business & Society: Government response to call for views on corporate responsibility* (April 2014), available at https://www.gov.uk/government/uploads/ system/uploads/attachment_data/file/300265/bis-14-651-good-for-business-and- society-government-response-to-call-for-views-on-corporate-responsibility.pdf (accessed 11 November 2014).

[8]   HM Government, *Good Business: Implementing the UN guiding principles on business and human rights* (CM 8695, September 2013), available at https://www.gov.uk/government/uploads/system/uploads/attachment_data/file/236 901/BHR_Action_Plan_-_final_online_version_1_.pdf (accessed 11 November 2014).

developments demonstrate the extent to which CSR is on the public and political agenda.

CSR has been analysed in different academic disciplines such as Management Studies, Economics, Politics and Law from a range of perspectives and methodologies. However, the link between law and CSR remains unclear and contentious. In particular, business leaders continue to understand CSR as going beyond legal requirements. This approach is followed by the UK government. In its response to call for views on corporate responsibility the government states that CSR is 'by definition voluntary'.[9] This understanding is often based on the fact that a great deal of CSR activity is self-regulation, such as private CSR standards which are, inter alia, developed by corporations themselves or private actors (e.g. NGOs), sometimes acting alone, and sometimes in conjunction with corporations.[10] Much of the legal literature has focused on international law, for example by analysing the role of the UN or the OECD.[11] It is argued here that the literature on CSR and the law has, so far, largely neglected the contribution that private law makes or could make to the promotion of CSR. In fact, private law plays an increasing role in relation to CSR, for instance, through the incorporation of these private CSR standards into business relationships (e.g. contracts), the duty for directors to promote the success of the company for the benefit of its members as a whole in s172 (1) Companies Act 2006 and the liability of companies for violations of CSR principles in tort.

This book focusses on private law for four reasons. First of all, as indicated, the existing literature on CSR and the law has primarily concentrated on international law. So far, private law seems to have been largely side-lined despite its increasingly important role for the legal regulation of CSR, for example in company law. Secondly, while much of the literature on CSR and the law is interdisciplinary and/or based on socio-legal perspectives (e.g. reflexive governance which is a process-oriented legal theory that looks at the learning and exchange of different

---

[9] Department for Business Innovation & Skills, *Corporate Responsibility: Good for Business & Society: Government response to call for views on corporate responsibility* (April 2014) 3.

[10] R Mushkat, 'Corporate social responsibility, international law, and business economics: Convergences and divergencies' (2010) 12 *Oregon Review of International Law* 55.

[11] Zerk, *Multinationals and Corporate Social Responsibility: Limitations and Opportunities in International Law* (CUP 2006) 27.

social subsystems),[12] the focus here allows an in-depth analysis of the existing and possible legal effects of CSR in English private law in order to contribute a legal perspective to the ongoing discussion about CSR and the law. Thirdly, the CSR instruments of international governing bodies, such as the UN, are predominately soft law recommendations and guidelines, whereas private law provides individuals with remedies for breach of their rights. Private law could therefore be a tool to legally enforce CSR commitments. Fourthly, the UN Guiding Principles emphasise the importance of home state regulation of multinational corporations.[13] The home state is considered to be the state in which the multinational corporation is incorporated.[14] In contrast, the host state is the state in which the multinational enterprise, either directly or through its subsidiary, operates.[15] The focus on home state regulation in the Guiding Principles suggests that national private law, which is closely linked to national legal systems, could play an important role for the future regulation of CSR.

II. THE SCOPE OF THE BOOK

The book will analyse four areas of private law which have been chosen due to their relevance for the promotion of CSR. These areas are: First, company law and corporate governance; secondly, contract law; thirdly, consumer law; and fourthly tort law. Company law and corporate

---

[12]   C Scott, 'Reflexive governance, meta-regulation and corporate social responsibility: The "Heineken effect"' in N Boeger, R Murray and C Villiers (eds), *Perspectives on Corporate Social Responsibility* (Edward Elgar 2008) 174.

[13]   There is no agreed definition of the term 'multinational enterprises'. The OECD Guidelines on Multinational Enterprises state that a clear definition was not required for the purpose of the guidelines, but then say the following about multinational enterprises: 'These usually comprise companies or other entities established in more than one country and so linked that they may co-ordinate their operations in various ways. While one or more of these entities may be able to exercise a significant influence over the activities of others, their degree of autonomy within the enterprise may vary widely from one multinational enterprise to another. Ownership may be private, state or mixed.' See OECD Guidelines for Multinational Enterprises (OECD 2000), Guideline I Concepts and Principles, para 3, available at http://www.oecd.org/dataoecd/56/36/192 2428.pdf (accessed 11 November 2014).

[14]   B Cragg, 'Home is where the halt is: Mandating corporate social responsibility through home state regulation and social disclosure' (2010) 24 *Emory International Law Review* 735, 751.

[15]   ibid.

governance are the basis for the CSR engagement of companies, for example, through directors' duties or reporting duties. Contract law is used here as many companies incorporate their CSR commitments into their (global) supply chain contracts, for example, the contracts that an English company forms with its suppliers that are based abroad. Moreover, consumer law is analysed, as it might provide consumers with tools to enforce compliance of companies with their publicly adopted CSR commitments. Finally, as the violation of CSR principles can in some circumstances also constitute torts, for example negligence, tort law is included as the fourth private law area.

The selection of the four areas of private law is based on the particular role that they already play or could play for the promotion of CSR. It is not suggested that other areas of private law are not relevant. In particular, employment law could also be discussed in the context of CSR. However, CSR often refers to the conduct, directly or indirectly, of Western multinational companies in developing countries. English employment law would only apply within territorial boundaries of England and Wales. This book, on the contrary, intends to show, with the areas discussed here, that domestic private law can also have an impact on the promotion of CSR outside England and Wales, where English companies are involved, either directly or indirectly through their subsidiaries or their suppliers in global supply chains.

Even though CSR is a global issue, this book focuses on English law. The reason for this choice is that this work concentrates on private law which is closely embedded in national legal systems. Moreover, as English law is often the law of choice in international trade and as many common law jurisdictions share common features with English law, the analysis is of significance beyond England and Wales. The primary research questions of this book are to what extent English private law already promotes CSR and to what extent English private law could better promote CSR. With these linked research questions, it is intended to show both the weaknesses and the strengths of private law in the promotion of CSR. As CSR is particularly relevant in relation to the conduct of Western companies in developing countries the analysis of these research questions also addresses the regulation of global supply chains.

The word 'promote' is not a legal term.[16] It is used here to describe the role that English private law plays in the support, encouragement and

---

[16] To 'promote' is defined in the Oxford Dictionary of English, inter alia, as 'support', 'active encouragement' and 'further progression', see http://oxford dictionaries.com/ (accessed 20 October 2014).

further progression of CSR. In a legal context, the promotion of CSR could, inter alia, mean the following: Requiring, facilitating, enabling, incorporating and enforcing CSR. The aspect 'requiring' means that private law could, for example, through directors' duties or reporting duties, require directors to pursue CSR principles. Moreover, private law could also facilitate or enable the pursuing of CSR commitments, for instance, through discretion given to directors in directors' duties that they may pursue objects advancing the interest of all stakeholders of the company and not just the shareholders. Through contract law mechanisms, private law could enable companies to incorporate CSR commitments into their contracts with others. Finally, private law could provide tools to enforce CSR principles, for example, through the use of consumer law, the enforcement of contractual CSR obligations or through liability in tort law. In short: The term 'promotion' is used here to denote that private law advances the socially responsible conduct of companies.

Due to the focus of this book it is necessary to adopt a working definition of private law.[17] The general assumption seems to be that private law is a residual area, that is, the area of the law that is not public law. It is said that private law is, though much used by lawyers, only rarely defined in common law systems.[18] According to a common definition, public law is concerned with relations between the individual and the state as well as the distribution of power between public institutions and a range of non-governmental organisations.[19] Lord Woolf identifies the function which is performed as the essential criterion for distinguishing between public law and private law. If the function is a governmental activity, then it is public law.[20] He defines private law as the system which protects the private rights of private individuals or the private rights of public bodies. Cane follows a similar approach, but simply calls the activity 'private activity' and 'public activity'. The classification of an area of law into either public law or private law depends on a value judgment about whether the performance ought to be controlled by public or private law principles.[21] Hedley notes that private law would often be described as 'the law between private individuals that

---

[17]   See for the discussion about the public/private divide in English law: D Oliver, *Common Values and the Public-Private Divide* (Butterworths 1999) 9; Lord Woolf, 'Droit public – English style' (1995) *PL* 57, 61.

[18]   S Hedley, 'Is private law meaningless?' (2011) 64 *Current Legal Problems* 89.

[19]   Oliver (n 17) 14.

[20]   Woolf (n 17) 62.

[21]   P Cane, *Administrative Law* (OUP 2011) 18.

is contrasted with the law involving organs of the state which is public law'.[22] Hedley's definition mirrors the one suggested by Lord Woolf which looks at the function performed as the distinguishing factor between private law and public law. This book will adopt the definition used by Lord Woolf as it clearly identifies private law with its reference to the rules which regulate private rights between private individuals. This definition encompasses those areas of law that are traditionally understood as private law, that is, contract law, tort law and property law, but it also allows for expanding the scope of private law to cover areas such as company law, consumer law and commercial law. This definition accords with Oliver's classification of several areas of law as private law, namely tort, contract law, company law and restraint of trade.[23] On the basis of this definition, the areas of law analysed in this book are all private law (i.e. company law and corporate governance, contract law, consumer law, tort law).

The aim of the book is to reveal the central position of private law in the regulatory framework of CSR. This position is, so far, not sufficiently reflected in the literature. The analysis of the four substantive areas of private law, brought together, will build on the existing literature which has so far only discussed the relationship between singular aspects of private law with CSR such as torts law or company law. On the basis of this approach, links will be drawn between the different areas of private law, for example, the influence of corporate theory on company law and corporate governance and the engagement of a company with CSR, for example, its voluntary incorporation of CSR policies into supply contracts. Overall, the analysis of the different areas of private law will show how English private law contributes or could make a better contribution to the promotion of CSR.

Moreover, the analysis in this book will also help to answer the secondary research question, which is to what extent English private law contributes or could contribute to the implementation of the UN Guiding Principles on Business and Human Rights into English law. The UN Guiding Principles are intended to be implemented by countries and companies.[24] The UK government has made a political commitment to

---

[22] Hedley (n 18).

[23] Oliver (n 17) 15.

[24] Office of the United Nations High Commissioner for Human Rights, *New Guiding Principles on Business and Human Rights endorsed by the UN Human Rights Council*, available at http://www.ohchr.org/en/NewsEvents/Pages/Display News.aspx?NewsID=11164 (accessed 10 October 2014).

the Guiding Principles.[25] The publication of its National Action Plan in September 2013 started its work on the implementation of the Guiding Principles. An updated version is planned to be published by the end of 2015 which means that the discussion regarding the principles continues.[26] Due to the overlap between CSR and the Guiding Principles, the analysis in this book will also provide answers to the question to what extent English private law could be used by the UK government for the implementation of the Guiding Principles.

The book will be organised in the following way: It will start with a brief account of the regulatory framework of CSR by looking at different regulatory levels; International law, EU law, domestic law and private regulation. It will then focus on the analysis of the four substantive areas of private law: Company law and corporate governance, contract law, consumer law and tort law. Key issues in company law and corporate governance are the discussions about the purpose of the corporation (e.g. shareholder value versus a pluralist model), the duty to promote the success of the company for the benefit of its members as a whole,[27] the reporting about non-financial information in the strategic report,[28] the role of shareholders in enhancing the socially responsible conduct of companies and the composition of the board. Contract law is important for the promotion of CSR through supply chain contracts. This issue is topical due to various reports about human rights abuses by suppliers of well-known Western companies. Several Western companies, including UK businesses, commonly incorporate CSR policies into their supply chain relations with their suppliers.[29] This chapter provides a detailed

---

[25] UK Trade & Investment, 'Business and Human Rights': 'The Government is fully committed to implementing the Guiding Principles as part of its strategy on business and human rights and expects UK businesses to operate at all times in a way respectful of human rights whether in Britain or overseas', see http://www.ukti.gov.uk/de_de/export/howwehelp/overseasbusinessrisk/item/print/308520.html?null (accessed 16 October 2014). UK Trade & Investment is a UK government department that works in the area of international trade promotion.

[26] HM Government, *Good Business: Implementing the UN Guiding Principles on Business and Human Rights* (CM 8695, September 2013).

[27] s172 (1) Companies Act 2006.

[28] s414A Companies Act 2006.

[29] E Pedersen and M Andersen, 'Safeguarding corporate social responsibility (CSR) in global supply chains: How codes of conduct are managed in buyer-supplier relationships' (2006) 6 *Journal of Public Affairs* 228, 237; B Jiang, 'Implementing supplier codes of conduct in global supply chains: Process explanations from theoretic and empirical perspectives' (2009) 85 *Journal of Business Ethics* 77, 78.

analysis of the contract law rules pertaining to the incorporation of CSR into supply contracts. Consumer law is chosen as one of the four substantive areas of private law as many companies make their CSR commitments public while consumers increasingly consider corporate responsibility in their purchase and consumption behaviour (described by the term 'ethical consumerism').[30] Consumer law and CSR overlap where consumers are protected against false information about the CSR practices of companies. This chapter analyses whether consumer law protects consumers in the situation where companies are in breach of their publicly announced CSR commitments, for example, if a company violates the principles of a code of conduct to which it has signed up and which it has published on its website. Finally, CSR and the law of torts overlap where tort law protects the interests that CSR requires companies to pursue, such as the adherence to human rights or the protection of the environment. The violation of CSR principles can therefore constitute torts such as negligence. This chapter will also address challenges of using tort law as an instrument for the promotion of CSR, for example, the existence of corporate group structures consisting of a parent company and several subsidiaries.

The threads of the analysis of the four areas of private law are then drawn together in a chapter which discusses both the contributions that private law makes to the promotion of CSR and the limitations that it has. Within the discussion of the limitations and the strengths of private law in the promotion of CSR, this chapter also addresses the question to what extent English private law could contribute to the implementation of the UN Guiding Principles on Business and Human Rights into English law. The discussion in this chapter leads to a list of substantive recommendations for changes to English law that result from the analysis. The final chapter of the book applies the findings of the substantive chapters to the example of the Savor Building collapse in Bangladesh in 2013. The purpose of this case study is to illustrate the opportunities and limitations of private law in the promotion of CSR in the context of a real-life scenario. The case study will further contribute to the book's recommendations for changes to English law.

---

[30]　See N C Smith, 'Consumers as drivers of corporate social responsibility' in A Crane, A McWilliams, D Matten et al. (eds), *The Oxford Handbook of Corporate Social Responsibility* (OUP 2008) 281; M Carrington, B Neville and G Whitwell, 'Why ethical consumers don't walk their talk: Towards a framework for understanding the gap between the ethical purchase intentions and actual buying behaviour of ethically-minded consumers' (2010) 97 *Journal of Business Ethics* 139.

III. THE DEBATE ABOUT THE DEFINITION OF CSR

Although the term Corporate Social Responsibility is widely used, it is far from clear how it is defined.[31] In fact, there is no generally accepted definition of CSR and the growing academic and public interest in the concept of CSR has only added to the number of existing definitions.[32] It is often said that the debate about the definition of CSR is exacerbated by the interests of the different groups involved with CSR.[33] Horrigan observes that CSR has 'many different definitions, grounded in many different standpoints from which it can be approached'.[34] Nevertheless, a clear definition of CSR and related concepts is important in order 'to avoid talking at cross-purposes'.[35] This section will therefore seek to define CSR for the purpose of this book.

The Confederation of British Industry (CBI) defines CSR as 'the acknowledgement by companies that they should be accountable not only for their financial performance, but also for the impact of their activities on society and/or the environment'.[36] Notably, the CBI definition adds that CSR is 'voluntary', 'business-driven' and often goes 'well beyond' what is required by legislation. The long-standing definition of the European Commission used until its 2011 communication on CSR corresponded with this approach, as it defined CSR as 'a concept whereby companies integrate social and environmental concerns in their business operations and in their interactions with their stakeholders on a

---

[31] B Horrigan, *Corporate Social Responsibility in the 21st century: Debates, Models and Practices Across Government, Law and Business* (Edward Elgar 2010) 34. It is important to note that some authors refer to 'corporate responsibility' only thus omitting the word 'social'. Insofar as this book engages with or refers to literature which uses 'corporate responsibility', it will be examined in the same way as literature that refers to Corporate Social Responsibility, as the majority of authors still seem to have the same concept in mind. Moreover, Corporate Social Responsibility is the most widely used term. See for a discussion about the use of the term Corporate Responsibility: Zerk (n 11) 32.

[32] See for a discussion about definitions of CSR: C Villiers, 'Corporate law, corporate power and corporate social responsibility' in N Boeger, R Murray and C Villiers (eds), *Perspectives on Corporate Social Responsibility* (Edward Elgar 2008) 91–3.

[33] Zerk (n 11) 29.

[34] Horrigan (n 31) 34.

[35] N Boeger, R Murray and C Villiers 'Introduction' in N Boeger, R Murray and C Villiers (eds), *Perspectives on Corporate Social Responsibility* (Edward Elgar 2008) 1.

[36] Confederation of British Industry (CBI), *Issue Statement: Corporate Social Responsibility* (2001).

voluntary basis'.[37] This approach continues to be followed by the UK government which describes CSR as 'voluntary action'.[38] These definitions have in common that they define CSR as a voluntary undertaking. CSR is characterised as corporate actions above and beyond legal obligations. There appears to be a distinction between CSR and the law. The effect of these definitions is that law and CSR are separate concepts. In terms of the content of CSR, these definitions focus on the social and environmental impact of corporations.

However, the view that CSR is, by definition, a voluntary matter is far from settled. Doubts have been raised whether or not CSR can still be considered to be purely voluntary, arguing that research has shown that CSR produces a variety of legal effects.[39] There are several broader definitions in the academic literature which are more open to the question whether or not CSR is purely a voluntary commitment, for example, the definition provided by Sheikh who defines CSR as 'the assumption of responsibilities by companies, whether voluntarily or by virtue of statute, in discharging socioeconomic obligations in society'.[40] Other scholars have followed this approach. For example, Zerk applies a broader approach to CSR. In her view, CSR refers to the notion that 'each business enterprise, as a member of society has a responsibility to operate ethically and in accordance with its legal obligations and to strive to minimise any adverse effects of its operations and activities on the environment, society and human health'.[41] She concludes that the reason for the controversies about how to define CSR might be that these definitions are often presented 'with an agenda in mind'. Hereby Zerk indicates that business organisations and NGOs often argue for either a voluntary or mandatory understanding of CSR in order to promote their political agenda in this respect.

---

[37] European Commission, 'Green Paper: Promoting a European framework for Corporate Social Responsibility', COM (2001) 366 final, 20.

[38] Department for Business Innovation & Skills, *Corporate Responsibility: Good for Business & Society: Government response to call for views on corporate responsibility* (April 2014) para 1.1.

[39] C Glinski, 'Corporate codes of conduct: moral or legal obligation' in D McBarnet, A Voiculescu and T Campbell (eds), *The New Corporate Accountability: Corporate Social Responsibility and the Law* (CUP 2007) 147.

[40] S Sheikh, *Corporate Social Responsibilities: Law and Practice* (Cavendish 1995) 15.

[41] Zerk (n 11) 32.

Acknowledging that no clear consensus has yet been reached about what exactly CSR means, Campbell and Vick define CSR in the following way:

> At a minimum the term implies an obligation on the part of large companies to pursue objectives advancing the interests of all groups affected by their activities – not just shareholders but also employees, consumers, suppliers, creditors and local communities. These interests are not just economic, but also include environmental, human rights and 'quality of life' concerns. The obligation to be socially responsible is usually conceived of as being over and above the minimum requirement imposed on companies by formal legal rules, although this is not invariably the case.[42]

It is an important aspect of this definition that, while it acknowledges that CSR is often perceived of as being voluntary, it also includes statutory CSR obligations. The strength of this approach is that it recognises that, for example, mandatory legislation sometimes addresses issues which are part of the CSR agenda, such as bribery and corruption offences. The core of these different definitions is a shared belief that companies have a responsibility for the public good.[43] There is, by and large, a consensus about the aims of CSR – to make corporations advance the interests of those who are affected by their activities, focusing in particular on the social and environmental impact of their work.

This book adopts the definition from Campbell and Vick for three reasons.[44] First, this definition names various groups (stakeholders) affected by a corporation. Secondly, it explicitly includes economic, environmental and human rights issues into the ambit of CSR, thus clarifying that these are specific issues that are encompassed by CSR in any case. Thirdly, it is an advantage of this definition that, while it acknowledges that CSR is traditionally often perceived of as being voluntary, it also states that it can be mandatory. This approach reflects the situation that there are statutory legal requirements which overlap with CSR, for example, the duty to promote the success of the company pursuant to s172 (1) Companies Act 2006. This definition thus supports one of the core arguments of this book, namely that CSR is, at least in

---

[42]   K Campbell and D Vick, 'Disclosure Law and the market for corporate social responsibility' in D McBarnet, A Voiculescu and T Campbell (eds), *The New Corporate Accountability: Corporate Social Responsibility and the Law* (CUP 2007) 242.

[43]   M Blowfield and A Murray, *Corporate Responsibility: A Critical Introduction* (OUP 2008) 13.

[44]   See Campbell and Vick (n 42).

part, law. Notably, the position that CSR is purely voluntary seems to be losing ground, as evidenced, inter alia, by the fact that, in its 2011 communication on CSR, the European Commission puts forward a new definition of CSR that no longer classifies CSR as 'voluntary'. According to the Commission's new definition CSR is 'the responsibility of enterprises for their impacts on society'.[45]

IV. BRINGING LAW TO CSR: THE REGULATORY FRAMEWORK OF CSR

This section will highlight key regulatory instruments that are important from a CSR point of view by looking at the following levels: International law, European Union law, domestic legislation in English law and private regulation. This outline will demonstrate the significance of private law for CSR in its broader contexts thus forming the background to the subsequent chapters that analyse the promotion of CSR through different areas of private law. It is neither intended nor possible to extensively analyse the whole regulatory framework of CSR.

This book adopts a broad understanding of regulation as 'all mechanisms of social control or influence affecting behaviour from whatever source, whether intentional or not'.[46] This definition potentially encompasses different forms of regulation including the traditional state-based regulation. This approach is in line with those who see regulation as a concept that includes law, but is not limited to law.[47] This broad understanding of regulation is important as CSR is particularly based on private regulation, for example codes of conduct developed by corporations themselves or third parties such as non-governmental organisations.

---

[45] European Commission, 'Communication from the Commission to the European Parliament, the Council, the European Economic and Social Committee and the Committee of the Regions: A renewed EU strategy 2011–14 for Corporate Social Responsibility' COM (2011) 681 final, para 3.1.

[46] J Black, 'Decentring regulation: Understanding the role of regulation and self-regulation in a post-regulatory world' (2001) 54 *Current Legal Problems* 103, 129.

[47] Horrigan (n 31) 59.

A. International Law Level

The CSR instruments of international governing bodies, such as the UN, are predominately soft law recommendations and guidelines.[48] In the international law context, 'soft law' is used to denote 'principles and policies which have been negotiated and agreed between states, or promulgated by international institutions, but which are not mandated by law or subject to any formal enforcement mechanisms'.[49]

i. United Nations

An important UN source of CSR is the UN Global Compact which was launched in September 2000 by the UN Secretary-General Kofi Annan. He asked business leaders to voluntarily 'embrace and enact' principles of the Compact. The UN Global Compact was not created by states through a negotiated international treaty, but it was initiated by the UN Secretary-General together with business actors and UN agencies. Members of the UN Global Compact are corporations, employers' and employees' organisations, state institutions and civil society organisations.[50] Since its launch it has grown to more than 12,000 participants, including over 8,000 businesses in 145 countries around the world.[51] It was the underlying aim to provide for simple means of becoming a member of the Global Compact.[52] The Global Compact contains ten principles on human rights, labour standards, environmental protection and fighting corruption. The Global Compact was not intended to be a 'regulatory instrument'.[53] It is not a code of conduct.[54] Still, corporations who have subscribed to it are required to submit examples of how they

---

[48]   Cragg (n 14) 744.

[49]   Zerk (n 11) 70; For a general introduction see D L Shelton, 'Soft law' in D Armstrong (ed.), *Routledge Handbook of International Law* (Routledge 2009) 68.

[50]   See UN Global Compact, Global Compact Participants, available at http://www.unglobalcompact.org/ParticipantsandStakeholders/index.html (accessed 10 November 2014).

[51]   ibid.

[52]   W Kaleck and M Saage-Maass, 'Corporate accountability for human rights violations amounting to international crimes: the status quo and its challenges' (2010) 8 (3) *Journal of International Criminal Justice* 699, 714.

[53]   See UN Global Compact, http://www.unglobalcompact.org/AboutTheGC/index.html (accessed 9 November 2014).

[54]   Zerk (n 11) 259.

have complied with the principles on an annual basis.[55] The Global
Compact has been subject to criticisms due to the lack of sanctions
against corporations who do not comply with the principles. It has been
argued that corporations only agreed to the Global Compact 'after it had
been degraded to a toothless instrument'.[56] These criticisms eventually
led to a control mechanism that enables the Global Compact to exclude
members who severely violate the principles.[57] And, in fact, the UN
reports that, as of September 2013, it has in total delisted more than
4,600 business members for failure to meet the UN Global Compact's
mandatory annual reporting requirement, also known as the Communication on Progress (COP) policy.[58]

The UN Sub-Commission for the Promotion and Protection of Human
Rights published in 2003 the 'Norms on the Responsibility of Transnational Corporations and Other Business Enterprises with regard to
human rights obligations'.[59] The underlying idea was that the Norms
should be adopted by the member states. However, as the Norms tried to
impose legally binding obligations on transnational companies, they were
viewed rather critically by several member states and rejected.[60] NGOs,
on the other hand, welcomed them.[61] The difference between the Norms
and previous CSR initiatives is that they sought to extend the reach of
international law to transnational corporations by directly imposing
obligations upon them.[62] It was essentially the aim of the Norms to
impose on companies the same human rights duties as states have

---

[55] See UN Global Compact, http://www.unglobalcompact.org/AboutTheGC/
integrity.html (accessed 9 November 2014).

[56] N Weiß, 'Transnationale Unternehmen – weltweite Standards? eine Zwischenbilanz des Global Compact' (2002) 2 *MenschenRechtsMagazin* 82, 88.

[57] UN Global Compact, Integrity Measures, No. 4, available at http://
www.unglobalcompact.org/AboutTheGC/IntegrityMeasures/index.html (accessed
9 November 2014).

[58] United Nations Global Compact, Monthly Bulletin, October 2013, available at: http://bulletin.unglobalcompact.org/t/r-59330408B8779E362540EF23F3
0FEDED (accessed 5 November 2014).

[59] UN Doc. E/CN4/Sub.2/2003/12/Rev.2 of 26 August 2003.

[60] See generally about the debate D Kinley, J Nolan and N Zerial, 'The
norms are dead! Long live the norms! The politics behind the UN human rights
norms for corporations' in D McBarnet, A Voiculescu and T Campbell (eds), *The
New Corporate Accountability: Corporate Social Responsibility and the Law*
(CUP 2007) 459.

[61] ibid.

[62] Cragg (n 14) 746.

accepted under treaties.[63] Due to the controversy about the Norms, the UN Commission on Human Rights finally failed to adopt the document.[64]

Following the failure of the Norms, the UN Secretary-General of that time, Kofi Annan, subsequently appointed Professor John Ruggie of Harvard University as Special Representative on the issue of human rights and business (SRSG).[65] During his six-year mandate, Ruggie engaged in an extensive consultation process and reported six times.[66] Ruggie criticised the Norms for 'intermingling the respective roles of states and business'.[67] In his 2008 report, Ruggie proposed a three-pillar framework for corporate accountability for human rights, which he describes as 'Protect, Respect and Remedy'. The framework 'rests on differentiated but complementary responsibilities'.[68] Ruggie's work during his mandate led to the Guiding Principles on Business and Human Rights which were published in 2011.[69] The Guiding Principles were

---

[63] J Ruggie, 'The construction of the UN "protect, respect and remedy" framework for business and human rights: The true confessions of a principled pragmatist' (2011) 2 *EHRLR* 127.

[64] O Amao, 'The foundation for a global company law for multinational corporations' (2010) 21 (8) *ICCLR* 275, 281.

[65] UN Secretary-General, 'Secretary-General Appoints John Ruggie of United States Special Representative on Issue of Human Rights, Transnational Corporations, Other Business Enterprises' (28 July 2005), UN Doc SGA/A/934, available at http://www.un.org/News/Press/docs/2005/sga934.doc.htm (accessed 9 November 2014).

[66] See Ruggie's reports in 2006, 2007, 2008, 2009, 2010 and 2011, available at http://www.business-humanrights.org/SpecialRepPortal/Home (accessed 8 November 2014).

[67] J Ruggie, 'The construction of the UN "protect, respect and remedy" framework for business and human rights: the true confessions of a principled pragmatist' (2011) 2 *EHRLR* 127.

[68] J Ruggie, *Protect, Respect and Remedy: A Framework for Business and Human Rights,* (7 April 2008), para 9, available at http://www.reports-and-materials.org/Ruggie-report-7-Apr-2008.pdf (accessed 9 November 2014).

[69] Report of the Special Representative of the Secretary-General on the issue of human rights and transnational corporations and other business enterprises, John Ruggie, *Guiding Principles on Business and Human Rights: Implementing the United Nations 'Protect, Respect and Remedy' framework*, 21 March 2011, available at http://www.ohchr.org/Documents/Publications/GuidingPrinciples BusinessHR_EN.pdf (accessed 9 November 2014).

endorsed by the United Nations Human Rights Council in June 2011.[70] Human rights are an important element of the CSR agenda.[71] The Guiding Principles have therefore been called 'a landmark in the CSR debate'.[72] The UN Guiding Principles are organised in three pillars: the state duty to protect human rights, the corporate duty to respect human rights, and the need for access to effective remedy mechanisms when abuses occur. The Guiding Principles distinguish between the duties of states and the responsibilities of companies in order to indicate that respecting rights is not an obligation that current international human rights law generally imposes directly upon companies.[73] The introduction to the Guiding Principles emphasises that the normative contribution of the Guiding Principles lies not in the creation of new international law obligations, but in elaborating the implications of existing standards and practices for states and businesses.[74]

The Guiding Principles are intended to be implemented by countries and by companies.[75] In its 2011 Communication on CSR, the EU Commission has stressed that it seeks to support the implementation of the Guiding Principles and it has invited EU member states to develop national plans by the end of 2012 for the implementation of the UN Guiding Principles into domestic law.[76] The UK government consequently published its National Action on the implementation in September 2013.[77] As the

---

[70] Office of the United Nations High Commissioner for Human Rights, *New Guiding Principles on Business and Human Rights endorsed by the UN Human Rights Council*, available at http://www.ohchr.org/EN/NewsEvents/Pages/Display News.aspx?NewsID=11164&LangID=E (accessed 9 November 2014).

[71] See: K Buhmann, 'Integrating human rights in emerging regulation of corporate social responsibility: The EU case' (2011) 7 (2) *International Journal of Law in Context* 139, 142.

[72] Ames (n 4) 15.

[73] Ruggie (n 63) 129.

[74] J Ruggie, Introduction to the Guiding Principles, para 14.

[75] Office of the United Nations High Commissioner for Human Rights, *New Guiding Principles on Business and Human Rights endorsed by the UN Human Rights Council*, available at http://www.ohchr.org/en/NewsEvents/Pages/Display News.aspx?NewsID=11164 (accessed 10 November 2014).

[76] European Commission, 'Communication from the Commission to the European Parliament, the Council, the European Economic and Social Committee and the Committee of the Regions: A renewed EU strategy 2011–14 for Corporate Social Responsibility', COM (2011) 681 final, para 4.8.2., available at http://eur-lex.europa.eu/LexUriServ/LexUriServ.do?uri=COM:2011:0681:FIN:EN: PDF (accessed 9 November 2014).

[77] HM Government, *Good Business: Implementing the UN Guiding Principles on Business and Human Rights* (Cm 8695, September 2013).

Guiding Principles highlight, inter alia, the importance of home state regulation for the protection of human rights from business conduct, of course, national private law could be an important part of this home state regulation. Private law could therefore be used by the UK government to implement the Guiding Principles into English law.

ii.　Organisation for Economic Co-operation and Development

Another important international initiative for CSR are the OECD Guidelines for Multinational Enterprises which were first published in 1976[78] and most recently updated in 2011.[79] The negotiators of the Guidelines were the participating countries of the OECD, business associations, trade unions and some civil society organisations.[80] The Guidelines contain voluntary recommendations on human rights, employment, industrial relations, the environment, bribery and consumer interests. The Guidelines make direct reference to some important international instruments such as the Universal Declaration of Human Rights and the ILO Declaration on Fundamental Principles and Rights at Work. These recommendations only address corporations whose headquarters are in states which adhere to the OECD Guidelines. Complaints can therefore only be brought against companies from those countries. It has been regarded as positive though, that the OECD Guidelines apply 'both to the Member States in charge of implementing them and to the multinational enterprises whose activities these Guidelines are supposed to govern (whether they operate on the territory of a member country or are based there)'.[81] The OECD Guidelines have in recent versions involved the creation of National Contact Points as a 'follow-up' mechanism.[82] The National Contact Points are responsible for encouraging adherence to the principles. They mediate disputes in case of alleged non-adherence to the Guidelines. Complaints can be filed before such a National Contact Point. Civil society organisations have had access to this complaint

---

[78]　Organisation for Economic Cooperation and Development (OECD) Guidelines for Multinational Enterprises (1976) 15 I.L.M. 9.

[79]　The OECD Guidelines for Multinational Enterprises. The text of the revised version of the OECD Guidelines for Multinational Enterprises is available at http://www.oecd.org/document/28/0,3746,en_2649_34889_2397532_1_1_1_1,00.html (accessed 12 November 2014).

[80]　Amao (n 64) 280.

[81]　Y Queinnec, *The OECD Guidelines for Multinational Enterprises: An Evolving Legal Status* (Sherpa 2007) 6.

[82]　I Bantekas, 'Corporate social responsibility in international law' (2004) 22 *Boston University International Law Journal* 309, 319.

procedure since 2000. The UK National Contact Point is a non-judicial mechanism that does not have powers of enforceability and cannot impose sanctions on non-complying companies, but it can investigate complaints.[83]

iii. International Labour Organization

The International Labour Organization's (ILO) Tripartite Declaration of Principles Concerning Multinational Enterprises and Social Policy (Tripartite Declaration) aims 'to encourage the positive contribution which multinational enterprises can make to economic and social progress and to minimise and to resolve the difficulties to which their various operations give rise'.[84] It was published in 1978 and amended in 2001 and 2006.[85] The amended version makes reference to the ILO's 1998 Declaration on Fundamental Principles and Rights at Work.[86] The Tripartite Declaration contains fundamental principles in the fields of employment, training, working conditions and industrial relations. The ILO Tripartite Declaration is comparable to the OECD Guidelines insofar as it is intended to be non-binding.[87] The Declaration consequently lacks an enforcement mechanism for its provisions.[88]

B. European Union Level

The EU addressed the CSR agenda later than the UN, OECD and ILO.[89] The European Commission summarised its view on CSR in a Green Paper entitled 'Promoting a European Framework for Corporate Social Responsibility', published in 2001. As indicated above, the Commission defined CSR in this Green Paper as a 'voluntary concept'.[90] The Green

---

[83] See C Pedamon, 'Corporate social responsibility: A new approach to promoting integrity and responsibility' (2010) 31 *Company Lawyer* 172, 176.

[84] ILO Tripartite Declaration (1978) 17 ILM 422, para 2.

[85] See http://www.ilo.org/empent/Publications/WCMS_094386/lang–en/index.htm (accessed 9 November 2014).

[86] Adopted at the 86th session of the International Labour Conference, Geneva, 18 June 1998.

[87] Kaleck and Saage-Maass (n 52) 710.

[88] Amao (n 64) 280.

[89] See S Sheikh, 'Promoting corporate social responsibilities within the European Union' (2002) 13 (4) *ICCLR* 143.

[90] European Commission, 'Green Paper: Promoting a European Framework for Corporate Social Responsibility' COM (2001) 366 final, 20.

Paper focuses on the 'business case' for CSR.[91] The aim of the Green
Paper was to start a debate on CSR, rather than 'making concrete
proposals for action'.[92] Hence, the Green Paper recommends companies
to subscribe to existing international CSR standards, rather than develop
their own ones.[93]

Following the global financial crisis, the Commission released a new
communication on CSR in 2011 which contains an action agenda for the
period 2011–14.[94] The CSR policy outlined in the communication
addresses a number of factors that, in the Commission's view, 'will help
to further increase the impact of its CSR policy', including improved
company disclosure on social and environmental information.[95] Among
the points in the communication is the notion that public authorities
should 'where necessary' complement voluntary CSR policies through
regulation that, for example, promote transparency or create market
incentives for responsible business conduct.[96] With this point the Commission underlines its deviation from its previous insistence that CSR
was purely voluntary (as also indicated in the Commission's new
definition of CSR, mentioned above). Moreover, the Commission seeks
to improve self- and co-regulation processes and it has launched a
process with enterprises and other stakeholders in this respect.[97] However, the communication does not significantly deviate from the Commission's previous CSR policies overall. In particular, the Commission does
not propose the introduction of any specific Europe-wide CSR regulation.

---

[91]   See generally S MacLeod, 'Reconciling regulatory approaches to Corporate Social Responsibility: The European Union, OECD and United Nations
compare' (2007) 13 *European Public Law* 671, 681.

[92]   European Commission, 'Green Paper: Promoting a European framework
for Corporate Social Responsibility' COM (2001) 366 final, 23; see the discussion in A Voiculescu, 'The other European framework for Corporate Social
Responsibility: From the Green Paper to new uses of human rights instruments'
in D McBarnet, A Voiculescu and T Campbell (eds), *The New Corporate
Accountability: Corporate Social Responsibility and the Law* (CUP 2007) 379.

[93]   European Commission, 'Green Paper: Promoting a European framework
for Corporate Social Responsibility' COM (2001) 366 final, 9, 16.

[94]   European Commission, 'Communication from the Commission to the
European Parliament, the Council, the European Economic and social committee
and the committee of the regions: A renewed EU strategy 2011–14 for Corporate
Social Responsibility' COM (2011) 681 final, available at http://ec.europa.eu/
enterprise/policies/sustainable-business/corporate-social-responsibility/index_en.
htm (accessed 9 November 2014).

[95]   ibid, para 2.

[96]   ibid, para 3.4.

[97]   Ibid. para 4.3.

Towards the end of the 2011–14 communication, the Commission sought stakeholders' views on the impact of its strategy and suggestions for the future development of its CSR policy.[98]

A potentially significant milestone at the European level is the increase of CSR reporting duties through the Directive on disclosure of non-financial and diversity information by large companies and groups which was adopted by the European Parliament and the Council in 2014.[99] The Directive will require large companies with more than 500 employees to disclose relevant and material environmental and social information in their annual reports.[100]

C. Domestic Legislation in English Law

There is no specific CSR Act in domestic English law. However, one can find sections in the Companies Act (CA) 2006 which have relevance for CSR. These will be discussed in the chapter on company law and corporate governance and will therefore only be indicated here. The new directors' duty in s172 CA 2006 ('Duty to promote the success of the company') states that a director must act in the way he considers, in good faith, would be most likely to promote the success of the company for the benefit of its members as a whole. The section enumerates several factors to which directors should have regard when making their decisions, such as the likely consequences of any decision in the long term, the interests of employees and the impact on the environment. The list is non-exhaustive. This provision embodies the 'enlightened shareholder value theory' that underlies the Companies Act 2006.[101]

The second part of the CA 2006 which is relevant for CSR is the strategic report contained in s414A CA. The strategic report requires directors to report on their strategy and their business model. The

---

[98] European Commission, Press Release: 'EU Corporate Social Responsibility policy: The Commission seeks stakeholders' views on achievements and future challenges' (29 April 2014), available at http://europa.eu/rapid/press-release_IP-14-491_en.htm (accessed 12 November 2014).

[99] European Commission, 'Statement: Disclosure of non-financial information: Europe's largest companies to be more transparent on social and environmental issues' (Brussels 29 September 2014), available at http://europa.eu/rapid/press-release_STATEMENT-14-291_en.htm (accessed 14 November 2014).

[100] And who, during the financial year, exceed on their balance sheet dates either a balance sheet total of EUR 20 million or a net turnover of EUR 40 million.

[101] Horrigan (n 31) 229.

strategic report comes first in the directors' report. The purpose of the strategic report is 'to inform members of the company and help them assess how the directors have performed their duty to promote the success of the company under section 172 CA'.[102] The proposed EU Directive on non-financial information disclosure will increase the reporting on CSR that is required of companies.

Another means to hold corporations liable in private law is through torts law. A company is vicariously liable in tort for the wrongful acts of an agent or employee acting within the scope of his authority or in the course of his employment. Tort law and CSR overlap where tort law provides causes of action for corporate conduct that constitutes violations of CSR principles. Different causes of action in tort such as negligence, private nuisance or battery could therefore provide remedies vis-à-vis companies that have violated CSR principles.

Domestic law can also play a role in terms of CSR through the use of consumer protection laws and competition laws to hold corporations accountable for false advertisement.[103] Claims based on consumer law or competition law could be made against a company that violates commitments that it has made in a code of conduct, for example where a company pledges in a code of conduct to respect human rights in its business practice, but is actually involved in the commission of international crimes.[104] Moreover, the rules provided by English contract law are already used by companies in their supply chain contracts to incorporate CSR standards.[105] As companies understand their supply chain as an area of reputational risk, they increasingly incorporate CSR obligations into the contracts with their suppliers.[106]

Corporations can also be criminally liable for violations of CSR principles, for example, for the use of physical force against employees.[107] Companies can commit crimes, although some offences cannot be

---

[102]   s417 (2) CA.

[103]   See C Glinski, 'Corporate codes of conduct: Moral or legal obligation?' in D McBarnet, A Voiculescu and T Campbell (eds), *The New Corporate Accountability: Corporate Social Responsibility and the Law* (CUP 2007) 126.

[104]   Kaleck and Saage-Maass (n 52) 718.

[105]   D McBarnet and M Kurkchiyan, 'Corporate social responsibility through contractual control? Global supply chains and "other-regulation"' in D McBarnet, A Voiculescu and T Campbell (eds), *The New Corporate Accountability: Corporate Social Responsibility and the Law* (CUP 2007) 59.

[106]   ibid, 63.

[107]   See for an overview of the criminal liability of corporations: D French, S Mayson and C Ryan, *Mayson, French & Ryan on Company Law* (28th edn, OUP 2011–12) para 19.8.4. The criminal liability of corporations is discussed in the

committed by companies due to their nature. If criminal liability is to have a wide reach, it is necessary that the acts of the company's employees, agents or officers are attributed to the company.[108] The Corporate Manslaughter and Corporate Homicide Act 2007 (CMCHA) makes corporate manslaughter an offence, provided that the company's activities are managed or organised in a way that causes a person's death and amounts to a gross breach of a relevant duty of care owed by the company to that person.[109] English multinational corporations also face liability under the UK Bribery Act which came into force in 2011.[110] Common to all cases of bribery outlined in the Act is the offer or taking of a 'financial or other advantage'.[111] The Bribery Act creates four offences: paying bribes, receiving bribes, the offence of bribing a foreign public official and the failure of a commercial organisation to prevent bribery. The Act has a near-universal jurisdiction, allowing for the prosecution of an individual or company with links to the UK, regardless of where the crime occurred. Section 7 makes it an offence for commercial organisations which have business in the UK to fail to prevent bribery on their behalf. This offence does not only apply to the organisation itself; individuals and employees may also be guilty.

---

context of CSR in: A Voiculescu, 'Changing paradigms of corporate criminal responsibility: Lessons for corporate social responsibility' in D McBarnet, A Voiculescu and T Campbell (eds), *The New Corporate Accountability: Corporate Social Responsibility and the Law* (CUP 2007) 399.

[108] The leading case regarding the rules of attribution is now *Meridian Global Funds Management Asia Ltd v Securities Commission* [1995] 2 BCLC 116, PC. Lord Hoffmann held that it is for the court to ask whose act or knowledge or state of mind is for the purpose of that rule intended to count as the act, knowledge or state of mind of the company, applying the usual canons of interpretation, taking into account the language of the rule (if it is a statute) and its contents and policy. Before this decision the leading rule for the attribution was the identification theory with the 'directing mind and will of the company' test, established in *Lennard's Carrying Co Ltd v Asiatic Petroleum Co Ltd* [1915] AC 705, 713. According to this test, the directing mind and will must 'be sought in the person of somebody who for some purposes may be called an agent, but who is really the directing mind and will of the corporation, the very ego and centre of the personality of the corporation.' In *Tesco Supermarkets v Nattrass* [1972] AC 153 it was held that the identification of the directing mind and will is usually the board of directors and not junior management.

[109] s1 (1) CMCHA.

[110] Bribery Act 2010, available at www.legislation.gov.uk/ukpga/2010/23/pdfs/ukpga_20100023_en.pdf (accessed 12 November 2014).

[111] G Sullivan, 'Legislative comment: The Bribery Act 2010: Part 1: An overview' (2011) *Criminal Law Review* 87, 89.

Although the Bribery Act is criminal law and hence not private law, it is important for the book for two reasons. First, it supports the view taken here that CSR is, at least in part, law, given that the prevention of bribery is one of the aims of CSR. Secondly, the existence of the Bribery Act raises the issue of whether there is also civil liability for bribery.[112]

D. Private Regulation

Private regulation describes normative settings which are not provided for by state-based decision-making, but by voluntary decisions of non-public actors such as corporations or NGOs which create general rules beyond single contracts.[113] Private CSR regulation, inter alia, consists of codes of conduct and labelling schemes. Private regulation plays an increasingly important role for CSR. The general proliferation of private regulation in CSR in recent years is due to the influence of non-state actors, such as NGOs or corporations themselves. NGOs, in particular, are said to have transformed CSR 'from a fringe concern to a mainstream policy issue'.[114] NGOs document cases and monitor adherence to CSR standards. For example, when producers meet the standards of private regulatory initiatives, they receive a certificate or label.[115]

The area of private regulation is not homogenous, as CSR standards and codes of conduct are not only developed by corporations themselves, but also at industry level or by NGOs. This has led to calls to 'disentangle' the private sphere.[116] Abbott and Snidal have developed a conceptual map to classify the different private regulatory regimes. They have created a 'governance triangle' by distinguishing between three major actors, the state, companies and non-governmental organisations

---

[112]   The High Court discussed this recently in the case *Fiona Trust & Holding Corp v Privalov* [2010] EWHC 3199 (Comm).

[113]   D Schiek, 'Private rule-making and European governance – issues of legitimacy' (2007) 32 *European Law Review* 443, 444.

[114]   Zerk (n 11) 95.

[115]   A Marx, 'Global governance and private regulation of supply chains – types, trends and challenges' (Antwerp Management School, Working Papers, 2010) 2.

[116]   See D Vogel, 'The private regulation of global corporate conduct' in W Mattli and N Woods (eds), *The Politics of Global Regulation* (Princeton University Press 2009) 156; F Cafaggi, 'New foundations of transnational private regulation' in C Scott, F Cafaggi and L Senden (eds), *The Challenge of Transnational Private Regulation – Conceptual and Constitutional Debates* (Wiley-Blackwell 2011) 31.

which develop rules and standards, either separately or together.[117] Seven zones are distinguished within this triangle, depending on how many parties are involved in defining standards: Three zones consist of initiatives where one actor develops the standards (e.g. OECD Guidelines for Multinational Enterprises, industry-driven initiatives and NGO-driven initiatives), a further three zones consist of initiatives where two actors develop the standards (cooperation between NGOs and the state, initiatives between international authorities and companies such as the UN Global Compact) and one zone contains initiatives developed by the three parties.[118] An example of the latter is the 1977 Declaration of the International Labour Organizations, for it involves all three parties. The focus of this conceptual map is on who develops the initiatives.

There is an abundance of private CSR standards available for companies to choose from, some of them are commonly used such as the ISO 26000 standard 'Guidance on social responsibility'[119] or the Ethical Trading Initiative Base Code.[120] While it is not possible to discuss the various CSR standards in this section, the analysis in the following chapters will refer to some of them, such as the Ethical Trading Initiative Base Code.

V. CONCLUSION

The overview of the regulatory framework of CSR in this chapter has shown that CSR and law, at least have the potential to overlap in various ways, for example, the duty for directors to promote the success of the company for the benefit of its members as a whole in s172 (1) CA or the strategic report in s414A CA. The overview therefore supports the view taken here that CSR is, at least in part, law. The outline of the regulatory framework of CSR has particularly shown that private law plays or at

---

[117] K W Abbott and D Snidal, 'Governance triangle' in W Mattli and N Woods (eds), *The Politics of Global Regulation* (Princeton University Press 2009) 50.

[118] ibid.

[119] International Organisation for Standardisation, ISO 26000 *Guidance on social responsibility*, available at http://www.iso.org/iso/iso26000 (accessed 10 November 2014). See for a discussion: A Johnston, 'Constructing Sustainability Through CSR: A critical appraisal of ISO 26000' (University of Oslo Faculty of Law Research Paper No. 2011–33), available at http://papers.ssrn.com/sol3/papers.cfm?abstract_id=1928397 (accessed 12 November 2014).

[120] Ethical Trading Initiative Base Code, available at http://www.ethicaltrade.org/eti-base-code (accessed 11 November 2014).

least could play a significant role for CSR. Apart from direct overlaps between CSR and company law and tort law, private law also provides tools for the incorporation of CSR commitments into contracts and for its enforcement, for example, by companies and consumers.

2. Company law, corporate governance and corporate social responsibility

I. INTRODUCTION

English company law and corporate governance have in recent years been subject to substantial changes through the enactment of the Companies Act (CA)[1] 2006. The global financial and economic crisis caused several reviews of the system of corporate governance in English and European Union company law.[2] A particular feature of the Companies Act 2006 is its endorsement of the enlightened shareholder value theory.[3] This change was intended to promote a long-term approach to doing business, which includes a range of stakeholders, rather than purely focusing on shareholders.[4] This aim of the enlightened shareholder value approach overlaps with the concept of CSR, which implies an obligation on the part of large companies to pursue objectives advancing the interests of all groups affected by their activities – not just shareholders but also stakeholders such as employees, consumers, suppliers, creditors and local communities.[5] It has therefore been argued that the revised Companies Act

---

[1]   In the following, unless indicated differently, the abbreviation 'CA' will refer to the Companies Act 2006.

[2]   See Walker, *A Review of Corporate Governance in UK Banks and Other Financial Industry Entities, Final Recommendations* (November 2009); European Commission, 'Corporate governance in financial institutions and remuneration policies' COM (2010) 284; BIS Department for Business, Innovation & Skills, *A long term focus for Corporate Britain: Summary of responses* (2011); EU Commission, 'The EU corporate governance framework' COM (2011) 164 final.

[3]   See for example: A Keay, 'Tackling the issue of the corporate objective: An analysis of the United Kingdom's "Enlightened shareholder value approach"' (2007) 23 *Sydney Law Review* 23.

[4]   B Horrigan, *Corporate Social Responsibility in the 21st Century: Debates, Models and Practices Across Government, Law and Business* (Edward Elgar 2010) 229.

[5]   K Campbell and D Vick, 'Disclosure law and the market for corporate social responsibility' in D McBarnet, A Voiculescu and T Campbell (eds), *The*

has several potential CSR implications.[6] This potential link raises the question to what extent English company law and corporate governance promote or could be further developed to better promote the socially responsible conduct of companies.[7]

The potential significance of company law and corporate governance for CSR was also emphasised in the 2011 final report of the UN Special Representative on the issue of human rights and business (SRSG) John Ruggie. Principle 3 of the UN Guiding Principles on Business and Human Rights recommends that states should, inter alia, ensure that company law does not constrain, but enables respect for human rights.[8] The commentary to this principle makes the criticism that there is 'a lack of clarity in corporate and securities law regarding what companies and their officers are permitted, let alone required, to do regarding human rights'.[9] Moreover, the implications of corporate and securities laws for human rights 'remain poorly understood'.[10] As human rights are an important element of the CSR agenda, this principle shows the potential importance of company law and corporate governance for the promotion of CSR.

New Corporate Accountability: Corporate Social Responsibility and the Law (CUP 2007) 242.

[6]   ibid, 229.

[7]   It is important to note that the Companies Act applies to the whole of the United Kingdom and not just to England and Wales. However, for reasons of consistency in this book, which focusses on English private law, this chapter will refer to English company law. See s1299 CA2006: 'Except as otherwise provided (or the context otherwise requires), the provisions of this Act extend to the whole of the United Kingdom.'

[8]   Principle 3, UN Guiding Principles on Business and Human Rights.

[9]   John Ruggie, *Guiding Principles on Business and Human Rights: Implementing the United Nations 'Protect, Respect and Remedy' Framework*, available at http://www.business-humanrights.org/SpecialRepPortal/Home/Protect-Respect-Remedy-Framework/GuidingPrinciples (accessed 4 November 2014). The comments made by Ruggie refer to company law generally and are not related to a specific national company law.

[10]   ibid.

II. THE CORPORATE PURPOSE AND CSR

A. Linking the Concepts of CSR and Corporate Governance

This chapter focusses on both company law and corporate governance as these are related, but different concepts. The scope of corporate governance is wider.[11]

Corporate governance is commonly understood as 'the set of processes, customs, policies, laws and institutions affecting the way a company is directed, administered or controlled'.[12] This is a short version of the definition of corporate governance, promulgated by the Cadbury Committee which is regarded as the 'the most authoritative definition of corporate governance in the UK'.[13] With regard to its scope, corporate governance focuses on the ownership, direction and control of companies.[14] According to the definition of CSR adopted here, CSR is about

---

[11] Du Plessis notes that the meaning of corporate governance has 'surprisingly not been the topic of many in-depth studies in the past', see: J Du Plessis, 'Corporate law and corporate governance lessons from the past: Ebbs and flows, but far from "the end of history ...": Part 1' (2009) 30 (2) *Company Lawyer* 43–51. The following are considered to be sources of company law: Primary legislation (Companies Act 2006), secondary legislation, rule-making by legislatively created bodies, for instance, the UK Corporate Governance Code, the common law of companies and the company's own constitution. The sources of corporate governance overlap with these, but are more diverse. They also encompass codes, reports and statements of good corporate governance codes prepared, inter alia, by industry groups or individual institutional investors.

[12] R Smerdon, *A Practical Guide to Corporate Governance* (4th edn, Sweet & Maxwell 2007) 1.

[13] J Birds et al. (eds) *Boyle & Birds' Company Law* (8th edn, Jordans 2011) para 11.3. This is the definition used by the Cadbury Commission (1992): 'Corporate governance is the system by which companies are directed and controlled. Boards of directors are responsible for the governance of their companies. The shareholders' role in governance is to appoint the directors and the auditors and to satisfy themselves that an appropriate governance structure is in place. The responsibilities of the board include setting the company's strategic aims, providing the leadership to put them into effect, supervising the management of the business and reporting to shareholders on their stewardship. The board's actions are subject to laws, regulations and the shareholders in general meetings.' The UK Corporate Governance Code also refers to this definition.

[14] K J Hopt, 'Comparative Corporate Governance: The State of the Art and International Regulation' (2011) European Corporate Governance Institute, Law Working Paper 170/2011, 6, available at http://ssrn.com/abstract_id=1713750 (accessed 3 October 2014). Hannigan therefore addresses the following topics in

wider relationships with various stakeholders, not just shareholders.[15]
CSR requires companies to advance the interests of the different stakeholders, for example, the employees and the local community. These
interests are not purely economic. Horrigan makes an important point
about how one's approach to corporate governance defines the relation
between corporate governance and CSR.

> The variety of standpoints from which we might conceive the point of
> corporate governance from the outset inevitably affects the approach we take
> to define what corporate governance means. In turn, this affects how we
> characterise the relation (if any) between corporate governance and CSR.[16]

This observation highlights that there is interdependence between corporate theory, corporate governance and CSR. Corporate theory is the
theoretical framework underlying the system of company law and corporate governance.[17] It is important for the relationship between corporate governance and CSR as it, in Horrigan's words, describes 'the
standpoint from which we conceive the point of corporate governance'.[18]
Millon notes that 'corporate theory can be used to legitimate or criticise
corporate doctrine'.[19] However, he also points out that the actual extent to
which 'normative claims ... are perceived to follow in a determinate way
from the underlying positive assertion is controversial'.[20] Corporate
theory deals with the question in whose interest corporations are run. It
thus determines what the purpose of the company is. The purpose of the
company has an effect on the scope of corporate governance, including

---

her book on Company Law under the heading 'Corporate governance': Directors' duties, shareholders' rights and remedies as well as the composition of the
board, see B Hannigan, *Company Law* (3rd edn, OUP, Oxford 2012).

[15]   Campbell and Vick define CSR in the following way: 'At a minimum the
term implies an obligation on the part of large companies to pursue objectives
advancing the interests of all groups affected by their activities – not just
shareholders, but also employees, consumers, suppliers, creditors and local
communities. These interests are not just economic, but also include environmental, human rights and 'quality of life' concerns. The obligation to be socially
responsible is usually conceived of as being over and above the minimum
requirement imposed on companies by formal legal rules, although this is not
invariably the case.' Campbell and Vick (n 5) 242.

[16]   Horrigan (n 4) 175.

[17]   See for a discussion of the significance of corporate theory: D Millon,
'Theories of the corporation' (1990) *Duke Law Journal* 201, 241.

[18]   Horrigan (n 4) 175.

[19]   Millon (n 17) 241.

[20]   ibid, 241, 243–51.

directors' duties.[21] The underlying corporate theory therefore has an impact on the question whether a company may pursue social and environmental goals.

The underlying corporate theory therefore influences the ability of the system of corporate governance to promote CSR. The theoretical model of the company and CSR can positively correlate with each other or be in conflict with each other depending on the respective position of shareholders and non-shareholders in the model. If the corporate theory focusses on the (short-term) interests of shareholders, then it does not have a positive impact on CSR.[22] However, if the promotion of stakeholders' interests is within the scope of the theoretical framework (e.g. in a pluralist model of the company), then corporate governance can better promote CSR.[23]

Despite these potential overlaps between corporate governance and CSR, the link between the two concepts has, so far, not been widely explored in the academic literature. Horrigan therefore notes that the connection between the two 'does not meet with universal acclaim'.[24] Yet, these two concepts are not 'mutually exclusive'.[25] The various points where CSR and corporate governance meet, for example, the duty to promote the success of the company in s172 CA, demonstrate that corporate governance can be an important tool in the promotion of CSR. The CSR agenda should, therefore, include corporate governance within its focus. Mitchell even argues that 'the most likely way for proponents of CSR to achieve their goals is to recast their issues as issues of corporate governance'.[26]

The following section will briefly review the three theories about the objective of the company that have dominated the discussions in the preparation of the Companies Act 2006, namely the shareholder value theory, the stakeholder value theory and the enlightened shareholder

---

[21] A Keay, *The Enlightened Shareholder Value Principle and Corporate Governance* (Routledge 2013) 14.

[22] However, CSR can be pursued to promote the reputation and, consequently, the sales of a company (often referred to as 'the business case for CSR').

[23] C Nakajima, 'The importance of legally embedding corporate social responsibility' (2011) 32 *Company Lawyer* 257, 258.

[24] Horrigan (n 4) 174.

[25] Nakajima (n 23) 258.

[26] L E Mitchell, 'The board as a path toward corporate social responsibility' in D McBarnet, A Voiculescu and T Campbell (eds), *The New Corporate Accountability: Corporate Social Responsibility and the Law* (CUP 2007) 280.

value theory.[27] The enlightened shareholder value theory underlies the Companies Act 2006. It will therefore be looked at in terms of its implications for CSR.

B. The Background to the Adoption of the Enlightened Shareholder Value Theory

There was a considerable debate about corporate theory in the Company Law Review Steering Group[28] during the discussions about the new Companies Act 2006, as the hitherto prevailing shareholder value doctrine had come under criticism in English law.[29] The Company Law Review Steering Group contrasted the shareholder value theory (also referred to as the Anglo-American model) with the pluralist approach (also referred to as the stakeholder value model, represented, for instance, by Germany and Japan)[30] and a third model, the so-called 'inclusive approach' (also referred to as the enlightened shareholder value theory), which it finally adopted in its White Paper.[31]

---

[27] The 'stakeholder value theory' was referred to as the 'pluralist model' in the review process of English company law that led to the Companies Act 2006. Johnston suggests classifying the two main economic theories that have dominated the long-running shareholder versus stakeholder debate under the headings of the agency model and the productive coalition model, see: A Johnston, 'After the OFR: Can UK shareholder value still be enlightened?' (2006) 4 *EBOLR* 817, 821.

[28] In 1998 the Department of Trade and Industry launched a process of reviewing the Companies Act 1985 with the aim of reforming it. The Company Law Review was made up of a Steering Group, essentially consisting of lawyers and businessmen, and several working groups. See for an overview of the company law review process: Keay (n 21) 65–84.

[29] Johnston (n 27) 817. The Company Law Review Steering Group acknowledged that the shareholder value model had been in operation in English company law, see: Company Law Review, *Modern Company Law for a Competitive Economy: The Strategic Framework* (DTI 1999) paras 5.1.4–5.1.7.

[30] S Wen, 'The magnitude of shareholder value as the overriding objective in the UK: The post-crisis perspective' (2011) 26 (7) *Journal of International Banking Law and Regulation* 325, 326.

[31] For reasons of consistency, the 'pluralist approach' will be referred to as the 'stakeholder value theory' and the 'inclusive approach' as the 'enlightened shareholder value theory' in this book.

i.   The shareholder value theory

The shareholder value doctrine is based on an agency model which has strongly influenced debates about corporate governance in the United States and the United Kingdom.[32] The basis for this agency model lies in Berle and Means' observation known as 'separation of ownership and control'.[33] They identified the situation that the ownership of the company and its control had become divided between the shareholders of the company and its management whereas, originally, it was united in the person of the entrepreneur.[34] As the group of shareholders had increasingly become diverse and geographically dispersed, it experienced difficulty in the exercise of control over the management. In practice, it was often the managers who had gained effective control over the company (the situation is also referred to as 'managerialism'). The identification of this phenomenon initiated the corporate governance debate. The agency theory argues that the directors are the agents of the shareholders.[35] Consequently, the management should be exclusively accountable to the shareholders (who are their principals) and primarily strive to maximise their profit.[36] It has been argued that the preoccupation of this model with shareholders' rights would benefit the company (and society) as it ensures accountability and therefore reduces the likelihood that the board could act in a self-serving way.[37]

Under this model the company is treated as a nexus of contracts, which means that the corporate entity is regarded as a 'legal fiction' created out of explicit and implicit private contracts.[38] According to this theory, the shareholders are the company's residual claimants as the other corporate constituencies have fixed claims, for example, employment contracts. The shareholders are the only constituents whose interest (i.e. dividend) is not secured, for example, by an explicit contract such as a loan agreement. For this reason they only receive what is left (the so-called

---

[32]   A Johnston, *EC Regulation of Corporate Governance* (CUP 2009) 21.

[33]   A Berle and G Means, *The Modern Corporation and Private Property* (Transaction Publishers 1991, originally published in 1932).

[34]   ibid.

[35]   E Fama, 'Agency problems and the theory of the firm' (1980) 88 *Journal of Political Economy* 288.

[36]   S Sheikh and W Rees (eds), *Corporate Governance & Corporate Control* (Cavendish 1995) 10; *Hutton v West Cork Railway Co. Ltd.* [1883] 23 Ch. D. 654, 673.

[37]   H Hansmann and R Kraakman, 'The end of history for corporate law' (2001) 89 *Geo.L.J.* 439, 448.

[38]   W Allen, 'Contracts and communities in corporation law' (1993) 50 *Wash. & Lee L. Rev* 1395, 1400.

'residual earnings') after the company has fulfilled all its other contractual obligations.[39] The shareholders therefore bear the risk of the company as their claim will be the last to be fulfilled, although they have provided the investment.[40] This situation is used as the justification for rewarding the shareholders by way of giving them control over the company and is the reason why directors must work in their interest, that is, by the principle of maximising shareholder value.[41] In this model, shareholders become the owners of the company, or at least of the business, through the purchase of shares.[42] The shareholder value model is said to be clear and certain, as it provides a yardstick to measure the performance of directors.[43]

It has been argued that the shareholder value theory made claims that a company should act in a socially responsible manner irrelevant.[44] Drawing upon the idea that 'the manager is the agent of the individuals who own the corporation', Friedman argues that a director who acts in a socially responsible way would become a 'public employee', although, in fact, he is an 'employee of a private enterprise'.[45] Such a manager would impose taxes on the shareholders.[46] So, with this version of corporate theory, corporate governance and CSR do not overlap with each other as CSR is beyond the scope of corporate governance.

ii. The stakeholder value theory

The stakeholder value theory, also known as the pluralist model or the productive coalition model,[47] proposes that a company should be run in

---

[39]   F Easterbrook and D Fischel, *The Economic Structure of Corporate Law* (Harvard University Press 1991) 25.

[40]   D Fisher, 'The enlightened shareholder value – leaving stakeholders in the dark: Will section 172 (1) of the Companies Act 2006 make directors consider the impact of their decisions on third parties?' (2009) 20 *ICCLR* 10, 11.

[41]   Hansmann and Kraakman (n 37) 449.

[42]   H Hansmann, 'Ownership of the firm' (1988) 4 *Journal of Law, Economics and Organisation* 267.

[43]   See for a discussion of this point: Keay (n 21) 18–20.

[44]   Millon (n 17) 225.

[45]   M Friedman, 'The social responsibility of business is to increase its profits' *New York Times* (New York 13 September 1970) § 6 Magazine.

[46]   ibid.

[47]   M Blair and L Stout, 'A team production theory of corporate law' (1999) 85 *Virginia Law Review* 247.

the interest of all its stakeholders rather than just the shareholders.[48] This theory can therefore be characterised by its recognition of all stakeholders' interests.[49] All parties affected by the activities of the company should be given a place in corporate decision making, albeit differentiated in nature and degree.[50] Directors have the obligation to balance conflicting interests of all stakeholders and they should not automatically give priority to the shareholders.[51] The underlying idea of this approach is that the company functions as a social institution whose conduct has an important impact on people's lives. The proponents of the stakeholder value theory emphasise that individuals owe obligations to each other in a community independent of contract.[52] Senior managers are seen as the trustees of the corporation's assets which they strive to sustain. According to this model, companies should seek to maximise the total creation of wealth instead of purely maximising profit.[53] Supporters of the stakeholder value theory question the theoretical underpinnings of the shareholder value theory. In particular, it is disputed that shareholders 'own' the company.[54] The argument is that, by purchasing shares, shareholders would acquire a title to the shares but not to the company. They can therefore not 'own' the company. This argument would follow from the company's separate personality (as evolved in the case *Salomon v Salomon*[55]). Moreover, proponents of the stakeholder value theory argue that shareholders are not the only constituents who invest in the

---

[48]   R Freeman, *Strategic Management: A Stakeholder Approach* (Pitman/Ballinger 1984).

[49]   The term stakeholder is unclear. Freeman has defined stakeholders as 'any group or individual who can affect or is affected by the achievement of the organisation's objectives', see: Freeman (n 48) 246. See for an overview of the discussion: (n 21) 47.

[50]   J Dean, 'Stakeholding and company law' (2001) 22 *Company Lawyer* 66, 69.

[51]   Company Law Review, *Modern Company Law for a Competitive Economy: The Strategic Framework* (DTI 1999) para 5.1.13.

[52]   D Millon, 'Communitarians, contractarians, and the crisis in corporate law' (1993) 50 *Wash. & Lee L.Rev.* 1373, 1382.

[53]   J Kay and A Silberston, *Corporate governance*, available at http://www.johnkay.com (accessed 13 November 2014).

[54]   P Ireland, 'Company law and the myth of shareholder ownership' (1999) 62 *MLR* 32.

[55]   *Salomon v Salomon & Co* [1897] AC 22.

firm and have a stake in it.[56] For example, employees invest in training
which is tailored to the needs of the firm or suppliers invest in machines
which produce goods needed by a specific company to which they supply
goods (called 'firm-specific investment').[57] The stakeholder value theory
is based on the idea that the interests of these stakeholders should not be
subordinated to those of the shareholders, as the company benefits from
the investments of all its stakeholders.[58]

Blair and Stout view the public corporation as 'a team of people who
enter into a complex agreement to work together for their mutual gain'.[59]
In their view, all members of the team have agreed to give up control
rights and, consequently, no member of the team is a principal of the
other team members.[60] The corporation operates under a 'mediating
hierarchy'.[61] Blair and Stout focus on the central position of the board of
directors who are given the control rights over the company.[62] The
directors are 'trustees for the corporation itself'.[63] They are 'mediating
hierarchs' who balance the competing interests of the various members of

---

[56]   G Kelly and J Parkinson, 'The conceptual foundations of the company: A
pluralist approach' (1998) *CfiLR* 174, 188.

[57]   ibid.

[58]   J Dean, 'Stakeholding and company law' (2001) 22 *Company Lawyer* 66,
69. Moreover, linked to this argument, it is important to take account of a recent
study that has researched from the year 1993 to 2009 the performance of 180
companies that have either voluntarily adopted sustainability mechanisms or that
have followed a traditional profit maximisation approach. The results from that
study show that in 2009 those companies which have voluntarily pursued CSR
matters (named as High Sustainability companies) have outperformed those that
have not, both in terms of stock market and accounting measures. The study
matched a sample of 180 companies. Ninety companies were classified as High
Sustainability companies due to their voluntary adoption of CSR policies. The
other 90 companies were classified as Low Sustainability firms because they had
not adopted policies guiding their impact on the society and the environment.
See: R Eccles, I Ioannou and G Serafeim, 'The impact of corporate sustainability
on organizational processes and performance' (2011) Harvard Business School
Working Paper, 12-035, available at http://papers.ssrn.com/sol3/papers.cfm?
abstract_id=1964011 (accessed 21 November 2014).

[59]   Blair and Stout (n 47) 278.

[60]   ibid, 277.

[61]   ibid, 278.

[62]   ibid, 276.

[63]   ibid, 281.

the team in a way that ensures the functioning of the productive coalition.[64]

With its emphasis on the team production process, this model of the company enables directors to pursue the interests of all groups affected by a company, that is, to act in a socially responsible way. The directors are given discretion to make decisions that benefit the team as a whole. Under this version of corporate theory, corporate governance and CSR are coterminous.[65] Corporate governance allows the promotion of CSR goals, as priority should not automatically be given to shareholders. The reason for pursuing CSR can be based both on the argument that it ensures the productive functioning of the team, as well as the idea that the company is a social institution.

iii. The enlightened shareholder value theory

Following a discussion of these two theories, the government's White Paper finally settled upon an approach which it calls the 'inclusive approach'.[66] This approach is known as the 'enlightened shareholder value theory'.[67] It was seen as a possible 'third way', an alternative to strict shareholder primacy on the one hand and the stakeholder value theory on the other hand.[68] The enlightened shareholder value theory continues to give primacy ultimately to the interests of shareholders, but it requires directors also to consider other factors related to the interests of various other stakeholders who are affected by the company.[69] This theory is premised on the belief that long-term profit maximisation can only occur through the fostering of co-operative relationships with the

---

[64] ibid.

[65] J Solomon and A Solomon, *Corporate Governance and Accountability* (John Wiley & Sons Ltd. 2003) 24.

[66] Company Law Review, *The White Paper: Modernising Company Law* (DTI 2002, Cm 5553-I and Cm 5553-II) para 3.3. See for an overview of the background to the adoption of the enlightened shareholder value model: Keay (n 21) Chapter 3.

[67] D French, S Mayson and C Ryan, *Mayson, French & Ryan on Company Law* (28th edn, OUP 2011–12) para 1.6.4.3. See for a detailed analysis of the enlightened shareholder value model: Keay (n 21).

[68] D Millon, 'Enlightened shareholder value, social responsibility and the redefinition of corporate purpose without law' in P M Vasudev and S Watson (eds), *Corporate Governance after the Financial Crisis* (Edward Elgar 2012) 69.

[69] J Ho, 'Is section 172 of the Companies Act 2006 the guidance for CSR?' (2010) 31 *Company Lawyer* 207, 209.

various non-shareholder constituents.[70] It is argued that this theory would better promote wealth generation and competitiveness for the benefit of all.

The enlightened shareholder value model is embedded in the shareholder value theory[71] as directors have to act in the collective best interest of shareholders.[72] However, the directors are also required to recognise the company's need to promote its relationships with employees and suppliers and its impact on the environment as well as the community.[73] This theory does not support purely short-term financial benefits, but rather promotes the pursuing of long-term gains.[74] The focus on short-term gains was a common criticism of British businesses in the 1980s and 1990s.[75] A study conducted by the Institute of Directors in 1999 found that many directors thought they were legally required to maximise short-term shareholder benefits to the detriment of long-term profit.[76] The Company Law Review Steering Group therefore identified directors' duties as well as corporate reporting duties to be important for the implementation of the enlightened shareholder value doctrine.[77] The enlightened shareholder value theory is said to be enshrined in the duty of directors to promote the success of the company in s172 (1) CA.[78] Although the enlightened shareholder value theory does not support an understanding of corporate governance and CSR as coterminous, as the stakeholder value theory does, Millon states that it 'resonates with notions of CSR'.[79] In Yap's view, the concept of CSR lies behind the

[70] L Roach, 'The legal model of the company and the company law review' (2005) 26 *Company Lawyer* 98, 99.
[71] A Keay, 'Section 172(1) of the Companies Act 2006: An interpretation and assessment' (2007) 28 *Company Lawyer* 106, 107.
[72] Company Law Review, *Modern Company Law for a Competitive Economy: Developing the Framework* (DTI 2000) para 2.22.
[73] Horrigan (n 4) 223.
[74] Company Law Review, *Modern Company Law for a Competitive Economy: Developing the Framework* (DTI 2000) para 2.22.
[75] Commission on Public Policy and British Business, *Promoting Prosperity: A Business Agenda for Britain* (Vintage 1997).
[76] Institute of Directors, *Good Boardroom Practice* (IOD 1999).
[77] Company Law Review, *Modern Company Law, Final Report* (DTI 2001) para 3.8.
[78] Wen (n 30) 330.
[79] D Millon (n 68) 68.

enlightened shareholder value principle.[80] Moreover, Horrigan argues that the reform of UK company law 'is pregnant with potential CSR implications'.[81]

With its emphasis on fostering relationships with all stakeholders, the enlightened shareholder model at least potentially opens up the scope of corporate governance for CSR. To what extent company law and corporate governance, within the enlightened shareholder model, actually promote the socially responsible conduct of companies will be analysed in the following part of the chapter. The analysis first addresses the two areas identified by the Company Law Review Steering Group for the implementation of the enlightened shareholder value approach, namely, directors' duties (s172 CA) and non-financial reporting (s414A CA). It then addresses two further areas of company law and corporate governance that can contribute to the promotion of CSR: Shareholders' remedies and the board.

III. DIRECTORS' DUTIES: THE DUTY TO PROMOTE THE SUCCESS OF THE COMPANY (S172 CA)

The duty to promote the success of the company in s172 (1) CA has been met with much interest both in academia and in practice since its implementation into the Companies Act 2006.[82] S172 (1) CA reads as follows:

> A director of a company must act in the way he considers, in good faith, would be most likely to promote the success of the company for the benefit of its members as a whole, and in doing so have regard (amongst other matters) to –
>
> (a) the likely consequences of decisions in the long term,
> (b) the interests of the company's employees,
> (c) the need to foster relationships with suppliers, customers and others,

---

[80] J L Yap, 'Considering the enlightened shareholder value principle' (2010) 31 *Company Lawyer* 35, 37.

[81] Horrigan (n 4) 229.

[82] See for example: A Keay, 'The duty to promote the success of the company: Is it fit for purpose in a post-financial crisis world?' in J Loughrey (ed.), *Directors' Duties and Shareholder Litigation in the Wake of the Financial Crisis* (Edward Elgar 2013) 50; J Loughrey, A Keay and L Cerioni, 'Legal practitioners, enlightened shareholder value and the shaping of corporate governance' (2008) 8 (1) *JCLS* 79; Ho (n 69) 207; Keay (n 71) 106.

(d) the impact of the company's operations on the community and the environment,

(e) the desirability of the company maintaining a reputation for high standards of business and

(f) the need to act fairly between members of the company.

Prior to this Act, directors' duties were not regulated within the Companies Act, but based on common law. It has been argued that the duty in s172 CA encapsulates in statute the enlightened shareholder value theory.[83] Accepting this interpretation, this section analyses to what extent this duty promotes CSR. The analysis of s172 (1) CA will first look at the overlap between the duty and CSR. It will then interpret the meaning of the individual components of s172 (1) CA which are: 'good faith', 'success of the company for the benefit of its members as a whole' and 'having regard to', and their effect on pursuing CSR aims. S172 CA will be analysed with regard to its wording, its review in the academic literature and with references to the case law. Finally, this section of the chapter will analyse the enforceability of s172 (1) CA.

A. Overlap between s172 CA and CSR

S172 (1) CA enlists a number of factors that a director must 'have regard to' when discharging his duty to promote the success of the company for the benefit of its members as a whole. The list of factors in s172 (1) CA explicitly refers to various stakeholders, such as the employees, the suppliers, and customers, as well as the community and the environment. Although several factors are given explicit mention in s172 (1) CA the list of factors is non-exhaustive, as indicated by the clause 'amongst other matters'. The list in s172 (1) overlaps with the definition of CSR adopted in this book, according to which companies have an obligation to pursue objectives advancing the interests of all groups affected by their activities – not just shareholders but also employees, consumers, suppliers, creditors and local communities.[84] This definition of CSR also refers to environmental, human rights and 'quality of life' concerns. So, on comparison, several of the factors that are referred to in s172 (1) CA are also expressly included in the CSR definition adopted here. These are employees, suppliers, customers and others, the impact on the community and environment. Hence, there is a considerable overlap between s172 (1) CA and CSR, although the two are not entirely coterminous.

---

[83] Yap (n 80) 37.
[84] Campbell and Vick (n 5) 242.

Although the list in s172 (1) CA does not expressly refer to creditors, they are mentioned in s172 (3) CA which stipulates that the duty in s172 (1) CA 'has effect subject to any enactment or rule of law requiring directors, in certain circumstances, to consider or act in the interests of creditors of the company'.[85]

The duty of directors to consider some of the factors now contained in s172 (1) CA is not entirely new, but a mere repetition of the previous legal situation.[86] Apart from the employees[87] and the creditors,[88] this point applies to the need to act fairly as between members of the company[89] and the obligation to have regard to the likely consequences of any decision in the long term.[90] These issues were recognised as interests a director needs to consider in the old common law. The factors that are indeed new are the need to foster business relationships with suppliers, customers and others,[91] the impact of operations on the community and the environment[92] and the desirability of maintaining a reputation for high standards of business conduct.[93] The effect of this expansion of factors in s172 (1) CA is that when directors discharge their duty to act in the best interest of the company, they must consider a wider spectrum of aspects than under the previous situation. The new duty is therefore considered to be more inclusive.[94]

Based on these considerations, it can be stated that the list of factors in s172 CA overlaps with many concerns of CSR, but that the inclusion of some of these considerations into the decision-making process is not entirely new for directors' duties. Nevertheless, due to the overlap between the list of factors in s172 (1) CA and CSR, it has been argued that CSR is 'implicit in s172'.[95] Ho opines that s172 provides the

---

[85]　This provision refers to the common law principle that directors of an insolvent company must consider the interests of its creditors. *West Mercia Safetywear Ltd v Dodd* [1988] BCLC 250.

[86]　Hannigan (n 14) para 9-29.

[87]　S309 Companies Act 1985.

[88]　*West Mercia Safetywear Ltd v Dodd* [1988] BCLC 250.

[89]　*Mutual Life Insurance Co of New York v Rank Organisation Ltd* [985] BCLC 11. This duty is now found in s172 (1) (f) CA.

[90]　*Gaiman v National Association for Mental Health* [1971] Ch 317, at 330. This duty is now found in s172 (1) (a) CA.

[91]　S172 (1) (c) CA.

[92]　S172 (1) (d) CA.

[93]　S172 (1) (f) CA.

[94]　Hannigan (n 14) para 9–29.

[95]　Yap (n 80) 37.

guidance for CSR.[96] The Ministerial Statements by Margaret Hodge claim that section 172 CA would 'mark a radical departure in articulating the connection between what is good for a company and what is good for society at large'.[97] She went on to give CSR a mention in this context by stating that 'Corporate social responsibility has developed and evolved over time'.[98] All of the factors considered so far suggest a clear correlation between s172 (1) CA and CSR. The question remains, however, to what extent this duty of directors in s172 CA actually promotes or has the potential to promote CSR. This issue will now be analysed by looking at the different components of the section.

B. Good Faith

The duty in s172 (1) CA requires a director to act in the way he considers, in good faith, would be in the best interest of the company. The relevant question for the promotion of CSR through this duty is what standard the courts apply to this test when assessing the issue if a director has breached his duty to promote the success of the company for the benefit of its members as a whole.

The wording of s172 (1) CA emphasises the terms 'he considers' and 'in good faith'. The inclusion of these two terms gives priority to the director's judgement. These terms put the emphasis on what the director considers, in good faith, to be in the best interest of the company, and not on the views of third parties, for instance the court. Through this emphasis, the section distinguishes between the considerations of the director and the court. This situation is in line with the approach which was taken to the previous common law duty to act bona fide for the company before the codification of directors' duties in the Companies Act 2006.[99] As s170 (4) CA stipulates a requirement to interpret the general duties in the same way as common law rules or equitable principles, it is likely that the courts will refer to the case law pertaining to the old common law duty to act bona fide for the company when interpreting the 'good faith' provision. The reason is that 'good faith' can be seen as a continuation of the previous 'bona fide' requirement. This interpretation was indicated in the case *Cobden Investments Ltd v RWM*

---

[96]   Ho (n 69) 210.

[97]   DTI, 'Companies Act 2006, Duties of company directors, Ministerial statements' Introduction by Margaret Hodge (2007) 1.

[98]   ibid.

[99]   A Keay, 'Good faith and directors' duty to promote the success of their company' (2011) 32 *Company Lawyer* 138, 139.

Langport Ltd[100] which was decided after the enactment of the Companies Act 2006 and where the judge said:

> The perhaps old-fashioned phrase acting '*bona fide* in the interests of the company' is reflected in the statutory words acting 'in good faith in a way most likely to promote the success of the company for the benefit of its members as a whole'. They come to the same thing with the modern formulation giving a more readily understood definition of the scope of the duty.[101]

The traditional approach to acting 'bona fide' is embodied in the case *Re Smith and Fawcett Ltd*[102] in which it was held that directors of a company must act '… bona fide in what they consider – not what a court may consider – is in the interest of the company, and not for any collateral purpose'. The test was discussed in the case *Regentcrest plc v Cohen* where the court emphasised that it would focus on 'the director's state of mind'.[103] This formulation of the court indicates that the test is a subjective one. This situation demonstrates that the courts are unwilling to interfere with the judgement of the directors 'with the benefit of hindsight'.[104] The interpretation of 'good faith' in s172 CA taken in *Cobden Investments Ltd v RWM Langport Ltd*[105] was followed in other recent decisions which were made after the enactment of the Companies Act 2006. In *Iesini v Westrip Holdings Ltd*,[106] the court held that it was not in the best position to make judgements about the weight of the considerations in s172 CA except in very clear cases as these are commercial issues and the directors' subjective judgements would prevail in these circumstances.

The courts are therefore not likely to second-guess decisions by the directors with regard to how to promote the success of the company. This finding has ramifications for the importance given to the interests of the various stakeholders, listed in s172 (1) CA. As the good faith test is firmly grounded in subjectivity, the key point for assessing how directors have discharged their duty is their subjective opinion as to whether a

---

[100]   [2008] EWHC 2810 (Ch) [52].
[101]   *Cobden Investments Limited v RWM Langport Ltd, Southern Counties Fresh Foods Limited, Romford Wholesale Meats Limited* [2008] EWHC 2810 (Ch) [52].
[102]   [1942] Ch 304 [306].
[103]   [2001] 2 BCLC 80 [105].
[104]   Ibid [106]–[107].
[105]   [2008] EWHC 2810 (Ch).
[106]   [2009] EWHC 2526.

decision was meant to promote the best interest of the company. It will therefore be difficult to find directors to be in breach of their s172 (1) CA duty as long as they can convince the judge that they acted in good faith in their decision making. This situation is a severe limitation of the enforcement of the duty to consider the interests of the various stake-holders through s172 (1) CA. In turn, it means that although s172 (1) CA overlaps with the concept of CSR, it is doubtful if CSR will be promoted through this duty. It rather remains in the discretion of directors to consider how to balance the interests of the various stakeholders and how much weight to give to these in the decision-making process.

C.   Success of the Company for the Benefit of the Members as a Whole

The next issue is what the term 'success of the company for the benefit of its members as a whole' means for the pursuing of CSR goals. The directors must have regard to the list of factors in s172 (1) CA when working towards promoting the success of the company. The question is to what extent CSR forms part of the goal of promoting the 'success' of the company. Keay points out that there is no indication in s172 (1) CA as to the meaning of what fulfils the requirement 'success of the company'.[107] He suspects that this is because directors can fulfil their duty to promote the success of the company under the same precondi-tions as the 'good faith' requirement, that is, when they believe their action to do so, even if it does not do so objectively.

The Guidance on Key Clauses in the Company Law Reform Bill states that:

> the decision as to what will promote success, and what constitutes such success, is one for the directors' good faith judgment. This ensures that business decisions on, for example, strategy and tactics are for the directors and not subject to decisions by the courts, subject to good faith.[108]

Guidance as to what constitutes 'success of the company' can be found in the case law pertaining to the common law prior to the Companies Act 2006. In fact, the 'new' duty in s172 CA has its origins in the previous common law fiduciary duty for directors to act bona fide in what they

---

[107]   Keay (n 71) 109.
[108]   DTI, Guidance on Key Clauses to the Company Law Reform Bill (2005) para 63.

consider to be in the best interests of the company.[109] In this common law duty, the interest of the company was interpreted as meaning the shareholders as a general body. The notion of promoting the interests of the various stakeholders of the company was not included in this concept. This interpretation led to the idea of enhancing shareholder value.[110] The shareholder-centricity of English company law can be traced back to the origins of English company law which evolved out of partnership law in the nineteenth century.[111] At that time the shareholders were considered to be 'the company' (i.e. the joint stock company), as there was not yet any conception of the company as an object separate from its shareholders. Despite this long history of shareholder-centricity of English company law, the focus of directors on maximising shareholder value has been particularly dominant in the US and the UK since the 1980s.[112] The concept of CSR with its focus on the interests of the stakeholders does not form part of this concept, unless it promotes the value of the shareholders.

Under the s172 (1) CA duty, directors must promote the success of the company for the benefit of its members as a whole. Membership of a company is normally based on shareholding.[113] The expression 'members as a whole' is understood by the courts as present and future shareholders.[114] This prioritisation of shareholders suggests that directors are only allowed to pursue CSR if it ultimately benefits the shareholders. CSR can therefore easily be reduced to a secondary issue in the directors'

---

[109] Hannigan (n 14) para 9-1.

[110] *Hutton v West Cork Railway Company* (1883) 23 Ch. D. 654; *Re Smith & Facett Ltd* [1942] Ch [304], [306]; *Second Savoy Hotel Investigation*, Report of the Inspector (1954) HMSO; *Parke v Daily News Ltd* [1962] Ch. 927; *Gaiman v National Association for Mental Health* [1971] Ch 317.

[111] Ireland (n 54) 39. See for an historical overview: P Ireland, 'Limited liability, shareholder rights and the problem of corporate irresponsibility' (2010) 34 *Cambridge Journal of Economics* 837.

[112] M Omran, P Atrill and J Pointon, 'Shareholders versus stakeholders: Corporate mission statements and investor returns' (2002) 11 *Business Ethics: A European Review* 318. It is said that the exclusive focus of corporations on shareholder value developed during the Reagan and Thatcher years, see: W Lazonick and M O'Sullivan, 'Maximizing shareholder value: A new ideology for corporate governance' (2000) 29 *Economy and Society* 13, 14.

[113] French, Mayson and Ryan (n 67) para 14.2.

[114] See *Gaiman v National Association for Mental Health* (1971) Ch [317], [330].

decision-making process. Parliamentary debates about the new Companies Act acknowledged that success is usually measured by the long-term increase of shareholder value, but it may also be fulfilled by pursuing other goals, if that is the purpose of the firm.[115] The Company Law Review Steering Group declared that it inserted 'success of the company for the benefit of its members as a whole' into the provision in order to emphasise that the directors do not work to favour the individual interests of members, but for the interests of the members as an association.[116]

Although there has so far not been much case law about the new duty in s172 CA, it seems that the courts, by and large, considered it to be merely the codification of the previous duty to act bona fide in the best interest of the company.[117] This finding suggests that 'success of the company' is a continuation of the duty under the old common law to work in 'the best interests of the company' with the ultimate goal of the directors' decisions being the promotion of the benefit of the shareholders. Stakeholders and hence the concept of CSR are not given a prominent role in the term 'success of the company'. Although CSR might be implicit in s172 (1) CA,[118] this duty of directors is limited in its ability to promote CSR. The impact of CSR on the directors' decision making will be limited to those instances where there is a clear business case for pursuing CSR objects.

D.   Having Regard for the List of Factors

Despite the significant overlap between the list of factors in s172 (1) CA and the concept of CSR, the question remains what role do these factors play in the decision-making process of directors. This issue depends on how one interprets the duty of directors to 'have regard to' the list of factors.

The first issue in relation to the phrase 'having regard to' is that the list of factors in s172 (1) CA does not contain any guidance about how directors should balance between the different factors. There is a lack of clarity about the weight given to the various considerations. This is particularly a problem in the case of competing interests, for example,

---

[115]   HL Deb, vol 678, GC 255-8 (6 February 2006).

[116]   The Company Law Review, *Modern Company Law for a Competitive Economy: Developing the Framework* (DTI 2000) para 3-51.

[117]   *Re West Coast Capital (LIOS) Ltd* [2008] CSOH [72]; *Cobden Investments Ltd v RWM Langport Ltd* [2008] EWHC 2810 (Ch).

[118]   Yap (n 80) 37.

where a decision favours one factor (e.g. the environment), but disadvantages another factor (e.g. the employees).[119] It is also not made clear in the provision if directors are obliged to choose the factor that is likely to be most beneficial for shareholders in a particular situation.[120] However, seeing that 'success of the company' is interpreted to favour the interests of shareholders it seems that every factor may only be taken into account insofar as it ultimately favours the interests of the company's members, that is, the shareholders.

The second issue is that s172 (1) CA only requires directors to 'have regard to' the factors while they discharge their duty to promote the success of the company for the benefit of the members as a whole. 'Having regard to' is a very vague concept which does not mandate more than to consider the factors enlisted in s172 (1) CA. It seems that the relationship between the 'success of the company for the benefit of its members as a whole' and 'having regard' to the list of factors is one of subordination. The analysis of 'success of the company' in the previous part has shown that directors must ultimately strive to enhance shareholder value when they work towards the promotion of the success of the company. The same finding applies in relation to the provision 'having regard to'. Directors must 'only' have regard to the list of factors in s172 (1) CA while they promote the interests of the members as a whole, that is, the shareholders.

Thirdly, the little case law that exists about s172 (1) CA further adds to the cautious view taken here about the role of the stakeholders listed in s172 (1) CA in the directors' decision-making process. The case *R. (on the application of People & Planet) v HM Treasury*[121] is important for the analysis about how directors must 'have regard to' the list of factors. Here, the High Court had the opportunity to consider the scope of the duty in s172 CA and the importance of the interests of the stakeholders. The case was brought against the government as it had bought a stake of about 84 per cent of the shares of the Royal Bank of Scotland (RBS).[122] The government's ownership of RBS was arranged through a limited company, UK Financial Investments Ltd (UKFI).[123] RBS is a significant provider of financing to the energy industry. This situation led to a

[119] ibid.
[120] A Keay, 'Enlightened shareholder value' (2006) *LMCLQ* 335, 352.
[121] [2009] EWHC 3020 (Admin) (QBD (Admin))
[122] J Treanor, *RBS axes 3,700 jobs as taxpayer stake hits 84 per cent*, The *Guardian*, 2 November 2009, available at http://www.guardian.co.uk/business/2009/nov/02/rbs-slash-costs-cuts-jobs (accessed 13 November 2014).
[123] UKFI Annual Report 2008/9, 46.

challenge by activists of the student network People & Planet which
works in the areas of poverty, human rights and the environment. People
& Planet disagreed with HM Treasury Policy regarding UKFI's management of RBS on the basis of the statutory norms regarding the protection
of the environment in s172 (1) CA.[124] Due to the peculiarities with the
government owning the shares, the litigation in this case was not based
on a shareholder derivative action, but on judicial review. The government agreed to a policy document in which it decided not to intervene in
the day-to-day management decisions. This approach confirmed a commercial approach as the best way for UKFI to achieve its objectives. The
court rejected the application for permission to bring judicial review
proceedings. It argued that to go beyond the commercial approach would
'cut across the fundamental legal duty of boards to manage their
companies in the interest of all their shareholders'.[125]

Notably, the court held that had the government sought to impose its
own policy on combating climate change and promoting human rights on
the board of RBS, this would have 'cut across the duties of the RBS
Board as set out in s172 (1)'.[126] UKFI could properly seek to influence
the board of RBS to have regard to environmental and human rights
considerations in accordance with its duty under s172 CA 2006, but this
would be a step too far for the Treasury. This decision is significant as
the court noted that, if shareholders seek to influence the decisions of
the management, they could only influence directors to act within the
constraints of s172 CA (which means the shareholder prerogative). The
limit of enforcing the consideration of the list of factors in s172 (1) CA is
therefore the promotion of shareholder value. Consequently, CSR considerations may only be pursued to the extent that these promote the
business case. Secondly, the court pointed out that there is then a risk of
litigation by minority shareholders who could complain that the value of
their shares had been detrimentally affected.[127] This argument further
supports the interpretation of the previous point that the stakeholder-
oriented considerations to which a director must have regard in s172 (1)
CA are subordinated under the interests of the shareholders. Following
the High Court's decision, one should be cautious as to the effect of
s172 (1) CA on the promotion of CSR.

---

[124] S Copp, 's172 of the Companies Act 2006 fails people and planet?'
(2010) 31 (12) *Company Lawyer* 406.
[125] *R. (on the Application of People and Planet) v HM Treasury* [2009]
EWHC 3020 (Admin), [13e].
[126] ibid, at para 34.
[127] ibid.

The analysis of the meaning of 'having regard to' has shown that the interests of the members are given priority over the various stakeholders referred to in the non-exhaustive list of factors in the second part of s172 (1) CA.[128] Effectively, this means that the concept of CSR is not considered as an end in itself, but only as a means to an end, namely to increase shareholder value. The term 'having regard to' subordinates CSR under the goal of enhancing shareholder value. The interests of shareholders are prioritised through the phrase 'having regard to' as these factors are only considered as aspects a director must consider when pursuing the ultimate goal of promoting the interests of the company's members.

E. Enforceability

Having analysed the different components of s172 (1) CA with regard to their effect on the promotion of CSR, the question remains how enforceable claims about an alleged breach of this duty are. The principal position is that the proper claimant in respect of a wrong allegedly done to the company is the company ('proper plaintiff rule').[129] It is therefore up to the management to decide whether or not to pursue a claim. The only group which could have a right to bring proceedings in the case of an alleged breach of the s172 CA duty are shareholders. They can bring a derivative action pursuant to s260 CA. This action will be analysed below.

It is notable that the various groups listed in s172 (1) CA are not given legal standing. One can therefore argue that the provision lacks teeth in terms of the enforcement of the interests of these groups. This situation is likely to have a limiting effect on the promotion of CSR through s172 (1) CA. The reason is that the board of directors and the shareholders, as the only groups who have standing to bring a claim for an alleged breach of s172 (1) CA, are usually more concerned with the protection of their

---

[128] Pedamon criticises that the board's final decision might ignore all factors listed in s172 (1) CA as long as it can justify that it has at least considered them. This would reduce the consideration of the interests of the various stakeholders 'to a box-ticking exercise'. See C Pedamon, 'Corporate Social Responsibility: A new approach to promoting integrity and responsibility' (2010) 31 (6) *Company Lawyer* 172, 175. Keay points out that there is no explanation given whether directors should consider stakeholder interests per se or only insofar as they benefit shareholders, Keay (n 120) 352.

[129] *Foss v Harbottle* (1843) 2 Hare 461; see Hannigan (n 14) para 18-13.

interests, that is, the promotion of shareholder value. As the various stakeholders listed in s172 (1) CA cannot bring a claim for an alleged non-consideration of their interests, it is less likely that their interests are enforced at all, unless socially minded shareholders litigate. The practical effects of s172 (1) CA for the promotion of CSR are therefore further limited.

The academic literature has consequently assessed the enforceability of s172 (1) CA in a rather cautious manner. Birds calls the effect of s172 CA 'likely to be educational rather than in any sense restrictive'.[130] In his opinion, business decisions taken in good faith will not be any more easily challengeable than they were prior to the CA 2006. This situation has been rightly called 'a right without a remedy'.[131] Keay therefore concludes that 'there is certainly an enforcement problem with the provision'.[132] He points out that there is an absence of significant case law with regard to this section even though the Companies Act has been in force for some years now.[133] On the basis of the analysis here, it seems that it is the way in which s172 (1) CA has been drafted, with its emphasis on good faith decisions of directors and its prioritisation of shareholder value, that is the principal reason for the lack of enforcement of the provision.

F.   The Promotion of CSR through s172 (1) CA

The analysis of s172 (1) CA provides a rather limited effect of this duty for the promotion of CSR. The priority attributed to shareholder value is a continuation of the legal situation prior to the enactment of the Companies Act 2006. In particular, the analysis of the requirements 'good faith' and 'success of the company' have revealed considerable conformity between the old common law duty to work bona fide in the interest of the company and s172 (1) CA. Where directors were previously required to work in the interest of the company, understood as meaning the shareholders as a general body, s172 (1) CA now stipulates that directors must promote the success of the company for the benefit of its members as a whole which are in fact the shareholders. This result demonstrates that CSR is only a secondary consideration for directors.

---

[130]   Birds et al. (n 13) para 16.5.1.
[131]   Fisher (n 40) 15.
[132]   A Keay (n 82) 95.
[133]   ibid, 86.

This outcome is further confirmed by the results of a recent evaluation of the Companies Act 2006, commissioned by the Department for Business Innovation & Skills (BIS).[134] The study showed that there is a need among business and stakeholders to add clarity and guidance for s172 CA in order to boost awareness and understanding to increase behavioural change.[135] The responses from businesses confirm the scepticism about the practical impact of s172 CA. Less than a fifth of companies overall which were aware of this duty agreed that it had affected the behaviour of directors and over three-fifths disagreed that the change had impacted the behaviour of directors.[136] A further important distinction is that among interviewees significantly more directors disagreed that the change had affected their behaviour (91 per cent) as opposed to non-directors (64 per cent). These results show that although there is high awareness of the changes made in relation to directors' duties in the CA 2006 (79 per cent were aware of this), only few directors have yet changed their decision-making process as a consequence of the new duty in s172 (1) CA. This evaluation provides for rather pessimistic reading from a CSR point of view, as the vast majority of directors have stated that they have not changed their decision making following the introduction of s172 CA, it is unlikely that they are going to pursue CSR goals to a greater extent than they have done in the past. This point further confirms the result of the analysis above: That the practical effects of s172 (1) CA for the promotion of CSR are limited.

In light of the findings of this section, it is doubtful if the enlightened shareholder value doctrine that underlies the s172 (1) CA duty really marks a shift away from the legal situation prior to the enactment of the Companies Act. At least directors have discretion in how they discharge this duty, including considerations above and beyond short-term shareholder gains. It is right that directors make 'good faith' decisions about the promotion of the interests of shareholders and the consideration of

---

[134] The evaluation is based on a quantitative telephone survey of 1001 businesses (amongst people in companies who are responsible for corporate governance) and in-depth interviews of 15 stakeholders. See: Department for Business Innovation & Skills, *Evaluation of the Companies Act 2006, Executive Summary* (2010), available at https://www.gov.uk/government/uploads/system/uploads/attachment_data/file/31657/10-1362-evaluation-companies-act-2006-executive-summary.pdf (accessed 13 November 2014).

[135] ibid.

[136] Department for Business, Innovation and Skills, *Evaluation of the Companies Act 2006, Volume One* (2010) 72 available at https://www.gov.uk/government/uploads/system/uploads/attachment_data/file/31655/10-1360-evaluation-companies-act-2006-volume-1.pdf (accessed 13 November 2014).

stakeholder interests which they can balance in different ways.[137] Nevertheless, this chapter has shown that this was already possible under the
common law duties prior to the Companies Act 2006. Directors can
promote CSR, if they believe that it promotes the benefit of the company
in the long run, but CSR remains subordinated under shareholder value.
Because shareholder value and the concerns of CSR are not always
coincidental and might well be in conflict, this subordination is a severe
limitation of the s172 (1) CA duty for the promotion of CSR.

Therefore, it appears unlikely that the duty to promote the success of
the company in s172 (1) CA will fundamentally change the way directors
run the company under the Companies Act 2006. S172 (1) CA can be
regarded as a general statement with limited practical effects. It is still
subject to what is called the 'historical magnitude of a corporation as a
vehicle for shareholder value maximisation'.[138]

IV. THE STRATEGIC REPORT (S414A CA)

The duty to promote the success of the company pursuant to s172 (1) CA
is linked with the strategic report in s414A CA which was previously the
business review in s417 CA. The enlightened shareholder value model
was implemented through s172 CA as well as the business review.[139] As
a result of the consultation process on the state of narrative reporting in
the UK the government replaced the business review by a strategic report
in 2013.[140]

A. Legislative Requirements for the Strategic Report

Companies are required to file a directors' report for each financial year
of the company, s415 (1) CA. Pursuant to s414A (1) CA the directors'
must prepare a strategic report, unless the company is entitled to the
small companies' exemption.[141] The purpose of this strategic report is to
inform members of the company and help them assess how the directors

---

[137] Ho (n 69) 212.
[138] Wen (n 30) 336.
[139] A Keay (n 21) 83.
[140] BIS, *The Future of Narrative Reporting: A new structure for narrative
reporting in the UK* (October 2012), available at http://www.bis.gov.uk/assets/
BISCore/business-law/docs/F/12-979-future-of-narrative-reporting-new-structure.
pdf (accessed 12 November 2014).
[141] s414B CA.

have performed their duty under s172 CA.[142] The strategic report is relevant for this chapter insofar as the list of factors in s172 (1) CA to which a director must have regard when making decisions overlap with CSR. The reporting duty therefore requires directors to inform members about how they have discharged their duty to promote the success of the company, including the pursuing of CSR goals. With this transparency, the strategic report can contribute to the promotion of CSR. The current legislative reform of narrative reporting at European level which seeks to improve the transparency of large companies on social and environmental matters will be addressed later in this section.[143]

The strategic report must contain a fair review of the company's business and a description of the principal risks and uncertainties facing the company.[144] The review is: (a) a balanced and comprehensive analysis of the development and performance of the company's business during the financial year; and (b) the position of the company's business at the end of that year.[145] In the case of a quoted company, s414C (7) CA further stipulates that the strategic report must, to the extent necessary for an understanding of the development, performance or position of the company's business: (a) include the main trends and factors likely to affect the future development, performance and position of the company's business; and (b), (i) include information about environmental matters (including the impact of the company's business on the environment), (ii) the company's employees, and (iii) social, community and human rights issues, including information about any policies of the company in relation to those matters and the effectiveness of those policies.[146]

It is important from a CSR point of view that, if the review does not contain information regarding the issues mentioned in s414C (7) (a) and (b) CA, it must only state which of these categories it does not contain. The fact that this section allows quoted companies to leave out information about environmental matters, employees as well as social, community and human rights issues, as long as the company declares that its

---

[142]   S414C (1) CA.
[143]   EU Commission, 'Commission moves to enhance business transparency on social and environmental matters' (Press Release, 16 April 2013), available at http://europa.eu/rapid/press-release_IP-13-330_en.htm (accessed 12 November 2014).
[144]   S414C (2) CA.
[145]   S414C (3) CA.
[146]   Human rights issues were added to social and community issues in the strategic report.

strategic report does not contain this information, degrades reporting about CSR to a voluntary exercise for directors. It is a clear weakness of the provision that it remains very vague about what is to be included into the strategic report.[147] Directors can make quite neutral statements due to the discretion that they have in the writing of the reports.[148] A notable change from the business review to the strategic report is that quoted companies will be required to disclose the number of women on the board, in senior executive positions and in the whole organisation.[149]

Research about the question regarding how the relationship between company boards and their investors has been affected by the non-financial reporting requirements under the strategic report and its predecessor, the business review, further questions the effectiveness of the new regime.[150] A study by Villiers and Aiyegbayo based on semi-structured interviews with key corporate governance actors, such as investor relations managers and corporate governance directors from institutional investment firms, shows that the business review makes little difference to the quality of reports.[151] According to Villiers and Aiyegbayo's study, companies are struggling to report effectively their non-financial key performance indicators.[152] As these are CSR issues such as environmental matters, this study supports the view taken in this section that the practical effect of non-financial information disclosure for the promotion of CSR is limited.

---

[147] Birds (n 13) para 11.6 regarding the business review.

[148] C Villiers, 'Narrative reporting and enlightened shareholder value under the Companies Act 2006' in J Loughrey (ed.), *Directors' Duties and Shareholder Litigation in the Wake of the Financial Crisis* (Edward Elgar 2013) 108.

[149] This idea was suggested by Lord Davies in his report about women on boards in the UK. The 2012 version of the UK Corporate Governance Code requires that a separate section in the annual report section 'should include a description of the board's policy on diversity, including gender, any measurable objectives that it has set for implementing the policy, and progress on achieving the objectives'. These requirements for the strategic report are found in s414C (8) (c): 'In the case of a quoted company, the strategic report must include – (c) a breakdown showing at the end of the financial year – (i) the number of persons of each sex who were directors of the company; (ii) the number of persons of each sex who were senior managers of the company (other than persons falling within sub-paragraph (i)); and (iii) the number of persons of each sex who were employees of the company.

[150] C Villiers and O Aiyegbayo, 'The enhanced business review: Has it made corporate governance more effective?' (2011) *JBL* 699, 700.

[151] ibid, 712.

[152] ibid.

This outcome is further exacerbated by the fact that it is difficult to hold directors accountable for breaches of their reporting duty. Pursuant to s463 CA, directors are only liable for false and misleading statements or the omission of anything required to be in the report under the condition that the director knew that the statement was untrue or misleading or if he was reckless as to whether it was untrue or misleading and he knew the omission to be dishonest concealment of a material fact.[153] This section effectively restricts liability to cases of deceit. It cannot arise in negligence, which is the reason why it has been called a 'safe harbour provision'.[154] Moreover, the claimant is the company which can only sue in case of a loss suffered as a consequence of the false or misleading statement, something which is difficult to prove. This means that the stakeholders of the company who should benefit both from the considerations enlisted in s172 (1) CA and the reporting about the discharge of this duty are left without a remedy in cases where the directors do not report about matters of CSR at all.

B. The Limitations of the Strategic Report

The strategic report is considered to be what accountants call 'narrative reporting'.[155] Narrative reporting enables managers to explain the company's performance without numbers and to indicate the future direction of the company's business.[156] The duty to write a strategic report is part of the government's intention that companies acknowledge their social responsibilities.[157] However, what appeared to be a rather novel idea during the work of the Company Law Steering Group in the late 1990s and early 2000s has since then to some extent been overtaken by disclosure developments outside the Companies Act. In the meantime, the pressure on companies to publicly commit themselves to CSR has led to the widespread voluntary disclosure of CSR-related activities by companies which were not foreseen at the time of the Company Law

---

[153]   Under these circumstances the director is required to compensate the company for any loss suffered as a result of the misconduct, s463 (2) CA.

[154]   Hannigan (n 14) para 16-28.

[155]   French, Mayson and Ryan (n 67) para 9.9.6.

[156]   Villiers and Aiyegbayo (n 150) 702. See generally for a discussion of potential readers of corporate reports: C Villiers, *Corporate Reporting and Company Law* (CUP 2006) 85–92.

[157]   Hannigan (n 14) para 9-40.

Review.[158] It must be added, however, that this voluntary disclosure is not necessarily very effective.[159]

Reviews from corporate reporting agencies, accounting firms and governmental regulators are critical of the quality of narrative reporting in the UK, too.[160] PWC, for example, reviews annually the narrative reporting practice of the FTSE 350.[161] In a recent review they conclude that 'companies still fail to present a clear, credible and coherent picture of the direction of travel and short-term performance'.[162] They argue that many companies would only pay lip service to their sustainability goals. This argument is evidenced by their finding that around 40 per cent of FTSE 100 companies and around 60 to 70 per cent of FTSE 250 companies have significant progress to make in terms of their narrative reporting regarding external drivers, risks and sustainability reporting.[163] In its response to the consultation on the future of narrative reporting, PWC points out that its research would show that regulation appears to have an indirect positive impact on reporting by establishing the key principles for good quality reporting.[164] The Accounting Standards Board, an operating body of the Financial Reporting Council (FRC), reviewed the reports of a sample of 50 listed companies.[165] Notably, they

---

[158]   ibid.

[159]   See below: Comments made to the consultation by BIS Department for Business Innovation & Skills, *Summary of Responses: The future of narrative reporting – A consultation* (December 2010) 14, available at http://www.bis.gov.uk/Consultations/the-future-of-narrative-reporting-a-consultation (accessed 12 November 2014).

[160]   Accounting Standards Boards, *Full Results of a Review of Narrative Reporting by UK Listed Companies in 2008/2009* (October 2009), available at http://www.iasplus.com/en/binary/uk/0910narrativereportingfull.pdf (accessed 12 November 2014); Financial Reporting Council, *Rising to the Challenge: A review of narrative reporting by UK listed companies* (2009), available at https://www.frc.org.uk/Our-Work/Publications/ASB/Rising-to-the-Challenge/Rising-to-the-challenge.aspx (accessed 12 November 2014).

[161]   PWC, *A Snapshot of FTSE 350 Reporting: Compliance mindset suppresses effective communication* (2009), available at http://pwc.blogs.com/files/a-snapshot-of-ftse-350-reporting.pdf (accessed 12 November 2014).

[162]   ibid.

[163]   ibid.

[164]   PWC, Letter: 'The future of narrative reporting: Consulting on a new reporting framework', Letter dated 25 November 2011, available at http://www.pwc.co.uk/assets/pdf/future-of-narrative-reporting-final-pwc-comment-letter.pdf (accessed 12 November 2014).

[165]   Accounting Standards Boards, *Full Results of a Review of Narrative Reporting by UK Listed Companies in 2008/2009* (October 2009).

found out that only 20 per cent of the companies in their sample revealed best practice in terms of their disclosure of the CSR issues concerning environmental matters, employees as well as social and community issues.[166] 34 per cent were compliant in spirit whereas 40 per cent were either not compliant with the law or were compliant but the discussion was either generic or related to matters that were unimportant to the business.[167]

It appears from the studies about narrative reporting that the strategic report in its current form does not meet its aims. From a CSR perspective it is a particular limitation that the information about the environment, employees, as well as social, community and human rights issues, must only be included in the strategic report of quoted companies 'to the extent necessary for an understanding of the development, performance or position of the company's business'. This restriction is further exacerbated by the fact that quoted companies only need to state which of the information about, for instance, the environment or employees, their report does not contain. The consequence is a situation where the reporting about these aspects is rather limited, as evidenced by several studies about the quality of the reports of FTSE 100 and FTSE 250 companies. Given that the quality of voluntary CSR reports of companies is also seen critically by their readers in the survey on the future of narrative reporting by BIS, it seems as if the state of reporting on CSR issues is generally poor.

Like its predecessor the business review, the strategic report is too vague and leaves too much discretion for any effective reporting on stakeholder issues. The business review replaced the originally proposed Operating and Financial Review (OFR).[168] The main objective of the OFR was to provide 'more qualitative and forward looking reporting, in addition to information that is quantitative, historical or concerns internal company affairs'.[169] However, the government decided to abolish the

---

[166] ibid, 23–5.

[167] ibid.

[168] The OFR included reporting on, inter alia, the company's purpose, strategy and principle drivers of performance; an account of the company's key relationships, with employees, customers, suppliers and others, on which such success depends; the company's environmental policies and performance, including compliance with laws and regulations; policies and performance on community, social, ethical and reputational issues.

[169] See for an overview of the background to the introduction of the business review and the withdrawal of the OFR: Keay (n 21) 147–56.

OFR as it was considered to increase the regulatory burden on companies.[170] This abolition of the OFR was received with criticisms.[171] Johnston criticises that the business review is less prescriptive than the OFR would have been and that the business review offers less guidance about its content.[172]

The approach of the government to encourage business to (voluntarily) disclose their CSR policies and activities rather than to legally require them to do so has so far only produced poor results. The strategic report is primarily aimed at shareholders, as s414C (1) CA states that 'the purpose of the strategic report is to inform members of the company'. It should help shareholders understand how the directors 'have performed their duty under section 172'. The focus of the review is on assessing the business from an investor's perspective.[173] The reporting about stakeholder issues, such as the environment, is left to the discretion of the company. Like the s172 (1) CA duty, the strategic report is firmly embedded in the goal of prioritising the interests of shareholders.[174] Both the duty to promote the success of the company for the benefit of its members as a whole and the strategic report are strongly limited in their ability to promote CSR.

C. The EU Directive on the Disclosure of Non-financial and Diversity Information

However, the reporting about CSR matters could be improved by the EU Directive regarding disclosure of nonfinancial and diversity information by certain large companies and groups. This Directive was proposed in April 2013.[175] The European Parliament and the Council adopted it in April 2014 and September 2014 respectively.[176]

---

[170] See K Campbell and D Vick (n 5) 257–8.
[171] See for example: Johnston (n 27) 817.
[172] ibid, 841.
[173] Horrigan (n 4) 259.
[174] ibid, 260.
[175] European Commission, 'Proposal for a Directive of the European Parliament and of the Council amending Council Directives 78/660/EEC and 83/349/EEC as regards disclosure of nonfinancial and diversity information by certain large companies and groups' COM (2013) 207 final, available at http://ec.europa.eu/internal_market/accounting/docs/non-financial-reporting/com_2013_207_en.pdf (accessed 19 October 2014).
[176] European Commission, 'Statement: Disclosure of non-financial information: Europe's largest companies to be more transparent on social and

In February 2013, the EU Parliament had adopted two resolutions in which it highlights the importance of company transparency on environmental and social matters.[177] The EU Parliament asked the Commission to bring forward a proposal on non-financial disclosure by companies. The impact assessment of the Commission on corporate reporting on nonfinancial information showed significant weaknesses both in terms of the quantity of information and the quality of information.[178]

The Directive will require large companies with more than 500 employees[179] to disclose relevant and material environmental and social information in their annual reports. The Directive stipulates that the annual report of these companies must include a non-financial statement containing information relating to at least environmental, social and employee matters, respect for human rights, anti-corruption and bribery matters.[180] This statement must include a description of the policy pursued by the company in relation to these matters, the results of these policies and the risks related to these matters and how the company manages those risks. Companies that do not pursue policies in relation to one or more of these matters shall provide an explanation for not doing so.[181] Moreover, the proposed Directive also requires companies to describe their diversity policy for their administrative, management and

environmental issues' (Brussels 29 September 2014), available at http://europa. eu/rapid/press-release_STATEMENT-14-291_en.htm (accessed 14 November 2014).

[177] The resolutions passed on 6 February are: First, Report on corporate social responsibility: Accountable, transparent and responsible business behaviour and sustainable growth (2012/2098(INI)); Committee on Legal Affairs, available at http://www.europarl.europa.eu/sides/getDoc.do?pubRef=-//EP//NON SGML+REPORT+A7-2013-0017+0+DOC+PDF+V0//EN&language=EN (accessed 14 November 2014); Secondly, Report on Corporate Social Responsibility: promoting society's interests and a route to sustainable and inclusive recovery (2012/2097(INI)); Committee on Employment and Social Affairs, available at http://www.europarl.europa.eu/sides/getDoc.do?pubRef=-//EP//NONSGML+ REPORT+A7-2013-0023+0+DOC+PDF+V0//EN&language=EN (accessed 14 November 2014).

[178] The Commission stated in its proposal for the Directive that it is estimated that only 2500 out of the total 42,000 EU large companies formally disclose non-financial information on a yearly basis. Moreover, the quality of information disclosed by companies does not adequately meet the needs of users.

[179] And who, during the financial year, exceed on their balance sheet dates either a balance sheet total of EUR 20 million or a net turnover of EUR 40 million.

[180] Article 1 (1) (a) of the Directive.

[181] ibid.

supervisory bodies with regard to aspects such as age, gender, geographical diversity, educational and professional background, the objectives of this diversity policy, how it has been implemented and the results in the reporting period.[182] The 'comply or explain' approach also applies to this reporting duty. The Commission envisages that companies will be required to publish their first reports in compliance with the Directive in 2017.[183]

The requirements of the Directive go further than the strategic report. First, contrary to the strategic report the Directive also explicitly requires reporting on anti-corruption and bribery matters. Secondly, rather than just requiring companies to report on CSR issues 'to the extent necessary for an understanding of the development, performance of position of the company's business' (the position under the strategic report), the Directive prescribes reporting of the policies, their results and risks whenever a company has a policy on these issues. Where a company does not have such a policy, it would need to give reasons for this situation, which applies the 'comply or explain' approach (that underlies the UK Corporate Governance Code) to CSR reporting. In contrast, the strategic report allows companies to state purely that they did not report on these issues. Therefore, the requirements of the Directive go beyond the current reporting system under the Companies Act. The Directive will consequently improve the reporting on CSR by large companies.[184] Thirdly,

---

[182]   Article 1 (2) of the Directive.

[183]   European Commission, 'Statement: Disclosure of non-financial information: Europe's largest companies to be more transparent on social and environmental issues' (Brussels 29 September 2014), available at http://europa. eu/rapid/press-release_STATEMENT-14-291_en.htm (accessed 14 November 2014).

[184]   The proposed Directive emphasises that in fulfilling their reporting duty under this directive companies may rely on national frameworks, EU-based frameworks and international frameworks such as the United Nations (UN) Global Compact, the Guiding Principles on Business and Human Rights implementing the UN 'Protect, Respect and Remedy' Framework, the Organisation for Economic Co-operation and Development (OECD) Guidelines for Multinational Enterprises, the International Organisation for Standardisation (ISO) 26000, the International Labour Organization (ILO) Tripartite Declaration of principles concerning multinational enterprises and social policy, and the Global Reporting Initiative. It is therefore intended to align CSR reporting under existing frameworks with the requirements of the Directive so that companies that already disclose CSR matters under existing frameworks do not repeat the reporting exercise. The proposed Directive exempts companies from the reporting duty under the Directive if they prepare a comprehensive report on CSR issues that address all the issues required under the Directive relying on national, EU-based

the diversity reporting under the Directive, too, goes beyond the requirements of the strategic report. Thus, the Directive has the potential to improve the status quo of CSR reporting in English law. Besides, as CSR is by its nature an international concern, it is a positive development if there is a level playing field for companies throughout the EU. The Directive is unlikely to make CSR reporting a primary concern for companies, but it will nevertheless improve the kinds of information that companies need to provide on their socially responsible conduct. While the reporting duty will not force companies to adopt CSR policies, it will nevertheless put the reporting on these matters on a comparable ground throughout the EU. Moreover, it will enable the public to identify those companies that do not have a CSR policy. The important issue that remains to be seen, however, will be the quality of reporting under the new reporting scheme with its continuance of the 'comply or explain' approach. The key issue for the success of the proposed reporting regime will be if companies use it as a genuine opportunity to reflect on their CSR policies and as an instrument to inform their investors as well as other stakeholders, or if companies only provide boilerplate statements.

V. SHAREHOLDERS' ENGAGEMENT AND THE DERIVATIVE ACTION

It is said that good corporate governance depends on both effective shareholder control and an effective board.[185] This section will analyse to what extent shareholders can contribute to the promotion of CSR within companies. The focus will be on two aspects: First, the role of institutional investors, as they are a powerful group of shareholders who have potential to influence the decision making of companies; secondly, the use of the derivative action pursuant to s260 (1) CA as a means to enforce CSR.

---

or international frameworks. This rule ensures that companies that already follow a CSR reporting framework will not be disadvantaged by having to repeat the same information.

[185]   Hannigan (n 14) para 5-43.

A. Institutional Investors

Several reviews of corporate governance have emphasised the importance
of institutional investors for the monitoring of the directors.[186] The reason
for this focus on institutional investors is that they hold approximately 40
per cent of the shares of quoted companies in the UK.[187] Due to this
power, discussions about corporate governance commonly focus on the
ability of institutional investors to monitor and engage with decisions of
the board. Shareholder activism is important for the promotion of CSR as
shareholders can influence the adherence of a company to social
issues.[188]

   However, the different reviews of institutional investors concur in their
critical assessment of the status quo, that is, the inadequate level of
engagement of institutional investors with their investee companies.[189]
Notably, the criticisms also repeat themselves. In 2001, the White Paper
on the company law reform already emphasised that a change in the
'traditional' attitude of institutional investors towards the companies in
their portfolios was necessary.[190] The 'traditional' attitude was understood as a lack of engagement with their portfolio companies, a focus on
short-term financial gains and the widespread use of an exit strategy (i.e.
selling of the shares) in case the investors were unhappy about the
direction of the company.[191] In the wake of the financial and economic
crisis, the role of institutional investors continued to be a matter of

---

[186] See for example Paul Myners, *Institutional Investment in the UK: A
Review* (the *Myners Report*) 2001; Company Law Review, *The White Paper:
Modernising Company Law* (DTI 2002, Cm 5553-I and Cm 5553-II) paras
2.43–2.44; Walker (n 2).
[187] Institutional shareholders accounted for 39.9 per cent of the UK ordinary
shares at 31 December 2008 with a combined value of £462.4 billion. Of these,
the largest holders were insurance companies (£154.9 billion) and pension funds
(£148.8 billion). It must be noted that the share ownership is less homogenous
than it was in the past as investors from outside the UK owned 41.5 per cent of
UK shares listed on the UK Stock Exchange. See Office for National Statistics,
Share Ownership Survey 2008, available at http://www.ons.gov.uk/ons/rel/pnfc1/
share-ownership – share-register-survey-report/2008/index.html (accessed 16
November 2014).
[188] D Millon, 'Shareholder social responsibility' (2013) 36 *Seattle University
Law Review* 911.
[189] See Company Law Review, *The White Paper: Modernising Company Law*
(DTI 2002, Cm 5553-I and Cm 5553-II) 36.
[190] ibid.
[191] ibid.

concern. For example, the 2009 Walker Review of corporate governance in UK banks devotes a whole chapter to the issue of the effective engagement of institutional investors with their portfolio companies.[192]

The discussions about the role of institutional investors eventually led to the development of the UK Stewardship Code in 2010.[193] It was revised in September 2012.[194] It is a set of principles which 'aims to enhance the quality of engagement between institutional investors and companies'.[195] It is addressed 'in the first instance to institutional investors, by which is meant asset owners and asset managers with equity holdings in UK-listed companies'.[196] Asset owners include pension funds, insurance companies, investment trusts and other collective investment vehicles.[197] Stewardship includes monitoring and engaging with companies on matters such as strategy, performance, risk and corporate governance, including culture and remuneration.[198] The UK Stewardship Code follows the 'comply or explain' approach of the UK Corporate Governance Code which means that investors who do not comply with provisions of the UK Stewardship Code shall explain that they have not done so and give reasons for this.[199] The UK Stewardship Code provides, inter alia, that institutional investors should monitor their investee companies, report about how they discharge this duty and that they should seek to exercise their voting rights. Principle 2 clarifies that it is the duty of institutional investors to act in the interests of their clients.[200] As part

---

[192] Walker (n 2) Chapter 5.

[193] Financial Reporting Council, The UK Stewardship Code (July 2010), available at http://www.frc.org.uk/Our-Work/Publications/Corporate-Governance/The-UK-Stewardship-Code.aspx (accessed 14 November 2014).

[194] Financial Reporting Council, The UK Stewardship Code (September 2012), available at http://www.frc.org.uk/Our-Work/Publications/Corporate-Governance/UK-Stewardship-Code-September-2012.aspx (accessed 14 November 2014).

[195] Preface of the 2010 version of the UK Stewardship Code. It is stated in the UK Stewardship Code that its origins lie in the Statement of Principles on the Responsibilities of Institutional Investors by the ISC which have since become a code, see ibid, 2.

[196] FRC, The UK Stewardship Code (September 2012), 'Application of the Code', 2.

[197] ibid, 'Stewardship and the Code', 1.

[198] ibid.

[199] ibid, 'Comply or Explain', 4.

[200] ibid, Principle 2 Guidance.

of their duty to monitor their investee companies (Principle 3), institutional investors should 'satisfy themselves that the company's board and committees adhere to the spirit of the UK Corporate Governance Code, including through meetings with the chairman and other board members'.

However, the effects of the UK Stewardship Code in terms of promoting CSR in investee companies are likely to be limited. Although the term 'stewardship' in the title appears to emphasise the responsibility of institutional investors, there is not much in the Code that is fresh. The duty to monitor investee companies is nothing new, in light of the guidelines previously published by the Institutional Shareholders' Committee.[201] In fact, there is a considerable continuity between the UK Stewardship Code and the previous documents by the Institutional Shareholders' Committee.[202] The explicit absence of references to the pursuit of CSR goals shows that the UK Stewardship Code does not mark a step towards the promotion of CSR. The comment in the guidance to principle 4, that the instances in which investors 'may want to intervene' include those 'that may arise from social and environmental matters', is rather vague. The absence of a principle with an express outline of CSR issues in the Stewardship Code is particularly disappointing, given that the new duty in s172 (1) CA refers to the interests of various stakeholders. This duty has not had any impact on these best practice guidelines for institutional investors. It is therefore not to be expected that the majority of institutional investors are promoting these interests as part of their shareholder engagement which means that the impact of the UK Stewardship Code for CSR is likely to be minimal.

On a practical note, it is important to consider that the overall share ownership of traditional institutional investors, such as insurance companies and pension funds (with a potentially higher interest in long-term success), is declining whereas that of hedge funds and overseas investors is increasing (there is a danger that these groups are less interested in the long-term success of their investee companies or CSR issues).[203] The

---

[201] See for a discussion of the relationship between '*The UK Stewardship Code*' and the '*Code on the Responsibilities of Institutional Investors*' produced by the Institutional Investor Committee: A Reisberg, 'The notion of stewardship from a company law perspective: Re-defined and re-assessed in light of the recent financial crisis?' (2011) 18 *Journal of Financial Crime* 126, 133.

[202] R Tomasic, 'Towards a new corporate governance after the global financial crisis' (2011) 8 *ICCLR* 237–49.

[203] Tomasic and Akinbami point out that the fact that foreign institutions will not be subject to the Code is a potential constraint on shareholder activism, see: R Tomasic and F Akinbami, 'Shareholder activism and litigation against UK

scepticism about the restricted ability of institutional investors to enhance greater CSR is also based on the fact that the division of power generally vests the power of management in the board of directors with only limited rights retained by the shareholders such as the statutory right to amend the articles,[204] to reduce the share capital[205] and to remove the directors.[206] At the moment, shareholders do not have much power to promote greater CSR in their investee companies. This sceptical assessment is further supported by the fact that the so-called 'shareholder spring' in 2012 focussed on directors' remuneration.[207] Whilst there was an intensive coverage in the press about the refusal of some institutional investors to accept the remuneration reports of some companies, the engagement of the investors did not expand to CSR matters such as the quality of corporate reports on CSR or their CSR record generally.[208] One also needs to consider that institutional shareholders such as pension funds are under pressure to pursue short-term investment strategies in order to meet their own ongoing contractual obligations.[209] Moreover, the fact that investment funds are required to ensure sufficient profitability in order to remain competitive on the market, further encourages short-term investment strategies.[210] In turn, such short-term investment strategies

---

banks – the limits of company law and the desperate resort to human rights claims?' in J Loughrey, *Directors' Duties and Shareholder Litigation in the Wake of the Financial Crisis* (Edward Elgar 2013) 151.

[204]   S21 CA.

[205]   SS617-619 CA.

[206]   S168 CA. See also Hannigan (n 14) para 8-6.

[207]   See for example: *Financial Times*, 'Boards wake up to a shareholder spring' (4 May 2012). The article refers to the examples of Aviva whose investors refused to approve its remuneration report as well as Barclays which experienced almost a 33 per cent disapproval of its remuneration report.

[208]   Moreover, the existence of a 'shareholder spring' has been questioned on the basis of statistical evidence which revealed that despite some public disapprovals of directors' remuneration reports the overall level of dissent in all votes on remuneration was higher than in 2011 and lower than in 2002 and 2003, see BBC News, 'The myth of a shareholder spring' (12 June 2012), available at http://www.bbc.co.uk/news/business-18407587 (accessed 1 November 2014).

[209]   Millon highlights that pension funds which are commonly perceived of as being long-term investors need to make sufficient returns on investment in order to meet their ongoing contractual obligations on a monthly basis. This need for cash is a driving force behind the reality of pursuing short-term investment strategies. Historically, public pension funds have assumed an annual return on investment rate of about 8 per cent. See for a discussion of the issue: D Millon (n 188) 911.

[210]   ibid, 934–7.

influence the way directors run their companies, often leading to the prioritisation of 'short-term earnings at the expense of potentially greater long-run firm value'.[211]

In summary, the contribution which institutional investors, within the framework of the UK Stewardship Code, can make to the promotion of CSR in their investee companies, is limited. Whilst the UK Stewardship Code further encourages institutional investors to fulfil their role to monitor their investee companies, it is unlikely to enhance greater social responsibility of companies.

B. The Derivative Action

Within the context of shareholder engagement, it is important to consider the derivative action pursuant to s260 CA as a possible means to promote CSR.

i. Analysis of the statutory derivative action

The derivative action is a claim brought by a member of the company in respect of a cause of action vested in the company and seeking relief on behalf of the company.[212] Pursuant to s260 (3) CA, a derivative claim may be brought only in respect of a cause of action arising from an actual or proposed act or omission involving negligence, default, breach of duty or breach of trust by a director of the company. This section further stipulates that a derivative claim may be against the director or another person (or both). The fact that a derivative action can be brought for breach of duty by a director is important for CSR as it brings breaches of s172 (1) CA into the ambit of the derivative claim.

Still, shareholders cannot initiate an action on behalf of the company that easily. They must apply to the court for permission to continue their claim[213] and they must pass a two-stage test. First, they must make a

---

[211]   ibid, 939.

[212]   S260 (1) CA. The other main remedy for shareholders is the unfairly prejudicial conduct remedy pursuant to s994 CA. However, this remedy is unlikely to be relevant in terms of promoting CSR, as it is predominately brought by members in a private limited company who seek relief (in the form of obtaining an order that their shares must be bought by the respondents at a fair price) on the basis that the company's affairs have been conducted in a manner that was unfairly prejudicial to his interests. The remedy is therefore primarily used to obtain relief for the claimant whereas the derivative action (s260 CA) that is analysed in this section is brought by a member of the company who seeks relief on behalf of the company, s260 (1) CA.

[213]   S261 (1) CA.

prima facie case; otherwise the court must dismiss the claim.[214] The second stage contains a non-exhaustive list of factors a judge must consider. S263 (2) CA contains a list of situations in which a court must refuse permission to continue with the derivative claim. According to this list, a court must refuse permission if it is satisfied that a person acting in accordance with s172 CA would not seek to continue the claim. Moreover, actual authorisation or ratification provides a complete defence to a derivative claim.[215] This authorisation may be done by the shareholders or by the directors. The ratification of acts of directors does not affect any rule of law as to acts which are incapable of being ratified by a company.[216] However, in fact, many breaches of duty by directors are ratifiable.

If none of the factors in s263 (2) CA apply, then the court has discretion to allow a claim to proceed.[217] S263 (3) CA provides guidance for the court's decision whether or not to grant permission to continue with the claim. According to s263 (3) (a) CA, the court must take into account whether the member is acting in good faith in seeking to continue the claim and pursuant to s 263 (3) (b) CA, the court must consider the importance a person acting in accordance with s172 CA (duty to promote the success of the company) would attach to continuing it. In considering whether to give permission, the court shall have particular regard to any evidence before it as to the views of members of the company who have no personal interest, direct or indirect, in the matter.[218]

In terms of the ability of the derivative action to enforce CSR, two of the conditions outlined deserve particular attention: First, breaches of directors' duties are a cause of action for a derivative action. This means that shareholders can bring a derivative action on grounds of alleged violations of CSR principles as these overlap with the list of factors in s172 CA. Secondly, when the courts decide whether or not to grant permission to continue with the claim they must consider the importance a person acting in accordance with s172 CA would attach to it. This

---

[214] S261 (2) CA.
[215] S263 (2) (b), (c) CA.
[216] S239 (7) CA.
[217] Hannigan argues that there is only limited scope for dismissing a claim under s263 (2) CA. In her view there will, in most cases, be no basis on which to dismiss the claim under s263 (2) CA. The consequence is that the court will then turn to s263 (3) CA for its decision whether or not to permit the claimant to continue with the claim, Hannigan (n 14) para 18-37.
[218] S263 (4) CA.

means that issues of CSR which are inherent in s172 CA can play a role in the way in which the courts assess the question whether or not to allow the shareholder to continue with their action.

The important question is if this new derivative action has a positive impact on pursuing CSR goals. One might assume that it does, considering the fact that, when the new statutory action was introduced, concerns were raised by business representatives that shareholder activists might overly use this new claim to challenge business actions on grounds of an alleged breach of the s172 CA duty.[219] It was argued then that a shareholder might, for example, challenge business decisions through a derivative action based on the claim that the directors did not have regard to the impact of the business decision on the community and the environment.[220] Adeyeye opines that derivative actions would be able to address CSR issues concerning both internal and external stakeholders.[221] In her view such claims can be used to enforce ethical behaviour of companies.[222] They might therefore be a tool to enforce the goals of CSR. In order to find out if Adeyeye's optimistic outlook on the derivative action as an instrument to promote CSR is justified, the case law will be considered. However, there is only very limited case law in this area, so far, which gives rise to doubts if this new cause of action does make a difference from a CSR point of view, given that the Companies Act came fully into force on 1 October 2007.

ii. Case law about the derivative action

The key question is how the courts will exercise their discretion whether or not to give permission to continue with the claim. Effectively, the courts need to decide if they should interfere with the decision of the board not to pursue the claim in the first place. This possibility potentially conflicts with the traditional reluctance of courts not to second-guess business decisions.[223] In *Franbar Holdings Ltd v Patel* the judge identified some reasons which a hypothetical director acting in accordance with s172 (1) CA would take into account when assessing the

---

[219]   See Hannigan (n 14) para 18-8.
[220]   S172 (1) (d) CA. See Hannigan (n 14) para 18-8.
[221]   A Adeyeye, 'The limitations of corporate governance in the CSR agenda' (2010) 31 *Company Lawyer* 114, 117. Internal stakeholders refer to those stakeholders inside the company (such as employees) and external stakeholders to those outside the company (e.g. human rights considerations, the environment and the community).
[222]   ibid.
[223]   Hannigan (n 14) para 18-56.

importance of continuing the claim.[224] These include: the prospect of the success of the claim, the ability of the company to make a recovery on any award of damages, the disruption which would be caused on the development of the company's business by having to concentrate on the proceedings, the costs of the proceedings and any damage to the company's reputation and business if the proceedings were to fail.[225] Notably, none of these factors refers to the interests of the stakeholders contained in the list of factors in s172 (1) CA. Instead, the factors mentioned by the court in *Franbar* about the assessment of the claim in light of s172 (1) CA are about financial considerations. Further factors were established in the subsequent decision in *Iesini v Westrip Holdings Ltd* which again focussed on financial aspects.[226] The judge pointed out that the weighing of the considerations was 'essentially a commercial decision'.[227] However, he also stated that s172 CA would only be used as a bar to derivative claims pursuant to s263 (2) (a) CA where the court is satisfied that no director acting in accordance with s172 CA would seek to continue the claim.[228] If some directors would, and others would not, seek to continue the claim, the case is one for the application of s263 (3) (b) CA.[229] Despite this slightly optimistic comment, the existing case law suggests that the decision about whether or not to permit continuation of the derivative claim is primarily based on financial concerns despite the fact that the yardstick for this decision, s172 (1) CA, requires directors to include the interests of various stakeholders in their decisions. The use of s172 (1) CA by the courts in this assessment of derivative claims is therefore firmly embedded in the goal of maximising shareholder value.

---

[224] [2008] B.C.C. 885 (Ch); [2008] EWHC 1534 (Ch).

[225] ibid [36].

[226] [2009] EWHC 2526 (Ch). The factors mentioned by the court are: 'The size of the claim; the strength of the claim; the cost of the proceedings; the company's ability to fund the proceedings; the ability of the potential defendants to satisfy a judgment; the impact on the company if it lost the claim and had to pay its own costs and the defendant's as well; any disruption to the company's activities while the claim was pursued; whether the prosecution of the claim would damage the company in other ways (e.g. by losing the services of a valuable employee or alienating a key supplier or customer) and so on.'

[227] ibid.

[228] Ibid, at [86]. The judge agreed with the decision in *Franbar* in this respect.

[229] Pursuant to s 263 (3) (b) CA, in considering whether to give permission (or leave) to continue the derivative claim, the court must consider the importance a person acting in accordance with s172 CA (duty to promote the success of the company) would attach to continuing the claim.

This pessimistic outcome from a CSR point of view is further exacerbated by the case *Stimpson v Southern Landlords Association*.[230] Here the court refused the application as it held that a hypothetical director acting in accordance with s172 CA would not continue the action. The significant aspect of the decision for this chapter is that the court held that it had to take into account the effect of the proposed actions on the former employees of the first defendant and that this was possible as the list in s263 (3) CA is non-exhaustive.[231] It therefore saw the effect on employees to be a consideration which is not part of the factors enlisted in s263 (3) CA, despite the explicit inclusion of s172 (1) CA with its referral to the interests of employees into s263 (3) (b) CA. This approach therefore separates the interests of employees and s263 (3) (b) CA although this section explicitly refers to s172 CA which, in turn, contains a list of factors including employees, the environment and the community. Gibbs therefore argues that the separation between s263 (3) CA, with its reference to s172 CA and employees, could put CSR merely at the discretion of the court when considering whether or not to allow a derivative claim to be further pursued.[232] When considering s172 CA through s263 (3) CA, the courts might then only assess it in terms of benefiting members as a whole, that is, the majority.[233] This assessment would leave out the list of factors contained in s172 (1) CA with its overlap with CSR issues from necessary considerations in s263 (3) CA. This situation means that insofar as the decision whether or not to permit a claim to be continued according to s263 CA is concerned, the courts seem to interpret s172 (1) CA as only focusing on shareholder value. The interests of the stakeholders contained in the list of the factors of the provision are left out of this approach. Courts can still include these considerations as in *Stimpson* with reference to the non-exhaustive nature of s263 (3) CA, but this severely limits the importance of these interests.

It might be that the rationale behind this approach is that allowing shareholders to decide via derivative actions which stakeholders to consider in the decision-making process would conflict with the rule that it is up to the majority of board members to make a decision.[234] The fact that employees as stakeholders which are internal to the company were

---

[230] *Stimpson v Southern Landlords Association* [2009] EWHC 2072 (Ch), [2010] B.C.C. [387].

[231] ibid [387], [402].

[232] D Gibbs, 'Has the statutory derivative claim fulfilled its objectives? The hypothetical director and CSR: Part 2' (2011) 32 *Company Lawyer* 76, 80.

[233] ibid.

[234] ibid.

taken into account by the court (though as a non-exhaustive aspect) might indicate that stakeholder interests internal to the company can form part of the test pursuant to s263 (3) CA. Gibbs, therefore, considers it more likely that stakeholder interests external to the company such as human rights, environment and the community are dismissed.[235] This situation contradicts Adeyeye's opinion who anticipated successful actions on the basis of these issues. *Stimpson*, therefore, further demonstrates that CSR does not play an important role insofar as the decision of the courts whether or not to permit derivative claims to be continued is concerned. This decision will effectively be a commercial one. In line with this approach, the judge based his decision to refuse the application to continue the claim in *Stimpson* also on financial considerations, as the court held that a hypothetical director acting in accordance with the s172 CA duty would not seek to continue the claim because the value of the claim was modest in reality.[236] The distinction between s172 (1) CA and the interests of employees in this case, as well as the emphasis on financial considerations, severely reduces the potential of the derivative claim for CSR goals.

iii.   The effect of the derivative action for CSR

This situation questions the ability of shareholders to use the derivative action to pursue CSR aims. This negative outcome for CSR is further exacerbated by the difficulty with successfully basing claims that directors have not sufficiently paid regard to CSR on s172 (1) CA. One can therefore conclude that the scope for the derivative action to be used to enforce CSR through alleged breaches of s172 (1) CA is very limited. The analysis here supports Keay's sceptical outlook on the impact of the new derivative action as he had expected such claims to be used in few situations only, for example, in case of a member who had invested in a company to pursue long-term gains, but where the directors are purely acting in the interest of short-term gains.[237] Even this idea seems questionable, given that s172 (1) CA gives much power to the directors to decide in a manner that they consider, in good faith, would be most likely to promote the success of the company. Further possible scenarios for Keay were derivative actions brought by employees who are also shareholders and who feel that the position of the employees has not been sufficiently included in the decision-making process or members

---

[235]   ibid.
[236]   *Stimpson v Southern Landlords Association* [2010] B.C.C. [387], [389].
[237]   Keay (n 71) 109.

who live in the local community and who fear that the community could be negatively affected by the impact of the corporation's work.[238] However, following the court's assessment of the derivative action in the *Stimpson* case, with its optional reference to employees, it is doubtful if such claims would be successful. First, even though these issues were not ruled out by *Stimpson* to be part of the court's considerations according to s263 (3) CA, it remains to be seen if they would actually be included. Secondly, even if such CSR considerations are included, the challenge remains to prove a breach of the duty in s172 (1) CA in the first place.

The discussion in this section shows that the concerns raised by business representatives at the time the Companies Act 2006 was drafted, that the combination of the new duty in s172 (1) CA and the statutory derivative action could lead to litigation about business decisions (referred to as 'judicial review of a commercial decision'),[239] seem to be unfounded so far. Quite the reverse, from a CSR perspective, the outcome is disappointing. The analysis in this section therefore confirms doubts which have been raised about the practical impact of the new derivative action in terms of promoting CSR goals.[240] In fact, the government had not anticipated a significant increase of derivative actions through the new statutory remedy.[241] The derivative action in its current form with the limitations (the two-stage test of the court to decide whether or not to give permission to continue the derivative claim) was intended to strike a balance between protecting the rights of shareholders on the one hand and leaving directors free to take business decisions in good faith on the other hand.[242] The traditional approach to shareholders' remedies that it is the company that is the proper person to sue (also known as the rule in *Foss v Harbottle*[243]) underlay the Parliamentary debates about the derivative action.[244] This rule is also based on the idea of majority rule.[245] Courts traditionally do not want to second-guess business decisions.[246] Although the rule in *Foss v Harbottle* was replaced with the statutory

---

[238]   ibid.
[239]   See for further discussion Hannigan (n 14) paras 9-35, 18-8.
[240]   See for example Keay (n 71) 109.
[241]   See 679 HL Official Report (5th series), cols GC4-5, 27 February 2006; 681 HL Official Report (5th series), col 883, 9 May 2006; HC Official Report, SC D (Company Law Reform Bill), 13 July 2006, cols 664-6.
[242]   681 HL Official Report (5th series), col 883, 9 May 2006.
[243]   *Foss v Harbottle* (1843) 2 Hare 461.
[244]   Hannigan (n 14) para 18-11.
[245]   ibid, para 18-14.
[246]   French, Mayson and Ryan (n 67) para 18.3.3.

derivative action in the Companies Act 2006, its underlying principles are still relevant for the courts' reluctance towards getting involved in business disputes as the position remains that the proper claimant in respect of a wrong done to a company is prima facie the company.[247] As this approach seems to continue to prevail in relation to shareholders' actions, there is not much to be expected from the derivative claim in terms of promoting CSR.

This analysis therefore agrees with Gibbs' argument that the new statutory derivative action does not appear 'to have altered tremendously for now'.[248] It is rather unlikely that the number of cases based on derivative actions is going to increase in the future.[249] The potential of shareholders' remedies to promote CSR is therefore limited.

VI. THE BOARD

The final part of this chapter will discuss the role and composition of the board for the promotion of CSR.

A. Non-executive Directors

Boards commonly consist of both executive directors and non-executive directors.[250] The difference between the two is that executive directors tend to devote their whole working time to the company whereas non-executive directors usually only spend part of their working time on the company and receive a smaller director's fee than their counter-parts.[251] Non-executive directors are often considered to be an effective means to ensure that the executive directors work in the interest of the company.[252] The UK Corporate Governance Code addresses the composition and the role of the board by stipulating that 'every company should be headed by an effective board which is collectively responsible

---

247 Hannigan (n 14) paras 18-12 to 18-15.
248 Gibbs (n 232) 82. See also the analysis of shareholder litigation by Tomasic and Akinbami who conclude that 'the prospects of successful litigation against directors of large public companies, such as directors of failed UK banks and financial institutions, are somewhat remote', see: Tomasic and Akinbami (n 203) 172.
249 E C Mujih, 'The new statutory derivative claim: A paradox of minority shareholder protection' (2012) 33 *Company Lawyer* 99, 100, 106.
250 French, Mayson and Ryan (n 67) para 15.2.3.
251 ibid.
252 ibid.

for the long-term success of the company'.[253] The Code further requires the company to have 'an appropriate combination' of executive and non-executive directors, in particular, independent non-executive directors.[254] The function of non-executive directors is specified by principle A 4 of the Code. It is their function to challenge the management and to contribute to the development of strategic proposals. Except for smaller companies (defined as those below the FTSE 350), at least half the board, excluding the chairman, should comprise non-executive directors determined by the board to be independent.[255] The board should determine whether the director is independent in character and judgment and whether there are relationships or circumstances which are likely to affect, or could appear to affect, the director's judgment.[256]

As it is their role to challenge the executive directors and to contribute to the strategy of the company, non-executive directors potentially hold an important position for the promotion of CSR. They are in the boardroom and can therefore critically engage with the decisions of the executive directors and add CSR considerations into the decision-making process. However, the fact that non-executive directors continue to be the subject of critical reviews,[257] demonstrates that they are obviously not always sufficiently exercising their function to monitor and to challenge the work of the executive directors. The economic and financial crisis has

---

[253] UK Corporate Governance Code, Section A: Leadership. The UK Corporate Governance Code was issued by the Financial Reporting Council in June 2010. The new edition of the Code was published in September 2014. The Code applies to premium listed companies and replaces the Combined Code on Corporate Governance. The Code contains standards of good practice in relation to board leadership and effectiveness, remuneration, accountability and relations with shareholders. Listed companies are required to report on how they have applied the main principles of the Code. They must confirm if they have complied with the Code's provisions. If they have not, they must provide an explanation for this (this is known as the 'comply or explain' system. For more information see the UK Corporate Governance Code (September 2014), available at   https://www.frc.org.uk/Our-Work/Publications/Corporate-Governance/UK-Corporate-Governance-Code-2014.pdf (accessed 14 November 2014).
[254] UK Corporate Governance Code, B 1: The Composition of the Board, Supporting Principles.
[255] ibid, B 1: The Composition of the Board, B 1.2.
[256] ibid, B 1: The Composition of the Board, B 1.1.
[257] Walker (n 2) para 2.2. (iv); See for example: D Higgs, *Review of the Role and Effectiveness of Non-Executive Directors* (DTI 2003), available at http://www.ecgi.org/codes/documents/higgsreport.pdf (accessed 14 November 2014).

revealed several examples of non-executive directors who have not sufficiently monitored the board.[258] When looking into the failure of Northern Rock, the Treasury Committee criticised the company's non-executive directors for their inability to restrain the CEO.[259] The non-executive directors failed to ensure that the company remained liquid and solvent and to prevent the unacceptable risks the company took.[260] In his review of corporate governance in UK banks and other financial industry entities, Sir David Walker questioned whether 'the long established conventional wisdom and practice that non-executive directors make an essential contribution to governance continues to be as realistic as previously envisaged'.[261] These examples underline that there are many instances where non-executive directors have not properly discharged their duties to monitor and critically challenge the decision-making process.[262] This issue is important here as non-executive directors have potential to put CSR on the agenda in the boardroom. However, whether they do this depends on the question of whether they fully engage with the running of the company.

The question of whether the duties of non-executive directors ought to be included in the Companies Act or remain in the UK Corporate Governance Code cannot be fully discussed here. Nevertheless, it is submitted here that it needs to be considered that the system based on 'comply or explain' has not prevented the failures of non-executive directors in the run-up to the current economic and financial crisis. It seems that the recent corporate governance failures, including the lack of sufficient monitoring by non-executive directors, mirror the situation in the early 1990s which occurred prior to the beginning of the whole corporate governance debate in the UK. Several reviews of corporate governance and the creation of codes of conduct since then do not appear to have achieved much in light of the scale of corporate governance failures. It is therefore doubtful if some amendments of the codes, as

---

[258] A Arora, 'The corporate governance failings in financial institutions and directors' legal liability' (2011) 32 *Company Lawyer* 3, 5.

[259] House of Commons Treasury Committee, *The Run on the Rock* (2008), available at http://www.parliament.the-stationery-office.com/pa/cm200708/cm select/cmtreasy/56/56i.pdf (accessed 14 November 2014).

[260] ibid.

[261] Walker (n 2) para 2.2 (iv).

[262] B Hannigan, 'Board failures in the financial crisis: Tinkering with codes and the need for wider corporate governance reforms: Part 2' (2012) 33 *Company Lawyer* 35, 41.

suggested in the Walker Review, do really suffice to improve the quality of the work of non-executive directors in UK boardrooms in a sustained manner.

These discussions reveal a rather critical view of the way in which many non-executive directors exercise their function at present. This situation has direct ramifications for the promotion of CSR in the boardroom. If non-executive directors do not devote enough time to their jobs or do not sufficiently challenge business decisions or contribute their positions to debates, then it is unlikely that they will achieve much for the promotion of CSR.

B.   The Composition of the Board

The composition of the board is closely connected with the question of what contribution non-executive directors can make to the promotion of CSR.[263] A more diverse board could potentially lead to a better inclusion of stakeholder interests in the decision-making process within the constraints of the system of company law and corporate governance analysed so far.

This idea has been taken up at European Union level. The European Commission's action plan on company law and corporate governance, published in December 2012, inter alia, addresses the improvement of transparency on board diversity with a particular focus on gender balance at board level. Prior to its Action Plan, the Commission published two Green Papers on corporate governance in listed companies and banks.[264]

---

[263]   Within the space of this chapter it is impossible to compare the one-tier board structure of English companies with two-tier systems such as the German corporate governance system (that has a managing board and a supervisory board). The German model generally provides for a stronger representation of employees in the decision-making process. In the German model, employees in German public limited companies (*Aktiengesellschaften*) make up to 50 per cent of the members on the supervisory board. Moreover, employees are involved in the decision-making process of companies through works councils. See for an introduction: F Schwarz, 'The German co-determination system: a model for introducing corporate social responsibility requirements into Australian law? Part 1' (2008) 23 *JIBLR* 125; F Schwarz, 'The German co-determination system: a model for introducing corporate social responsibility requirements into Australian law? Part 2' (2008) 23 *JIBLR* 190.

[264]   European Commission, 'Green Paper: The EU corporate governance framework' (COM 2011, 164 final), available at http://ec.europa.eu/internal_market/consultations/2011/corporate-governance-framework_en.htm (accessed 14 November 2014); European Commission, *Green Paper: Corporate governance*

The Green Paper on corporate governance in listed companies discusses boardroom diversity, in particular the inclusion of women and non-nationals in terms of their positive impact on the effective functioning of the board. The Commission emphasised that it considered 'group think' to be a realistic danger in the current composition of many boards. The Green Paper warns that a board consisting of executive directors with a similar personal and professional background is less likely to challenge traditional patterns of thought.

In this context it is interesting to consider the conclusions of an empirical investigation into the effects of the presence of outside directors and female directors on the company's CSR performance.[265] The study analysed more than 500 of the largest US-American companies in the aftermath of the Sarbanes-Oxley Act[266] which requires greater inclusion of outside directors on boards. The authors of the study argue that the empirical results show that greater presence of outside and female directors was related to better CSR performance of the company.[267] Whilst the potential effects of more diverse boards on the promotion of CSR cannot fully be discussed in the legal analysis here, it is worthwhile noting that boardroom diversity is increasingly regarded as an important issue for corporate governance. It is possible that a more diverse group of non-executive directors could lead to a better inclusion of CSR considerations to the decision-making process of the board. However, even if this might be the case, the directors would still have to work within the framework of s172 (1) CA and its emphasis on shareholder value.

VII. CONCLUSION

This chapter has shown that the system of corporate governance within the framework of the enlightened shareholder value doctrine has at least, in theory, the potential to promote CSR. Corporate governance and CSR

---

in financial institutions and remuneration policies (COM 2010, 284 final), available at http://ec.europa.eu/internal_market/company/docs/modern/com2010_284_en.pdf (accessed 14 November 2014).

[265] J Zhang, H Zhu and H Ding, 'Board composition and corporate social responsibility: An empirical investigation into the post-Sarbanes-Oxley Era' (2013) 114 *Journal of Business Ethics* 381.

[266] The Act requires companies listed on the major stock exchanges to have a majority of independent directors.

[267] Zhang, Zhu and Ding (n 265) 389.

overlap in different areas which are addressed here: the duty to promote the success of the company for the benefit of the members as a whole (s172 CA), the reporting duty (s414A CA), the derivative action (s260 CA) and the board. There is a strong correlation between the list of factors in s172 (1) CA and the concept of CSR. Nevertheless, the conclusions drawn from the different aspects of company law and corporate governance analysed in this chapter in terms of promoting CSR are rather disappointing. In particular, the duty in s172 (1) CA has so far not achieved much for the promotion of CSR. The present state of English company law contrasts with the announcements of the government about the long-term view that English company law would take, following the enactment of the Companies Act 2006 with the enlightened shareholder value model. In reality, not much has been achieved from a CSR point of view so far.

The various aspects analysed in this chapter all have severe shortcomings in the promotion of the socially responsible conduct of companies. CSR is too much left to the discretion of directors. One can critically ask what the real meaning of enlightened shareholder value is in English law, in light of the results of the legal analysis. The interests of stakeholders and the concept of CSR continue to be subordinated under the shareholder value prerogative. The ultimate beneficiaries of the company remain the shareholders with only discretionary consideration of other aspects. The analysis of the s172 (1) CA duty, the strategic report and the derivative action has demonstrated that English company law and corporate governance are still too embedded in the shareholder value model to effectively promote CSR. Moreover, it is doubtful if the recent focus on institutional investors is going to significantly change things for the better. The UK Stewardship Code contains only little recognition of social and environmental matters. Also, more generally, it is doubtful whether investors will go beyond scrutinising their investee companies and push for a stronger CSR policy. The conclusion of this chapter therefore is that, despite their overlap with CSR, English company law and corporate governance contribute only little to the promotion of CSR in practice. This situation is unlikely to change without a redirection of the corporate objective in English law to a more pluralistic understanding of the firm.

3. Contract law, global supply chains and corporate social responsibility

I. SUPPLY CHAINS AND CSR

In the course of globalisation, companies no longer completely produce their goods themselves within the boundaries of their resident country, but rather distribute their production to suppliers in different countries around the world through global supply chains.[1] Companies in the global North and West have increasingly outsourced parts of their production to suppliers in developing and transitional countries in order to reduce cost.[2] To that end they have developed sophisticated supply chains as a business tool.[3] The supply chain is defined as the series of companies, including suppliers, customers, and logistics providers which work together to deliver a value package of goods and services to the end customer.[4] Global supply chains function across different countries and different cultures.[5] This process of outsourcing to suppliers is particularly prevalent in labour-intensive production industries such as

---

[1]   See M Andersen and T Skjoett-Larsen, 'Corporate social responsibility in global supply chains' (2009) 14 *Supply Chain Management: An International Journal* 75, 77.

[2]   A Millington, 'Responsibility in the supply chain' in A Crane, A McWilliams, D Matten et al. (eds), *The Oxford Handbook of Corporate Social Responsibility* (OUP 2008) 363.

[3]   R Eltantawy, G Fox and L Giunipero, 'Supply management ethical responsibility: Reputation and performance impacts' (2009) 14 (2) *Supply Chain Management: An International Journal* 99.

[4]   M Maloni and M Brown, 'Corporate social responsibility in the supply chain: an application in the food industry' (2006) 68 *Journal of Business Ethics*, 35, 36.

[5]   C Muller, W Vermeulen and P Glasbergen, 'Pushing or sharing as value-driven strategies for societal change in global supply chains: Two case studies in the British-South African fresh fruit supply chain' (2012) 21 *Business Strategy and the Environment* 127, 129.

the garment industry and also in the food industry.[6] The buyers in these supply chains are often multinational companies.[7]

However, reports about human rights violations of employees of suppliers in the developing world, for instance through the use of child labour, unsafe working conditions or excessive working hours, have negatively affected the reputation of some Western companies which trade with these suppliers.[8] The collapse of the Rana Plaza Building in Bangladesh in April 2013, which killed more than 1100 people, dramatically highlighted the often-hazardous working conditions at supplier factories.[9]

Similarly, the pollution of the environment through poor production standards at the suppliers' factories[10] has become public causing a negative impact on the reputation of some of the Western companies which use supply chains.[11] The suppliers are often based in developing countries with weak legal standards in terms of human rights and/or a weak system of law enforcement.[12] The supply chain has therefore

---

[6] I Mamic, 'Managing global supply chain: the sports footwear, apparel and retail sectors' (2005) 59 *Journal of Business Ethics* 81.

[7] See the introduction into the concept of a 'multinational corporation': P Muchlinski, *Multinational Enterprises and the Law* (2nd edn, OUP 2007) 7–8. He opines that it may not be possible to define the term 'multinational corporation' with 'any degree of accuracy'. He states that an important feature of multinationals is their capacity to operate across national borders in terms of their business and managerial structure, their production and their trading.

[8] See, for example, *The Independent*, 'Leading article: The gruesome reality of sweatshops' (1 October 2010), available at http://www.independent.co.uk/opinion/leading-articles/leading-article-the-gruesome-reality-of-sweatshops-2094318.html?origin=internalSearch (accessed 16 November 2014); R Locke et al., 'Beyond corporate codes of conduct: Work organization and labour standards at NIKE's suppliers' (2007) 146 (1–2) *International Labour Review* 21.

[9] See for a comprehensive coverage of the Rana Plaza disaster and subsequent developments a special section in *The Guardian*, available at http://www.theguardian.com/world/rana-plaza (accessed 16 November 2014).

[10] David Barboza, 'Apple cited as adding to pollution in China', *The New York Times* (1 September 2011), available at http://www.nytimes.com/2011/09/02/technology/apple-suppliers-causing-environmental-problems-chinese-group-says.html?_r=1 (accessed 16 November 2014).

[11] C Soosay, A Fearne and B Dent, 'Sustainable value chain analysis – a case study of Oxford Landing from "vine to dine"' (2012) 17 *Supply Chain Management: An International Journal* 68.

[12] Millington (n 2) 364.

become increasingly scrutinised by NGOs, trade unions and consumers.[13] The UN Guiding Principles on Business and Human Rights refer to the responsibility of companies to 'seek to prevent or mitigate adverse human rights impacts' linked to their supply chain.[14] At the EU level, a document on responsible supply chain management was published in 2010, commissioned under the European Union's Programme for Employment and Social Solidarity – PROGRESS (2007–2013).[15]

As a consequence of this increasing interest in the supply chain, Western multinational companies, particularly those with well-known brands,[16] have come under increasing public and political pressure to show that they are socially responsible in their supply chain.[17] Many multinational companies therefore began to implement CSR policies into their supply chain.[18] To that end companies usually develop their own code of conduct or adopt a code developed by a third party which contains the company's policy on CSR and the principles it expects everyone within the company to uphold.[19] Many companies incorporate a

---

[13]   P Robinson, 'Do voluntary labour initiatives make a difference for the conditions of workers in global supply chains?, (2010) 52 *Journal of Industrial Relations* 561, 564.

[14]   Principle 13, UN Guiding Principles on Business and Human Rights, see: John Ruggie, *Guiding Principles on Business and Human Rights: Implementing the United Nations 'Protect, Respect and Remedy' Framework*, available at http://www.business-humanrights.org/SpecialRepPortal/Home/Protect-Respect-Remedy-Framework/GuidingPrinciples (accessed 16 November 2014).

[15]   M van Opijnen and Joris Oldenziel, *Responsible Supply Chain Management, Potential Success Factors and Challenges for Addressing Prevailing Human Rights and Other CSR Issues in Supply Chains of EU-Based Companies* (2010), available at http://ec.europa.eu/enterprise/policies/sustainable-business/files/business-human-rights/final_rscm_report-11-04-12_en.pdf (accessed 16 November 2014).

[16]   D Hoang and B Jones, 'Why do corporate codes of conduct fail? Women workers and clothing supply chains in Vietnam' (2012) 12 *Global Social Policy* 67, 68.

[17]   See J Leigh and S Waddock, 'The emergence of total responsibility management systems: J. Sainsbury's (plc) voluntary responsibility management systems for global food retail supply chains' (2006) 111 (4) *Business and Society Review* 409, 410.

[18]   Andersen and Skjoett-Larsen (n1) 77.

[19]   D Wells, 'Too weak for the job: Corporate codes of conduct, non-governmental organisations and the regulation of international labour standards' (2007) 7 *Global Social Policy* 51, 52. Pearson and Seyfang define these codes of conduct in the following way: '... codes of conduct are voluntary self-regulatory tools that are applicable to specific firms, or groups of firms, and thus to certain

CSR code of conduct into their supply chain contracts with their suppliers, although they do so differently and with different contractual effect.[20] The corporate codes of conduct are defined as documents which state a number of social and environmental standards and principles that a firm's suppliers are expected to fulfil.[21] This incorporation of the buyer's CSR policies into the supply contract is an interesting development, given that the codes of conduct of companies are often criticised for being non-binding.[22] Studies have analysed the proliferation of such CSR codes of conduct among the FTSE 100 companies.[23] A study published in 2010 shows that 77 out of the 100 constituent FTSE 100 firms had adopted such codes and many companies have policies about ethical sourcing which they integrate into the supply chain relations with their suppliers.[24] In light of the growing interest in CSR issues, it is to be expected that this number has increased further since then. In terms of content, most of these ethical sourcing policies stipulate requirements to uphold employee working conditions and health and safety at work, freedom of association, decent remuneration for employees, respect for

---

groups of workers at certain times, rather than applying to all citizens or workers in particular states', see R Pearson and G Seyfang, 'New hope or false dawn?: Voluntary codes of conduct, labour regulation and social policy in a globalising world' (2001) 1 *Global Social Policy* 48, 52

[20]   E Pedersen and M Andersen, 'Safeguarding corporate social responsibility (CSR) in global supply chains: how codes of conduct are managed in buyer-supplier relationships' (2006) 6 *Journal of Public Affairs* 228, 237.

[21]   Mamic (n 6) 81. These codes are established by individual companies, by industry associations, at national level (e.g. the Ethical Trading Initiative in the UK; the Department for International Development was involved into the development of this code), at regional level (e.g. Code of business conduct by the Asia-Pacific economic co-operation) or by international organisations. See for further information: L Preuss, 'Codes of conduct in organisational context: from cascade to lattice-work of codes' (2010) 94 *Journal of Business Ethics* 471, 472–3.

[22]   See C Pedamon, 'Corporate social responsibility: a new approach to promoting integrity and responsibility' (2010) *Company Lawyer* 172, 177

[23]   http://www.ftse.com/Indices/UK_Indices/Downloads/FTSE_100_Index_Factsheet.pdf (accessed 12 September 2014).

[24]   Preuss (n 21) 475: Preuss analysed the range of codes that constituent firms of the FTSE 100 index use. His findings show that 77 companies used a general company-wide code of conduct which often also include stipulations for suppliers, 43 companies had adopted ethical sourcing policies which specifically contain what companies expect from their suppliers in terms of CSR standards. Sixteen of the FTSE 100 companies were found to have specific codes which regulate the supply chain.

human rights and a commitment to environmental policies.[25] The principles are often based on well-known CSR standards such as the UN Global Compact, the ETI Base Code, the ILO Declaration on Fundamental Principles and Rights at Work or the UN Declaration of Human Rights.[26]

The incorporation of CSR into supply chain contracts has been extensively analysed in the management literature.[27] This chapter contributes to the existing literature a detailed contract law analysis of the incorporation of CSR policies into (global) supply chains. The purpose of this chapter is to answer the question to what extent English contract law promotes socially responsible behaviour in corporations.

CSR policies can only be enforced in contract law if the following is the case: First, CSR policies must become 'part' of the supply contracts and hence become enforceable (either by the Western company at the head of the supply chain or, for example, by an employee of the supplier, although the privity of contract doctrine makes the enforcement in supply chain contracts a complex issue). Secondly, the Western companies must be able to procure an appropriate remedy in contract law for these breaches. Thirdly, the Western companies (the buyers) must be sufficiently aware of breaches of these contractual terms pertaining to the CSR policies in order to at least consider using contract law to promote socially responsible behaviour among those companies in transitional economies where concerns about violation of CSR issues such as human rights are focused. The subsequent analysis will be structured in the order of these three preconditions.

II. JURISDICTION AND APPLICABILITY OF ENGLISH LAW IN INTERNATIONAL SUPPLY CONTRACTS

Due to the international nature of the supply contracts, it is necessary to establish under what circumstances English courts have jurisdiction and when English law is applicable.

It is likely that English companies (the buyers) will bring an action for breach of contract at English courts. English courts must apply the Brussels I Regulation in order to determine whether they can assume

---

[25] ibid, 483.
[26] See Andersen and Skjoett-Larsen (n1) 78.
[27] See for example, B Jiang, 'Implementing supplier codes of conduct in global supply chains: Process explanations from theoretic and empirical perspectives' (2009) 85 *Journal of Business Ethics* 77–92.

jurisdiction.[28] If the defendant is not domiciled in an EU member state, the general rule is that the court may apply its traditional rules of jurisdiction subject to Articles 22 and 23.[29] In most cases the defendant will be a supplier from a developing country and he will therefore not be domiciled in an EU member state. The parties can, pursuant to Article 23 (1) of the Regulation, decide that the courts of a member state have exclusive jurisdiction as long as one party to the contract is domiciled in a member state.[30] This is indeed the case in the contractual terms and conditions reviewed for this chapter in which they all contain a clause which stipulates that English courts have exclusive jurisdiction.[31] The reason for this situation is the strong bargaining power of the English companies as the buyers in these contracts.

When English courts are asked to hear an international contractual dispute, they have to apply the Rome I Regulation to determine the law governing the contract.[32] This Regulation governs choice of law in the European Union and is hence applicable to English courts in their decision as to which law governs a contract. For the Regulation to be applicable it is not necessary that the parties have a connection to the EU. What is required is that an action is brought at a court of an EU member state and that the case raises the question of which law is applicable. As with the choice of jurisdiction, the parties have freedom of choice to determine the law applicable to their contract.[33] The supply contracts

---

[28]   Council Regulation (EC) No 44/2001 of 22 December 2000 on jurisdiction and the recognition and enforcement of judgments in civil and commercial matters (or Council Regulation (EC) 44/2001).

[29]   Article 4 (1): 'If the defendant is not domiciled in a Member State, the jurisdiction of the courts of each Member State shall, subject to Articles 22 and 23, be determined by the law of that Member State.'

[30]   Section 7, Prorogation of jurisdiction, Article 23 (1): 'If the parties, one or more of whom is domiciled in a Member State, have agreed that a court or the courts of a Member State are to have jurisdiction to settle any disputes which have arisen or which may arise in connection with a particular legal relationship, that court or those courts shall have jurisdiction.'

[31]   For example, Rio Tinto's terms and conditions for purchase orders contain the following clause in its section 23 (a) Law: '... and the Supplier irrevocably and unconditionally submits to the exclusive jurisdiction of the English courts for all purposes in connection herewith'.

[32]   (Regulation (EC) No 593/2008 of the European Parliament and of the Council of 17 June 2008 on the law applicable to contractual obligations). Article 2 of the Regulation provides that the law specified by the Regulation shall be applied whether or not it is the law of a Member State.

[33]   Article 3 (1) of the Rome I Regulation. This provision means that parties have autonomy to decide among themselves which law should govern them.

analysed for this chapter all contained a choice of law clause in the buyer's general terms and conditions which determined English law as the applicable law for the contract.[34] Such a choice of law clause is likely to be included in most supply chain contracts due to the strong bargaining position of the buyer. Moreover, English law is generally the law of choice in international commercial contracts.[35]

English law does not draw a formal distinction between domestic and international sales contracts[36] which means that the law which will be analysed in this chapter is domestic English sales contract law despite the international nature of the supply chain contracts.

III. UNDER WHAT CIRCUMSTANCES CAN CSR POLICIES BECOME ENFORCEABLE CONTRACTUAL TERMS?

This section asks if and, if so, how the buyer's CSR policies become enforceable contractual terms.

The information about CSR in supply chain relationships retrieved from academic literature is complemented by small-scale research conducted for the purpose of this chapter. The websites of fifteen FTSE 100 companies[37] (the ten largest FTSE 100 companies measured by market capitalisation[38] plus five further companies from industries across the

---

[34] The effectiveness of the buyer's terms and conditions for the supply contract is a separate legal issue which is addressed below. It is assumed here.

[35] R Bradgate, *Commercial Law* (3rd edn, OUP 2005) para 1.4. The Law Society of England and Wales has even prepared a booklet for foreign businesses emphasizing the benefits of choosing English law for their commercial contracts. English law has therefore become an 'export product' in international trade. See: The Law Society of England and Wales, England and Wales: The jurisdiction of choice, available at http://www.lawsociety.org.uk/documents/downloads/ jurisdiction_of_choice_brochure.pdf (accessed 17 September 14).

[36] Bradgate (n 35) para 7.4. There are only few distinctions between domestic sales and international sales, for instance, s26 of the Unfair Contract Terms Act 1977 excludes 'international supply contracts' from the Act.

[37] The fifteen companies researched are: BHP Billiton, Royal Dutch Shell, HSBC, Vodafone Group, BP, Rio Tinto Group, GlaxoSmithKline, Unilever, British American Tobacco, BG Group, Marks & Spencer, BT Group, Burberry Group, Diageo and Tesco.

[38] As of 9 March 2011 these ten companies are: BHP Billiton, Royal Dutch Shell, HSBC, Vodafone Group, BP, Rio Tinto Group, GlaxoSmithKline, Unilever, British American Tobacco, BG Group; see http://www.telegraph.co.uk/

board which are known to have a supplier-base in developing countries)[39] were researched by this author in order to find out what CSR requirements they stipulate for their suppliers. This research had two aims: The first aim was to find out if and, if so, how CSR issues are incorporated into supply chain contracts between the UK-based multinational companies (the buyers) and their suppliers, for instance, through inclusion into the buyer's terms and conditions. The second purpose was to obtain contractual clauses which refer to CSR and which are used in the buyer–supplier contractual relations. This small-scale research of the way in which fifteen FTSE 100 companies incorporate CSR into their supply chain was necessary as the management literature seems to view the incorporation of CSR into supply chain contracts as given without describing the actual detail of how this is effected legally. The existing literature rather analyses the content of the CSR policies imposed on suppliers,[40] without examining if these duties have any effect in contract law.

All fifteen companies selected for the research here have made information available on their website pertaining to their CSR policies. Most of the companies explain the way they include CSR into their supply chain relationships with their suppliers, for example, through a reference to the buyer's CSR code of conduct in the standard purchase order forms. Several firms also provide their general terms and conditions which contain the CSR clauses and which they incorporate into their contracts with their suppliers. With the insights it offers into the practice of supply chain contracts, this material informs the legal analysis that follows.

This section analyses the ways in which buyers incorporate CSR into their supply contracts in order to determine if and, if so, how the corporate codes of conduct become part of the contracts (i.e. contractual terms) between the Western buyer and the supplier based in a transitional economy. The research of the fifteen companies shows four different

finance/markets/8371481/Top-ten-most-valuable-companies-in-the-FTSE-100-in-pictures.html (accessed 12 November 2014).

[39] These five companies are: Marks & Spencer, BT Group, Burberry Group, Diageo and Tesco.

[40] See A Tencati, A Russo and V Quaglia, 'Unintended consequences of CSR: Protectionism and collateral damage in global supply chains: the case of Vietnam' (2008) 8 (4) *Corporate Governance* 518; K Amaeshi, O Osuji and P Nnodim, 'Corporate social responsibility in supply chains of global brands: a boundaryless responsibility? Clarifications, exceptions and implications' (2008) 81 *Journal of Business Ethics* 223.

ways of incorporating the buyer's CSR policies into the supply chain relationship.

The first and most common mechanism of incorporation seems to be through the terms and conditions of the buyer which are incorporated into the buyer's purchase order forms. These terms and conditions either contain a reference to the buyer's code of conduct (e.g. Unilever and Rio Tinto)[41] or an express term which stipulates the buyer's CSR principles (e.g. GlaxoSmithKline).[42] An example of a reference to the buyer's code of conduct is the following term in Unilever's terms and conditions:

> Each supplier … acknowledges that it has reviewed Unilever's Responsible Sourcing Policy (**'RSP'**) and agrees that all of their activities shall be conducted in accordance with the RSP … The RSP can be accessed at the internet address … .[43]

The clause in Unilever's terms and conditions that refers to the company's CSR code of conduct is the contractual clause. The code of conduct is not a term of the contract, it is a reference document. It will help if the contractual term which refers to it is a condition, warranty or an innominate term (which is discussed later on and is important for the remedy the buyer can procure in case of a breach of the term) and whether or not the supplier is in breach of the term.

---

[41] Rio Tinto London Limited, *Purchase Order for the Supply of Goods, Terms and Conditions*, section 10 Compliance with law and policies: 'In supplying the Goods and associated services (if any), the Supplier will: (a) … ; (b) comply with Rio Tinto's policy titled "The Way We Work" that can be found at http://…', available at http://procurement.riotinto.com/documents/London_Purchase_Order_Terms_and_Conditions_for_Goods_(30_Sep_2014)_English_Version.pdf (accessed 16 November 2014); Unilever, *General Terms & Conditions of Purchase of Goods of Unilever Supply Chain Company AG ('Conditions')*, available at http://www.unilever.com/images/GTCs-Purchase-of-Goods.14.05.08_tcm13-326870.pdf (accessed 16 November 2014).

[42] GlaxoSmithKline, *Terms and Conditions of Purchase (Goods & Services)*, section 21: 'Ethical Standards and Human Rights: 21.1. Unless otherwise required or prohibited by law, Supplier warrants to the best of its knowledge, that in relation to the supply of Goods or Services under the terms of the Agreement: 21.1.1. it does not employ, engage or otherwise use any form of child labour …', available at http://www.gsk.com/media/279800/gsk-uk-terms-and-conditions-goods-and-services.pdf (accessed 16 November 2014).

[43] Unilever, *General Terms and Conditions of Purchase of Goods of Unilever Supply Chain Company AG ('Conditions')* section 13.

The alternative mechanism for incorporating CSR into the buyer's terms and conditions is through an express stipulation in the terms exemplified by GlaxoSmithKline:

> 21. Unless otherwise required or prohibited by law, Supplier warrants, to the best of its knowledge, that in relation to the supply of Goods or Services under the terms of the Agreement:
>
> 21.1.1. it does not employ, engage or otherwise use any child labour in circumstances such that the tasks performed by any such child labour could reasonably be foreseen to cause either physical or emotional impairment to the development of such child ...[44]

The difference to the previous example is that the CSR policy is in the contractual term without a reference to a further document. In both these cases the CSR policy of the buyer is contained in the buyer's terms and conditions. The reason for the use of general terms and conditions in purchase orders is that this incorporation saves the buyer a significant amount of time as he does not have to negotiate these contractual terms each time he orders goods.[45] Moreover, by using his terms and conditions, the buyer can include terms which are favourable for him.[46] In this situation, the buyer's CSR policies only become 'part' of the contract if his terms and conditions form part of the contract between the buyer and supplier which will be discussed below.

Secondly, the CSR code of conduct can be incorporated into a contract which is not based on standard terms and conditions, but whose terms were expressly negotiated. In this situation there are two ways of incorporating the buyer's CSR policies which are similar to the previous scenario: Either through reference to the buyer's code of conduct or through express stipulations in the contract. In this situation, the buyer's CSR policy becomes 'part' of the contract when the contract between the two parties is formed (see below).

Thirdly, some companies declare that they incorporate their CSR policies into their invitations to tender.[47] For the CSR policies to have

---

[44]   GlaxoSmithKline, *Terms and Conditions of Purchase (Goods & Services)*, section 21.

[45]   Bradgate (n 35) para 2.5.3.

[46]   ibid.

[47]   BT states that this is one of its ways of how it incorporates its CSR policy into its supply chain: 'Working with BT Generic Standards', 1. Introduction: Generic Standards will form part of the tenderer selection process and will be included in Invitations to Tender and form part of any subsequent contract. The inclusion of Generic Standards into Invitation to Tenders or contracts will be

contractual effects in this situation it is necessary that they are incorporated into the subsequent contract between buyer and supplier, either through the first or the second mechanism described above.

Finally, some companies state that they ask their suppliers to sign up to their code of conduct.[48] This mechanism creates contractual effects only if this signing of the code of conduct makes it a term of the contract. However, the privity of contract rule means that it is generally the parties to that contract who can enforce that contractual effect.

The following section analyses if and, if so, how the buyer's CSR policies become 'part' of the contract through these four mechanisms. It will follow the order used in this section with the incorporation of CSR through the buyer's terms and conditions taking priority due to their frequency.

A. Incorporation through the Buyer's Terms and Conditions

The buyer's terms and conditions, which are usually referred to on the buyer's purchase order form, must form part of the contract, that is, they must be properly incorporated into the contract. To do this, the buyer and supplier must first of all enter into a contract which presupposes that they reach an agreement, that is, offer and acceptance.[49] The basic rules as to the formation of contract are the same, irrespective of the type of commercial supply contract.[50] There are different kinds of commercial supply contracts such as the contract for the sale of goods, governed by

---

either through the Quality of Suppliers and Generic Standards clause, specifically drafted contract clauses or via inclusion in tender documents by buyers.'

[48] Vodafone, 'Checking Compliance: ... We ask our preferred and strategic suppliers to sign up to our Code of Ethical Purchasing and to ...', see: Vodafone, *Corporate Responsibility – Vodafone UK 2010/11*, available at http://www.voda fone.co.uk/cs/groups/configfiles/documents/contentdocuments/cr_report_2010_ 11.pdf (accessed 10 October 2014).

[49] The further requirements for the formation of contract, consideration and intention to create legal relations, are unproblematic in these supply chain contracts and will not be discussed in further detail here. There are no formal requirements for the contract. Consideration is rarely a problem in commercial contracts for the supply of goods or services as businesses do not tend to promise something for nothing, see Bradgate (n 35) para 2.2.1.

[50] In many cases the classification of the contract will not affect the obligations of the parties as the Sale of Goods Act 1979 and the legislation governing other supply arrangements are similar on certain points, such as implied terms as to quality, see R Bradgate and F White, *Commercial Law – Legal Practice Course Guides* (OUP 2009) para 9.4. The House of Lords has

the Sale of Goods Act 1979, or the contract for the supply of services, governed by the Supply of Goods and Services Act 1982.[51] However, neither of these statutes contains all the rules applicable to these types of contracts, as many rules governing these contracts can be found in the common law or in other statutes.[52]

Offers must contain all integral parts of the contract so that the offeree can just say 'yes'. For example, for contracts of sale of goods the following elements were held to be 'essential elements' of the contract although some terms can be implied into contracts, for example, default provisions under the Sale of Goods Act 1979: (a) the goods ordered should be described without ambiguity; (b) the purchase price and the terms of payment should be stated; and (c) the terms of delivery should be set out, including instructions for packing and invoicing, transportation and insurance.[53] The purchase order form is a commercial document issued by a buyer to a seller which indicates types, quantities, and agreed prices for products or services the seller will provide to the buyer.[54] The sending of a purchase order to a supplier is therefore considered to constitute a legal offer to buy products or services as the buyer makes an order.[55] The purchase order forms used by the buyers (the companies based in the UK) must contain all these essential elements of the contract in order to constitute a binding offer.

This offer must be accepted by the supplier (the seller). An acceptance is defined as any statement, by words or conduct, which clearly and

---

stated that it is undesirable to have unnecessary distinctions between different types of contract, see *Young & Marten Ltd v McManus Childs Ltd* [1969] AC 454.

[51] Further types of supply contracts which transfer ownership and possession of goods are gift, bailment, hire or barter. It usually makes no difference to the rights of the parties if the contract is one of sale or for work and materials. For further information see Bradgate and White (n 50) paras 9.4.6, 17.

[52] See for further information: Bradgate and White (n 50) para 9.1.1.

[53] C Murray, D Holloway and D Timson-Hunt, *Schmitthoff's Export Trade – The Law and Practice of International Trade* (11th edn, Sweet & Maxwell 2007) para 3-005.

[54] D Dobler and D Burt, *Purchasing and Supply Management, Text and Cases* (6th edn, McGraw-Hill 1996) 70.

[55] ibid. The classification of the purchase order as an 'offer' is also suggested by the terms and conditions of the buyers which are to be incorporated into the supply contract. For instance, GlaxoSmithKline's Terms and Conditions of Purchase (Goods & Services), section 2.2. states: '2. Status of these terms and conditions, … 2.2. The Purchase Order constitutes an offer by GSK to purchase Goods or Services specified therein in accordance with these Terms and Conditions …'.

unequivocally indicates that the person making it agrees to be bound by the terms of the offer.[56] When accepting, the offeree must not vary or add to the terms of the offer as this would constitute a counter-offer which rejects and terminates the original offer. It is not likely to happen in the supply situation here that the supplier would take the risk of changing the terms. The acceptance must usually be communicated to the offeror. Silence is generally held not to be able to amount to an acceptance although there are some exceptions to this rule.[57] However, the offeror can waive this requirement which means that acceptance can be by conduct.[58] In the example of a sale of goods contract, the seller may in this case accept an offer by dispatching the goods that the offeror ordered in the purchase order form. Acceptance of a purchase order by a seller usually forms a one-off contract between the buyer and the seller, so no contract exists until the purchase order is accepted. This system is used to control the purchasing of products and services from external suppliers.[59]

To form part of the supply contract, the general terms and conditions of the buyer which contain the CSR obligations must be incorporated into his offer (which is commonly the purchase order).[60] This incorporation can be done by printing the terms and conditions on offers. The text of the offer should at least contain a clear reference to the fact that terms and conditions of purchase are printed on the reverse of the offer or on an attached sheet or on a website.[61] The buyer must obtain the seller's agreement to the terms and conditions. To that end the seller should ideally agree in writing to the offer (countersign), for instance through

---

[56]   Bradgate (n 35) para 2.3.2.

[57]   Murray, Holloway and Timson-Hunt (n 53) para 3-008. *Felthouse v Bindley* (1862) 11 CB NS 869 is often referred to as the authority for this rule. However, there are some exceptions to this rule, for example: (1.) The offeree's silence can constitute acceptance where there has been a course of dealing whereby the offeree has taken the benefit of services offered; (2.) The offeree's silence will constitute acceptance where it is the offeree who is attempting to hold the offeror to the offeror's stipulation of silence. See for further information: J Poole, *Textbook on Contract Law* (11th edn, OUP 2012) 57–9.

[58]   Bradgate (n 35) para 2.3.2. For instance, GlaxoSmithKline's Terms and Conditions of Purchase (Goods & Services) stipulate the following in section 2.2. '... The Purchase Order and these Terms and Conditions shall be deemed to be accepted by Supplier on the earlier of: (a) Supplier issuing a written acceptance of the Purchase Order; or (b) Supplier doing any act consistent with fulfilling the Purchase Order, at which point the Agreement shall come into existence.'

[59]   Dobler and Burt (n 54) 70.

[60]   Murray, Holloway and Timson-Hunt (n 53) para 3-017.

[61]   ibid.

returning a countersigned acceptance form.[62] Agreement is also possible by conduct, if the other party despatches the goods which happens often in practice. A signed agreement is binding even if the party signing it has not understood or read it.[63] If the parties have not signed an agreement, no terms are incorporated unless the party which wants to incorporate them has drawn the terms to the attention of the party prior to, or at the same time of, the agreement.[64] These rules mean that for the terms and conditions of the buyer to take effect it is important that the offeror (the buyer) clearly refers to them and that the seller (the supplier) agrees to them, ideally by countersignature. Otherwise, the buyer's terms and conditions which contain his CSR policy will not be included into the contract.

It may be, however, that the buyer's terms and conditions do not become part of the contract due to a practice known as 'battle of the forms'.[65] A 'battle of forms' denotes the situation where one party notifies the other that their general terms apply to the contract, but the other party responds by saying that their general terms will apply.[66] Although such a 'battle of forms' usually occurs in relation to conflicting provisions about the retention of title and exclusion clauses, it is to be expected that the same would apply to conflicting CSR policies. It is the buyer who wants to incorporate his company's CSR code of conduct into his supply contracts whereas the seller might either have less burdensome CSR principles or not have a CSR policy in his terms and conditions at all. In the scenario here, a 'battle of forms' occurs when the buyer orders goods on his terms and conditions of purchase whereas the seller acknowledges the order on his own standard terms of sale.[67] The traditional approach of the English courts is that this situation is analysed in terms of offer and counter-offer.[68] That means where the buyer orders goods on a form which incorporate his standard terms and the seller acknowledges the order on a form that incorporates his terms, the

---

[62] ibid, paras 3-010, 3-011, 3-017.
[63] *L'Estrange v Graucob Ltd* [1934] 2 KB 394; *Chellaram & Co v China Ocean Shipping Co* [1991] 1 Lloyd's Rep 493.
[64] *Parker v South Eastern Ry* [1877] 2 CPD 416.
[65] R Lawson and S Singleton, *Commercial Contracts: A Practical Guide to Standard Terms* (Tottel Publishing 2006) para A1.17.
[66] ibid.
[67] Bradgate (n 35) para 2.3.4; J Adams, 'The battle of forms' (1983) *JBL* 297.
[68] *Butler Machine Tool Co Ltd v Ex-Cell-O Corpn* [1979] 1 All ER 965.

response by the seller will be a counter-offer rather than an acceptance.[69] The 'battle of forms' is usually won by the party who sends the last terms and conditions (commonly described as 'firing the last shot').[70] In that case the seller (supplier) would be in a favourable position to make their terms and conditions win the 'battle' by delivering the goods ordered with a delivery note which contains the seller's standard terms which the buyer may be deemed to accept by keeping the goods. This situation means that the seller's terms and conditions would prevail as they are the last general terms to reach the opposite party. It is possible that the counter-offer is accepted by conduct. In a 'battle of forms' the difficulty is to determine which standard terms apply. The buyers will often try to ensure acceptance of their standard terms by obtaining the signature of their suppliers that they consent to their terms.[71]

Although in theory, the law on 'battle of forms' appears relevant, it may not be in practice. In commercial practice, due to the strong economic bargaining power of the buyer in international supply contracts, one can expect that buyers can often impose their CSR policies on their suppliers as a prerequisite to trading and that no 'battle of forms' occurs at all. Multinational buyers from Western companies are usually in a position where they can choose between numerous potential suppliers. Their suppliers are therefore unlikely to enter into a 'battle of forms' with their buyers.

Occasionally, it is also possible that the parties start performing (i.e. supplying and paying) before a contract has, in fact, been concluded or that no contract has been concluded at all due to discrepancies in the declarations of the parties.[72] In that case, a court could or could not conclude that a contract came into being and depending on when it came into being a CSR policy may or may not be incorporated.

Finally, the rules on unfair contract terms cannot make invalid the CSR policies which are included in the buyer's terms and conditions. The reason is that the supply chain contracts analysed here consist of a

---

[69] R Bradgate, 'Formation of contracts' in A Grubb, *The Law of Contract* (3rd edn, LexisNexis Butterworths 2007) para 2.221.

[70] Bradgate (n 35) para 2.3.4.

[71] *Butler Machine Tool Co Ltd v Ex Cell-O Corpn* [1979] 1 All ER 965.

[72] Where parties commence performance before agreement is reached, it depends on the circumstances if a contract has been concluded in the end and if standard terms are incorporated, see *British Steel Corporation v Cleveland Bridge and Engineering Co Ltd* [1984] 1 All ER 504.

business-to-business situation whereas the unfair contract terms framework, by and large, focusses on business-to-consumer relationships.[73] S3
of the Unfair Contract Terms Act 1977 which applies to both business-
to-consumer and business-to-business contracts entered into on standard
terms only encompasses the exclusion and restriction of liability or
contractual performance. The rules on Unfair Contract Terms would
therefore not usually invalidate contractual CSR obligations. In any
event, it is important to note that international sales contracts are
normally excluded from the scope of the Unfair Contract Terms Act
1977.[74]

B. Incorporation of CSR Policy through an Expressly Negotiated Contract

In case the buyer does not use terms and conditions, but incorporates his
CSR policies into a negotiated contract, it is again necessary that the
parties are in agreement, that is, that there is an offer and an acceptance,
as in the previous scenario. In this case the CSR policies of the buyer are
only incorporated into the supply contract if the buyer has included this
policy into his offer and if the supplier has agreed to it and if the
contractual clauses referring to the buyer's CSR policy are then included
into the written agreement signed by the parties.

---

[73] The statutory framework consists of the following: The Unfair Contract
Terms Act 1977, The Unfair Terms in Consumer Contracts Regulation 1999, The
Sale of Goods Act 1979, The Supply of Goods and Services Act 1982 and The
Consumer Credit Act 1974.

[74] Unfair Contract Terms Act 1977, Section 26 excludes international supply
contracts. These are defined as: (a) being either a contract of sale of goods or
being a contract under or in pursuance of which the possession or ownership of
goods passes; and (b) it is made by parties whose places of business are in the
territories of different States (the Channel Islands and the Isle of Man being
treated for this purpose as different States from the United Kingdom). Moreover,
a contract falls into this category only if either: (a) the goods in question are, at
the time of the conclusion of the contract, in the course of carriage, or will be
carried, from the territory of one State to the territory of another; or (b) the acts
constituting the offer and acceptance have been done in the territories of different
States; or (c) the contract provides for the goods to be delivered to the territory of
a State other than that within whose territory those acts were done.

C.   Incorporation of CSR Policy through an Invitation to Tender

In the situation in which the buyer incorporates his CSR policy into an invitation to tender, it is again necessary for the CSR policy to be part of the agreement between buyer and supplier. The practice of some companies to issue invitations to submit a tender to supply or buy goods generally constitutes an invitation to treat.[75] Consequently, every person who submits a tender makes an offer and the party which invited tenders (here: the buyer) is in the position to make a choice between the offers.[76] In this case, the incorporation of CSR into the supply contract would depend on the terms of the supplier's offer. If this offer does not contain any CSR clause, then there is no contractual obligation on the supplier to comply with CSR duties. As the supplier makes the offer in this scenario, one would usually expect that the supplier does not include a CSR clause into the offer as it burdens him. However, if the invitee (the buyer) insists on the inclusion of his CSR policy into the subsequent contract by making it a condition of offers, then the CSR policy becomes part of the subsequent contract through the tender process. The potential supplier will then have to include the buyer's CSR policy into the terms of their offer in order to be recognised by the buyer. The declaration from BT that it includes its Generic Standards (which contain the company's CSR policy) into the tenderer selection process and into invitations to tender and that these standards form part of any subsequent contract reflects this legal situation. In that situation, the buyer's use of invitations to tender does not preclude the incorporation of the buyer's own CSR policy into the supply contract.

D.   Incorporation of CSR Policy through Signing up to the Buyer's Code of Conduct

Where the buyer makes his supplier sign up to his CSR code of conduct, the CSR policy can only be enforced in contract law if it is part of the supply contract. The problem with this method of signing up to the code of conduct is that it does not per se incorporate the buyer's code of conduct into the terms of the supply contract. If the seller signs up to the buyer's code of conduct, then the situation is legally comparable to the situation when the buyer himself signs up to codes of conduct. The

---

[75]   *Spencer v Harding* [1870] L.R. 5 CP 51. However, the invitee can bind himself to accept the best tender, *Harvela Investment Ltd v Royal Trust of Canada (CI) Ltd* [1986] A.C. 207.

[76]   Murray, Holloway and Timson-Hunt (n 53) para 3-004.

general view is that codes of conduct are not binding for the companies that adhere to them.[77] This view means for the supply chain relationship that if the supplier signs up to the buyer's code of conduct this signing up does not create any contractual effects. It is not part of the agreement and hence not part of the contract.

IV. THE CONTINUING INCORPORATION OF THE BUYER'S CSR POLICY INTO LONG-TERM CONTRACTUAL RELATIONSHIPS AND INFORMAL AGREEMENTS

The analysis in the previous section when the buyer's CSR policies become part of the supply contract raises the related question if the buyer's CSR policy remains part of subsequent informal contracts between the parties.

So far, the focus has been on the situation that buyer and supplier enter into a contract for every single order in written form. This situation might be different, however, when the two parties have traded with each other for some time. In commercial practice, contractual relationships between parties are often long-term.[78] Many businesses pursue long-term relationships for the supply of products.[79] Trading partners regularly use informal agreements among themselves such as oral agreements or e-mail exchanges.[80] Most commercial contracts tend to be rather informal as they are not clearly defined and are not formally written down.[81] The way contracts are formed also depends on particularities of the respective industries. Industries trading with perishable goods are more likely to use informal agreements. By contrast, industries trading with medical goods tend to employ comprehensively drafted contracts as the production and sale of medical goods is subject to much regulation.[82] It should also be

---

[77]   See Pedamon (n 22) 177. However, see Chapter 4 of this book which discusses the legal effects of CSR codes of conduct in consumer protection law.

[78]   Millington (n 2) 371.

[79]   ibid.

[80]   D McBarnet and M Kurkchiyan, 'Corporate social responsibility through contractual control? Global supply chains and "other-regulation"' in D McBarnet, A Voiculescu and T Campbell (eds), *The New Corporate Accountability: Corporate Social Responsibility and the Law* (CUP 2007) 68.

[81]   T Jenkinson and C Mayer, 'The assessment: Contracts and competition' (1996) 12 (4) *Oxford Review of Economic Policy* 3.

[82]   McBarnet and Kurkchiyan (n 80) 69.

remembered that long-term contracts are commonly considered through the prism of relational contract theory, although that is not necessarily the case.[83] Relational contract theory can apply to both short-term and long-term contract, but in many different ways.[84] One of the key issues affecting long-term contracts is the need to allow for sufficient flexibility to adjust to changes in the environment.[85] However, these issues are not relevant here, as the important question for this chapter is rather to what extent the long-term nature of many supply chain contracts affects the incorporation of CSR policies. The issue within long-term business partnerships is if the buyer's CSR policy, which was included in the initial supply contracts, either through incorporation of the buyer's terms or conditions or expressly outlined in a closely-defined written contract, continues to be part of subsequent informal contracts such as oral agreements.

   The English courts have been willing to incorporate terms into a contract by a prior course of dealing which was both regular and consistent.[86] This incorporation is also possible in verbal contracts when the parties previously had regular contractual relationships.[87] For a specific clause to be implied into the verbal agreement there is a need for it to have been included in several previous contracts.[88] The requirement 'regular' will not be met in the case of only some previous contracts. It is difficult to guess a minimum period of time and number of previous orders which would be sufficient for a court to constitute a 'prior course

---

[83] M Eisenberg, 'Relational Contracts', in J Beatson and D Friedmann (eds), *Good Faith and Fault in Contract Law* (Oxford 1995). For an introduction into relational contract theory see: D Campbell and P Vincent-Jones (eds), *Contracts and Economic Organisation, Socio-Legal Initiatives* (Aldershot 1996).

[84] See: I Macneil, 'Reflections on relational contract theory after a neo-classical seminar', in D Campbell, H Collins and J Wightman (eds), *Implicit Dimensions of Contract* (Hart Publishing 2003) 207–17.

[85] Important issues which are often discussed in the literature on long-term and relational contracts are the need to allow for flexibility and adjustments of the contracts to changing circumstances. See for an introduction into this topic: M Hviid, 'Long-term contracts and relational contracts', in B Bouckaert and G De Geest (eds), *The Encyclopaedia of Law and Economics vol III* (Edward Elgar 2000) 46.

[86] *McCutcheon v David MacBrayne Ltd* [1964] 1 All ER 430, [1964] 1 WLR 125, HL.

[87] R Austen-Baker, *Implied Terms in English Contract Law* (Edward Elgar 2011) para 5.34.

[88] The party which asks the courts to imply this specific clause would need to provide documentation that the clause had been incorporated into previous contracts.

of dealing', but one can assume that, on the basis of the case law, there ought to be a consistent previous dealing of at least a year with some orders per month.[89] It is therefore likely that in such circumstances courts would be prepared to imply the CSR policy into subsequent informal agreements (e.g. verbal contracts) which are not as detailed as to provide for the CSR policy of the buyer.

V. ENFORCEMENT AGAINST SUPPLIERS 'DOWN THE CHAIN'

As the concerns about lack of corporate social responsibility among firms in transnational economies apply in particular to those contractors at the end of the supply chain, the chapter needs to consider the question of whether the Western company at the 'head' of the supply chain could enforce a contract against firms further down the supply chain. In fact, a particular challenge which the supply chain poses for the promotion of CSR through contracts between the buyer and the supplier is that many suppliers use sub-contractors further down the supply chain to provide material or to complete a significant element of the contract.[90] A distinction is therefore often made in the literature on supply chains between different tiers of suppliers to describe this situation: First-tier suppliers, second-tier suppliers and so on.[91] The sub-suppliers are not party to the contract between the buyer and the supplier.

Due to the privity of contract doctrine, it is a general rule that third parties cannot be subjected to a burden by a contract to which they are

---

[89]   It depends on the facts of the particular case what constitutes a 'regular' course of dealing. The Court of Appeal held in *Hollier v Rambler Motors (A.M.C.) Ltd* [1972] 2 Q.B. 71; [1972] 1 All ER 399 that past dealings on three or four occasions over a period of five years is not sufficient to imply a term into a contract by course of dealing between the parties. This case is to be contrasted with the interpretation of 'regular' in *Henry Kendall Ltd v William Lillico Ltd* [1962] 2 AC 31 in which the House of Lords considered three or four dealing per month over a period of about three years as sufficient, which amounts to about a hundred contracts over this period. The threshold of what is 'regular' will be somewhere between these two cases.

[90]   A Agrawal, A de Meyer and L van Wassenhovez, *Managing Value in Supply Chain – Case Studies on The Sourcing Hub Concept* 1, available at http://papers.ssrn.com/sol3/papers.cfm?abstract_id=1888756& (accessed 16 November 2014).

[91]   ibid.

not a party.[92] Hence, no obligation can be placed upon them.[93] It is considered to be unreasonable to subject a third party to a burden in a contract to which he is not a party.[94] This issue is not regulated by the Contracts (Rights of Third Parties) Act 1999 which instead focusses on the rights of third parties. The Act does not allow enforcement of burdens imposed on third parties.[95] The supply chain contracts between the buyer and their seller can therefore not directly impose a duty on sub-suppliers to adhere to the code of conduct of the multinational company based in the UK. The buyer is therefore unable to sue sub-suppliers further down the supply chain as they are not parties to the contract. As a consequence of this legal situation there is a danger that the suppliers can evade their CSR obligations by employing a number of sub-contractors who do most of the work on their behalf.

However, if the buyer's general terms and conditions impose a duty on the first-tier supplier to implement the buyer's CSR policy further down its own supply chain (perpetual clause) then this term constitutes a contractual duty on the supplier to do so. If the first-tier supplier consequently incorporates the buyer's CSR policy into its contracts with its own sub-contractors, then it is able to sue its own contractors for breaches of this policy. If the first-tier supplier fails to incorporate the buyer's CSR policy into its contracts with its own contractors, then this failure constitutes a breach of the first-tier supplier's contractual duties to the buyer. In that case the buyer could sue its first-tier supplier for breach of contract. However, as indicated, the buyer could not directly sue the second-tier supplier to comply with its CSR policies as the second-tier supplier is not party to the contract between the buyer and the first-tier supplier.

The challenge of ensuring the incorporation of CSR obligations by suppliers into their sub-supplier contracts is also addressed in the CSR reports of multinational companies. Statements about the responsibility for the conduct of sub-suppliers are rather cautious as the multinational companies tend to emphasise the duty of their direct (first-tier) suppliers to implement similar CSR policies within their own supply chains. Vodafone, for instance, states that it requires its first level (direct) suppliers to confirm that they will comply with the company's code of ethical purchasing and that it would also 'encourage all suppliers to implement the standards across their whole business and within their own

---

92 McKendrick, *Contract Law* (8th edn, Palgrave Macmillan 2009) para 7.1.
93 Poole (n 57) para 11.2.
94 ibid.
95 ibid, para 11.3.4.

supply chain'.[96] Similarly, a previous version of Unilever's supplier code states that its direct suppliers are responsible for requiring their direct suppliers (sub-suppliers) to adhere to the principles of the code.[97] However, Unilever did not contain any clause in its terms and conditions or its supplier code which imposed a duty on its suppliers to establish a similar contractual CSR regime with their sub-contractors. In the guidelines to its supplier code, Unilever declared that it is aware of the fact that many of the CSR issues arise further down the supply chain and that first tier suppliers therefore have a responsibility to ensure that the principles are followed there, too.[98] In the successor of the supplier code, Unilever's Responsible Sourcing Policy, the company establishes 'mandatory requirements of doing business with Unilever' and benchmarks for suppliers that enable them to advance to 'best practice'. One 'best practice' benchmark is that the supplier has in place a code of conduct for their suppliers (i.e. sub-suppliers) that is consistent with Unilever's Responsible Sourcing Policy. Moreover, the suppliers are under a duty to communicate the requirements of the supplier's code to all their direct suppliers and to monitor compliance with it. Unilever acknowledges that 'achieving best practice will take time'.[99] Even the new regime, therefore, does not establish a mandatory requirement in relation to sub-suppliers. One can argue that there is, in practice, not much of a difference between the two supplier codes. Moreover, the fact that Unilever only refers to the direct suppliers of their suppliers demonstrates the limits of contract law in reaching beyond first tier suppliers.

Rio Tinto takes a different approach and expressly prohibits their suppliers to subcontract without its prior written authorisation.[100] More

---

[96]   Vodafone, *Responsible Supply Chain*, available at http://www.voda fone.com/content/index/about/sustainability/being_responsibleethicalandhonest/responsible_supplychain.html (accessed 20 October 2014).

[97]   Unilever, *General Terms & Conditions of Purchase of Goods of Unilever Supply Chain Company AG ('Conditions')*; Unilever, *Unilever's Supplier Code*, available at http://www.unilever.com/aboutus/purposeandprinciples/supplier-code/ (accessed 20 June 2014).

[98]   Unilever, *Supplier Code Guidelines*, available at http://www.unilever.com/sustainability/customers-suppliers/suppliers/guidelines/index.aspx (accessed 22 June 2014).

[99]   ibid, 11.

[100]   Rio Tinto, *Purchase Order for the Supply of Goods Terms and Conditions*, section 11: 'Assignment; Subcontracting: The Supplier shall not assign, delegate, novate, mortgage, charge, sub-let, subcontract or otherwise dispose of the Purchase Order or any interest, rights or obligations hereunder, in whole or in

cautiously, GlaxoSmithKline uses the following term in its terms and conditions of purchase:

> Supplier agrees that it is responsible for controlling its own supply chain and that it shall encourage compliance with ethical standards, and human rights by any subsequent supplier of goods and services that are used by Supplier when performing its obligations under the Agreement.[101]

The different examples of how the companies deal with sub-suppliers reflect the legal situation that contractual duties cannot be imposed against third parties who are not party to the contract. The carefully worded clause by GlaxoSmithKline that its suppliers 'shall encourage compliance' within their own supply chain as well as the statement by Vodafone that they ask their suppliers to 'encourage all suppliers to implement the standards … within their own supply chain' are in line with the fact that contractual parties (e.g. the multinational company based in the UK and its direct/first-tier supplier in the developing world) cannot enforce a burden imposed on a third party such as sub-contractors/second-tier suppliers.

Sub-contracting therefore poses a significant challenge for the promotion of CSR policies in the supply chain through contract law, especially if there are diversified suppliers and sub-suppliers. The more parties are involved in the production process, the easier it is that CSR obligations are circumvented, as the Western buyer cannot bind companies further down the supply chain that are not its contractual partners. The ability of contract law to promote CSR throughout the supply chain is therefore limited in practice. This situation is a major drawback of using contract law to promote socially responsible behaviour among corporations. However, this drawback can be mitigated if Western companies use their bargaining power to force their suppliers to ensure compliance with CSR standards further down the supply chain. Such a practice might arise due to growing public pressure and the reputational damage that reports about human rights abuses within the supply chain entails.[102]

---

part, including any performance or any amount that may be due hereunder, without the Buyer's prior written authorization.'

[101] GlaxoSmithKline, *Terms and Conditions of Purchase (Goods & Services)*, section 21.2.

[102] The increasing public pressure on multinational companies is evidenced, inter alia, by the recommendation of the UN Guiding Principles on Business and Human Rights that business enterprises should 'seek to prevent or mitigate adverse human rights impacts either through their own activities or as a result of their business relationships with other parties', see principle 13.

VI.   ENFORCEMENT OF THE CSR TERMS IN SUPPLY CHAIN CONTRACTS BY THIRD PARTIES

The incorporation of CSR policies into the supply contract also raises the question of whether third parties such as the supplier's employees are able to enforce the contract between the buyer and its supplier on the basis of the Contracts (Rights of Third Parties) Act 1999. This issue is particularly relevant in relation to the CSR terms in the contract which are potentially beneficial for third parties such as the supplier's employees or the local community.

At common law, the privity of contract doctrine stipulates that parties who are not party to the contract cannot enforce it, even if the contract was specifically entered into for their benefit.[103] However, this situation changed in English law with the Contracts (Rights of Third Parties) Act 1999. The Act was intended to overcome the common law's privity rules which were considered to be unjust and needlessly complex.[104] Section 1 of the Act provides that a person who is not actually a party to the contract may still enforce a term of the contract if he meets the test of enforceability in s1 (1) – (3) of the Act. This test requires that a term of the contract expressly provides that the third party may enforce a right in its own right or that a term purports to confer a benefit on that party.[105] The third party must be expressly identified in the contract by name, as a member of a class or as answering a particular description but need not be in existence when the contract is entered into.[106] If the third party meets this test, all remedies are available to him that would be available to the parties of the contract.[107] The third party can enforce his rights against the promisor of the term. In a supply contract, the CSR duties are

---

[103]   Lawson and Singleton (n 65) para A2.94. Authority for this rule can be found in *Dunlop Pneumatic Tyre Co. Ltd v Selfridge & Co Ltd* [1915] AX 847.

[104]   Law Commission, *Privity of Contract: Contracts for the Benefit of Third Parties*, No 242 (Cm. 3329, 1996) Part III.

[105]   S1 (1) Contracts (Rights of Third Parties) Act 1999. Notably the third party will be able to enforce the term of the contract even though he has not provided any consideration for his right. It is sufficient that the contract is supported by the considerations supplied by the original parties to the contract. It is argued that s1 of the Act is sufficiently clear to confer a right on a third party whether or not he had provided consideration, see McKendrick, *Contract Law* (n 92) para 7.7.

[106]   S1 (3) Contracts (Rights of Third Parties) Act 1999.

[107]   S1 (5) Contracts (Rights of Third Parties) Act 1999.

imposed on the supplier. For instance, the promisor of the right of employees to join a trade union is the supplier as their employer.

An express provision pursuant to s1 (1) (a) of the Act is provided if the contracting parties state that the third party 'shall have the right to enforce the contract'.[108] Alternatively, pursuant to s1 (1) (b) of the Act, the third party might derive a right from the supply contract if a contract term purports to confer a benefit on him. This option is applicable if 'on a true construction of the term in question its sense has the effect of conferring a benefit on the third party in question'.[109] In this case, the court did not consider it to be necessary that the predominant purpose or intent behind the term is that the subsection confers a benefit to the third party. On this basis it has been argued that the requirement that the term in question 'purports to confer a benefit' on the third party will not be difficult to meet.[110] Benefits conferred upon third parties in the CSR context could be duties on the supplier not to use child labour, not to make their employees work excessive working hours and to allow employees to join a Union.

In the documents from the companies reviewed for this chapter, there is no term that meets the requirements of s1 (1) (a) of the Act by expressly conferring upon a third party the right to enforce the contract. However, the second way for third parties to acquire an enforceable right in s1 (1) (b), that is, if a term 'purports to confer a benefit', is more likely to apply and to entitle third parties to enforce CSR clauses. The following provisions of GlaxoSmithKline's terms and conditions are an example of this situation:

... Supplier warrants ... :

21.1.2. it does not use forced labour in any form (prison, indentured, bonded or otherwise) and its employees are not required to lodge papers or deposits on starting work;
21.1.4. it does not discriminate against any employees on any ground (including race, religion, disability or gender).
21.1.7. it complies with the laws on working hours and employment rights in the countries in which it operates.
21.1.8 it is respectful of the employees right to join and form independent trade unions and freedom of association ...[111]

---

[108] McKendrick, *Contract Law* (n 92) para 7.6.
[109] *Prudential Assurance Co Ltd v Ayres* [2007] EWHC 775 (Ch); [2007] 3 All ER 946.
[110] McKendrick, *Contract Law* (n 92) para 7.6.
[111] GlaxoSmithKline, *Terms and Conditions of Purchase*, section 21: 'Ethical Standards and Human Rights'.

Upon a true construction of these terms one can argue that the supplier's declaration that it does not use forced labour in any form, that it does not discriminate against any employees on any ground, that it complies with the laws on working hours and employment rights and that it allows its employees the right to join a trade union are intended to confer a benefit on the employees. These exemplary terms provide clear benefits for the employees of the supplier who are also expressly identified as a class, hence meeting the test in s1 (3) Contracts (Rights of Third Parties) Act 1999.[112] Given the court's rather broad interpretation of 'purports to confer a benefit' on the third party, one can conclude that in this example, the employees of the supplier acquire an enforceable right due to s1 (1) (b) of the Act. The contractual obligations to comply with the laws on working hours, to grant its employees the right to join a trade union, not to discriminate on any ground and not to use forced labour in any form are imposed on the supplier as the promisor of these duties. Hence, in the example here, the third parties, the employees, are provided with a right of action against the supplier, their employer, due to the Contracts (Rights of Third Parties Act) 1999.

However, the Act enables the parties to the contract to expressly make clear that they do not intend to confer a right of action on a third party.[113] The contracting parties are allowed to exclude the conferment of a right of action upon third parties.[114] Section 1 (1) (b) is then disapplied by s1 (2) of the Act.[115] Where the parties indicate in the contract that they do not intend to confer an enforceable benefit upon a third party with the contract, the right that third parties might acquire from s1 (1) (b) Contracts (Rights of Third Parties) Act 1999 will not apply. The contractual parties are able to exclude the application of the Contracts (Rights of Third Parties) Act 1999 by third parties without the danger that this exclusion is considered to be an unfair term. The reason is that the

---

[112] McKendrick uses the example of a contract between A and B which extends a warranty given to A also to subsequent owners and/or tenants of a building. Employees are as identifiable as a group here and it can therefore be assumed that they would be classified as a member of a class. See McKendrick (n 92) para 7.6.

[113] S1 (2) Contracts (Rights of Third Parties) Act 1999. See also A Burrows, 'The Contracts (Rights of Third Parties) Act 1999 and its implications for commercial contracts' (2000) *LMCLQ* 540, 545.

[114] N Andrews, 'Strangers to justice no longer: the reversal of the privity rule under the Contracts (Rights of Third Parties) Act 1999' (2001) 60 *Cambridge Law Journal* 353, 373.

[115] T Roe, 'Contractual intention under section 1(1)(b) and 1(2) of the Contracts (Rights of Third Parties) Act 1999' (2000) 63 *MLR* 887.

supply contracts discussed here are exempt from the usual test for exclusion clauses pursuant to the Unfair Contract Terms Act 1977. S7 (4) of the Contracts (Rights of Third Parties) Act stipulates that s1 would not allow a third party to be treated as a contracting party for the purposes of any other Act. This includes the Unfair Contract Terms Act whose s3 test for exclusion or restriction of liability therefore does not apply if the buyer and supplier exclude the rights of third parties to enforce a term of the Act. Moreover, as indicated above, the Unfair Contract Terms Act 1977 does not apply to international sale of goods contracts.[116]

And, in fact, the terms and conditions of GlaxoSmithKline which have just been analysed in terms of providing rights to third parties also contain a term excluding the rights of third parties:

> 25.8. Except for any rights granted to GSK Affiliates, which the parties hereby designate as intended third party beneficiaries to the Agreement, no person who is not a party to the Agreement shall have any rights under the Contracts (Rights of Third Parties) Act 1999 to enforce any term.[117]

The terms and conditions of the other companies reviewed for this chapter all contain similar provisions such as the following clause in Rio Tinto's terms and conditions:

> No person who is not a party to the relevant contract or the Purchase Order shall have any right under the Contracts (Rights of Third Parties) Act 1999 to enforce any term of the Purchase Order.[118]

In actual fact, this exclusion of the rights of third parties is standard practice in commercial contracts[119] and it is therefore included in the model purchase agreements:

> Third parties: For the purposes of the Contracts (Rights of Third Parties) Act 1999 this Agreement is not intended to, and does not, give any person who is not a party to it any right to enforce any of its provisions.[120]

During the consultation process that led to the introduction of the Act, the Law Commission did not consider the easy exclusion of the rights of

---

[116] S26 (3) (b) Unfair Contract Terms Act 1977.

[117] GlaxoSmithKline, *Terms and Conditions of Purchase*, section 25: 'General'.

[118] Rio Tinto, *Purchase Order for the Supply of Goods Terms and Conditions*, section 12, 'Third Parties Excluded'.

[119] Poole (n 57) para 11.3.4.

[120] Section 21.12.

third parties to enforce terms that purport to confer a benefit on them to be problematic.[121] The discussions rather focused on the question whether or not the introduction of s1 (1) (b) would result in 'uncertainty'.[122] It was argued that the rebuttable presumption of enforceability for third parties would achieve a 'satisfactory compromise'.[123] However, the fact that the parties can relatively easily exclude the applicability of s1 (1) (b) of the Contracts (Rights of Third Parties) Act 1999 severely limits the power of the supply contracts to promote CSR among firms. The third parties, as the beneficiaries of the contractual CSR clauses, can acquire rights through s1 (1) (b) Contracts (Rights of Third Parties) Act that they then lose due to the standard exclusion of this Act in supply contracts. Viewed from their perspective, the compromise found in the Act is contradictory. It can be argued that contractual parties who promise to benefit third parties in a contract (through contractual CSR clauses) should expect to have these promises enforced by these third parties such as the employees of GlaxoSmithKline's suppliers in the example used above. This argument can be supported by the fact that the legislator expressly enabled third parties such as the supplier's employees to acquire a right if a contractual term purports to confer a benefit upon them and where they are identified as a member of a class (e.g. the employees of suppliers). Otherwise, contractual terms that pretend to enhance the position of third parties would only be general statements whose enforcement purely depends on the buyer and not on the intended beneficiaries themselves. At the moment, contract law can therefore be used as a tool to make public CSR commitments by entering into contractual CSR obligations that the intended beneficiaries, the third parties, are unable to enforce.

The current legal position means that the Contracts (Rights of Third Parties) Act 1999 has not significantly improved the situation of third parties as the intended beneficiaries of a greater socially responsible commitment of corporations. Quite the contrary, the possibility for the contractual parties to exclude the applicability of s1 (1) (b) of the Act contradicts the aim of the Act, namely to provide third parties with a right of enforcement. Third parties, such as the suppliers' employees that are expressly identified in a contractual clause, should have a right to enforce clauses that are beneficial for them, for example the right to join a trade union or not be forced to work excessive hours. While this

---

[121] See Law Commission, *Privity of Contract: Contracts for the Benefit of Third Parties*, No 242 (Cm. 3329, 1996) para 7.18 (iii).
[122] ibid.
[123] ibid, para 7.17.

contradiction in the Act is criticised, it is important to point out that it is still the contractual parties who choose to exclude the applicability of s1 (1) (b) Contracts (Rights of Third Parties) Act 1999 (and hence the enforcement of their CSR policies by the intended beneficiaries of these policies) in the first place. One can therefore criticise that many companies only pay lip service to CSR through supply contracts.

VII. WHAT REMEDIES ARE OR COULD BE AVAILABLE FOR BREACH OF CSR TERMS?

Once the buyer's CSR policy has become part of the supply contracts, the next issue in terms of promoting the socially responsible conduct of corporations is if the buyer (the Western company) is able to procure an appropriate remedy in contract law for the breach, that is, repudiation rather than damages. Repudiation of the contract is a particularly strong remedy as it provides the non-breaching party with the right to terminate further performance of the contract whereas the right to damages gives the innocent party a right to recover damages in respect of the loss suffered from the breach. The consequence of a right to terminate the contract is severe for suppliers as they can lose the contract with the buyer. This situation means that, if the buyers procure the right to terminate the contract rather than the right to claim damages for a breach of the CSR terms, then the socially responsible behaviour of the suppliers is given a particularly strong position through contract law.

The following section will analyse what remedies the buyers could procure for breaches of some of the contractual CSR clauses from the documents that were researched for this chapter. The analysis will focus on a small sample of companies which have provided their contractual documents such as their general terms and conditions for purchase order forms online. The three companies selected are Rio Tinto, GlaxoSmith-Kline and Unilever.[124] The contractual terms pertaining to CSR in the terms and conditions of these three companies are the object of the following analysis. There is, so far, no case law available that deals with the breach of CSR principles in supply contracts.

---

[124] Rio Tinto, *Purchase Order for the Supply of Goods, Terms and Conditions*; Unilever, *General Terms & Conditions of Purchase of Goods of Unilever Supply Chain Company AG ('Conditions')*; GlaxoSmithKline, *Terms and Conditions of Purchase*.

The kind of remedy which is available to the Western buyer here depends on the type of term which is broken.[125] The three types of terms are conditions, warranties and innominate terms.[126] A condition is an essential term of the contract which goes to the root or the heart of the contract (e.g. in the case of the purchase of a new car these are the terms as to the make of the car).[127] Conditions contain the main obligations and are central to the contract.[128] If a condition is broken, the breach is generally considered as repudiatory and the non-breaching party has the option of either terminating the contract for the future and to obtain damages for any loss suffered or affirming it and to recover damages for the breach.[129] A warranty is a lesser, subsidiary term of the contract (e.g. the colour of the car).[130] A breach of a warranty is not a repudiatory breach and the non-breaching party can only obtain damages, but not terminate or affirm.[131] Between these two types are innominate terms (also called 'intermediate terms'). They were introduced in *Hong Kong Fir Shipping Co Ltd v Kawasaki Kisen Kaisha Ltd*[132] as it was considered to be inflexible that breaches of contractual terms give only either rise to a termination or to damages depending on the classification of the terms.[133] Innominate terms are terms which cannot be categorised as being conditions or warranties, as they can be broken in a way that is so fundamental that it undermines the whole purpose of the contract (i.e. giving rise to repudiation) or in a way that is rather trivial and where, consequently, damages are an adequate remedy.[134] The assessment of the question if a breach of an innominate term gives rise to repudiation depends on the issue whether or not the nature of the breach deprives the

---

[125]   Poole (n 57) para 8.5.
[126]   ibid.
[127]   McKendrick (n 92) para 10.1.
[128]   Poole (n 57) para 8.5.2.1.
[129]   ibid, para 8.5.3.
[130]   McKendrick (n 92) para 10.1. S61 of the Sale of Goods Act 1979 defines warranties in the following way: '"warranty" (as regards England and Wales and Northern Ireland) means an agreement with reference to goods which are the subject of a contract of sale, but collateral to the main purpose of such contract, the breach of which gives rise to a claim for damages, but not to a right to reject the goods and treat the contract as repudiated'.
[131]   Poole (n 57) para 8.5.2.1.
[132]   [1962] 2 QB 26.
[133]   Poole (n 57) para 8.5.5.
[134]   E McKendrick, *Contract Law: Text, Cases and Materials* (4th edn, OUP 2010) 783.

non-breaching party of substantially the whole benefit of the contract.[135] The breach is repudiatory if the legal benefit of the contract has been removed from the non-breaching party. If it is repudiatory, then the non-breaching party has the right to terminate the contract, as in case of a breach of a condition. Innominate terms therefore give the courts greater remedial flexibility to focus on the consequences of the breach.[136] In essence, when assessing the type of a term, one must consider its 'commercial significance' for the contract as a whole.[137] It is therefore necessary to decide if the breach deprives the non-breaching party of substantially the whole benefit of the contract. It can be difficult to ascertain how serious the consequences of the breach must be before an innocent party is entitled to terminate.[138] The factors that courts include in their decision about the seriousness of a breach are, inter alia, the losses caused by the breach, the cost of making performance comply with the terms of the contract and the adequacy of damages as a remedy to the innocent party.[139] The decision depends on the facts of the individual case and on the effects of the breach.[140] It can, however, be difficult for courts to make this decision when a term has not previously been classified.[141] Innominate terms have therefore enjoyed a mixed reception in the case law.[142]

Another remedy which would promote CSR is specific performance. An order of specific performance is a remedy for breach of contract which compels the obligor to actually perform the agreed obligation rather than being exposed to a termination of the contract or having to pay damages as compensation for the breach.[143] However, whereas damages are available as a right upon breach of contract, the remedy of specific performance is only rarely awarded in English law.[144] It is an

[135] Poole (n 57) para 8.5.5.3.
[136] McKendrick (n 92) para 10.5.
[137] *State Trading Corporation of India Ltd v Golodetz Ltd* [1989] 2 Lloyd's Rep 277, 283.
[138] McKendrick (n 134) 783.
[139] ibid.
[140] In *Bunge Corporation New York v Tradax Export SA* [1981] 1 WLR 711.
[141] McKendrick (n 134) 784.
[142] See *Maredelanto Compania Naviera SA v Bergbau-Handel GmbH (The Mihalis Angelos)* [1971] 1 QB 164 and *Cehave NV v Bremer Handelsgesellschaft mbH (The Hansa Nord)* [1976] QB 44. An overview of the discussion can be found at: McKendrick (n 134) 783–94.
[143] Poole (n 57) para 10.2.
[144] McKendrick (n 92) para 21.9.

equitable remedy which is only available in the discretion of the courts.[145] Specific performance is traditionally regarded by the courts as a supplementary remedy which is only granted when damages are inadequate.[146] The scope of the specific performance remedy has been broadened in *Beswick v Beswick*[147] which held that specific performance could be awarded upon the basis of appropriateness rather than as a supplementary remedy. However, it is the duty of the non-breaching party to demonstrate that damages would be an inadequate remedy.[148]

Applying these principles to the companies chosen here, the first example is Rio Tinto:

10. Compliance with law and policies

In supplying the Goods and associated services (if any), the Supplier will: ... (b) comply with Rio Tinto's policy titled 'The Way We Work' that can be found at http://...

The contractual term in section 10 (b) of the terms and conditions stipulates compliance with the company's code of conduct. The code of conduct 'The Way We Work'[149] is a reference document. It is not part of the term itself. However, it is a point of reference to determine whether or not the supplier is in breach of his binding contractual commitment pursuant to section 10 (b) which is to be in compliance with the code. The code contains a variety of principles, for example, about the environment, human rights and bribery. The main purpose of the contract is supply and purchase. The issues addressed in the code do not address the main obligations of the contract of sale of goods such as payment and delivery, but they establish a duty on the supplier to adhere to a range of CSR principles. Therefore the term in section 10 (b) cannot be classified as a condition. However, given the significance of some of the principles in the code for the reputation of the buyer or, in case of bribery, potentially also for its liabilities, it would not be appropriate to classify

---

[145] ibid.

[146] Poole (n 57) para 10.2.

[147] *Beswick v Beswick* [1968] AC 58. However, it is argued that the more recent decision of the House of Lords in *Co-operative Ins. Society Ltd v Argyll Stores Ltd* [1998] A.C.1 indicates a return to a more restrictive approach of the courts to the granting of specific performance as a remedy.

[148] Poole (n 57) para 10.2.1.

[149] Rio Tinto, *The Way We Work: Our Global Code of Business Conduct*, (December 2009), available at http://procurement.riotinto.com/documents/The_way_we_work_-_English_-_Final.pdf (accessed 16 November 2014).

the term as a warranty either as this would only entitle the buyer to damages, but not to termination in case of a breach of the term.

The breach of this term can therefore be so severe that it undermines the purpose of the contract or it can occur in a way that is comparatively trivial. It therefore appears suitable here to classify the term as an innominate term. The reason for this classification is that otherwise, once classified, all breaches of the term would either only entitle Rio Tinto (the buyer) to damages (in case of a warranty) or would always entitle the company to termination (in case of a condition), even in case of trivial breaches. Given the diversity of the principles which are covered by the contractual term in question, it is preferable to have the flexibility which is offered by innominate terms. For example, Rio Tinto's principles on bribery in its code are strict: 'Rio Tinto prohibits bribery and corruption in all forms, whether direct or indirect'.[150] Pursuant to s7 of the Bribery Act 2010, Rio Tinto as a commercial organisation could be guilty of the offence of failing to prevent bribery by a person associated with it.[151] The associated person can be an employee, agent, subsidiary or supplier.[152] Pursuant to s11 (3) of the Act, commercial organisations, if convicted, are liable to pay a fine. One could therefore argue that the potential consequence of a breach of this principle (inter alia, liability under the Bribery Act 2010) can be of such commercial significance that it undermines the purpose of the contract. In serious cases (where the buyer might face a higher fine, if convicted) the breach of the principle

---

[150]   ibid, section 'Bribery and corruption', 19.

[151]   Pursuant to s7 (2) of the Bribery Act it is a defence for a commercial organisation to prove that it had in place adequate procedures designed to prevent persons associated with it from undertaking such conduct. Pursuant to s9 (1) of the Act the Secretary of State must publish guidance about procedures that relevant commercial organisations can put in place to prevent persons associated with them from bribing as mentioned in section 7 (1). The Ministry of Justice published the Guidance in March 2011. The Guidance, inter alia, recommends companies to use of anti-bribery terms and conditions in their supply contracts, see: Ministry of Justice, *The Bribery Act 2010: Guidance about Procedures which Relevant Commercial Organisations Can Put into Place to Prevent Persons Associated with Them from Bribing (Section 9 of the Bribery Act 2010),* (March 2011) para 39, available at https://www.justice.gov.uk/downloads/legislation/bribery-act-2010-guidance.pdf (accessed 16 November 2014).

[152]   S8 Bribery Act 2010. S8 (3) stipulates that 'associated person' may (for example) be an employee, an agent or subsidiary. The list is non-exhaustive, as indicated by 'for example'. Suppliers are generally considered to constitute an 'associated person' for the purpose of ss7, 8 of the Act. This understanding is outlined, for example, in the government's guidance how commercial organisations can prevent bribery committed by persons associated with them.

not to commit bribery could, consequently, deprive Rio Tinto of the benefit of the contract.

Although the breach does not affect the primary object of the contract, that is, supply and purchase, it can be argued that the potential liability that Rio Tinto could incur under the Bribery Act 2010 would justify classifying the breach as repudiatory in serious cases of bribery. Damages would then not be an appropriate remedy. In that case, the breach of the innominate term in Rio Tinto's terms and conditions could provide the buyer with the right to repudiation. However, it is likely that not every case of bribery by a supplier would provide the buyer with a right to repudiation, as the courts consider each breach of an innominate term in terms of its seriousness. Due to this flexibility of the courts it is difficult to predict under what circumstances breaches will be classified as repudiatory. Among the factors that the courts take into account when making that decision is the losses caused by the breach. The higher the potential fine due to the seriousness of the bribery, the more likely it will be that the breach will be considered as being repudiatory. In contrast, less severe cases of bribery will probably only give rise to damages.

An interesting comparison with bribery in this regard is the dealing with forced or child labour. At the time of writing, the Modern Slavery Bill is still under discussion by Parliament. However, the idea of creating an extraterritorial offence for supply chain slavery, based on the UK Bribery Act, was dismissed.[153] Rio Tinto's code of conduct also contains the principle not to use forced or child labour.[154] If one of the company's suppliers is found to be in breach of this principle, then this human rights violation is likely to have a significant negative impact on the reputation of Rio Tinto. In the absence of a criminal offence in English law such as the one in the Bribery Act it is doubtful if Rio Tinto would be deprived of the economic benefit of the supply contract. As will be shown in the chapter on tort law, where suppliers or subsidiaries of English companies commit torts (e.g. by abusing human rights), they will usually be liable themselves rather than the English company (i.e. the buyer in the supply chain). Rio Tinto would therefore rather face reputational damage than

---

[153] Draft Modern Slavery Bill Joint Committee, Report (8 April 2014), available at: http://www.publications.parliament.uk/pa/jt201314/jtselect/jtslavery/166/16602.htm. See also: Government Response to the Joint Committee on the draft Modern Slavery Bill (10 June 2014), available at https://www.gov.uk/government/uploads/system/uploads/attachment_data/file/318771/CM8889Draft ModernSlaveryBill.pdf (accessed 16 November 2014).

[154] Rio Tinto, *The Way We Work: Our Global Code of Business Conduct*, (December 2009), Section 'Employment', 12.

legal liability. Consequently, despite the significant reputational damage that human rights abuses can entail, it is likely that the breach of the innominate term here would result in the remedy of damages. However, in commercial practice, it is probable that Rio Tinto would not enter into new supply contracts with that supplier, following such a breach.

A clearer example of a breach that is likely to give rise to damages only is the following principle: 'forbid using inappropriate language in the workplace, including profanity, swearing, vulgarity or verbal abuse'.[155] Notably, this principle falls under the same heading as the prohibition of child labour and forced labour, namely 'employment' and it is only two bullet points away from these aspects. However, where the supplier is found to be in breach of this principle, it would not deprive the buyer of the economic benefit of the contract. In particular, the reputational risk vis-à-vis the customer is likely to be limited. It would therefore not seem to be proportional to treat such a breach as repudiatory.

These different examples – bribery, child/forced labour and the use of inappropriate language at the workplace – illustrate well the different situations which can lead to a breach of the term referring to CSR in Rio Tinto's terms and conditions. It depends on the facts if a breach of the term ought to be treated as repudiatory or not. The assessment of that issue depends on the question of whether the breach deprives the non-breaching (i.e. here the Western buyer) of the legal benefit of the contract. The classification of the term as an innominate term provides sufficient flexibility for the assessment of breaches of that contractual term. The remedies that Rio Tinto would obtain in case of breaches of the above examples are appropriate. However, the fact that serious cases of bribery by the supplier are likely to be considered to be repudiatory whereas the breaches of the other CSR duties are more likely to result in damages only suggests that legal liability (here through the Bribery Act 2010) in the home states of Western buyers enhances the position of CSR in supply contracts. The duty pertaining to bribery is, consequently, worded in a firm and verifiable manner.

The second company whose terms and conditions are analysed is GlaxoSmithKline. This company has taken a different approach. Instead of referring to its code of conduct, GlaxoSmithKline has expressly stipulated several CSR obligations upon the supplier in its terms and conditions:[156]

---

[155]   ibid.
[156]   GlaxoSmithKline, *Terms and Conditions of Purchase*.

21. Ethical Standards and Human Rights

21.1.   Unless otherwise required or prohibited by law, Supplier warrants, to the best of its knowledge, that in relation to the supply of Goods or Services under the terms of the Agreement:

21.1.1.   it does not employ, engage or otherwise use any child labour …

21.1.2.   it does not use forced labour in any form …

21.1.3.   it provides a safe and healthy workplace, presenting no immediate hazards to its employees …

21.1.8.   it is respectful of its employees right to join and form independent trade unions and freedom of association; and

21.1.9.   it complies with the GSK Anti-Bribery and Corruption Requirements set out in Annex A.

21.2.   Supplier agrees that it is responsible for controlling its own supply chain and that it shall encourage compliance with ethical standards and human rights by any subsequent supplier of goods and services …

21.3.   Supplier shall ensure that it has ethical and human rights policies and an appropriate complaints procedure to deal with any breaches of such policies.

These extracts show that GlaxoSmithKline has incorporated into its terms and conditions those aspects of socially responsible corporate behaviour that it requires from its supplier. The differentiation into several sub-points of section 21 allows for classifying all the terms individually. The fact that the supplier 'warrants' does not anticipate any classification of all the subsequent terms as warranties as it does not denote the terms as 'warranties' and as courts are not bound by the way parties have classified terms.[157] Several terms are strictly worded and breaches of them might be easy to prove. This assessment applies, for example, to the use of child labour and forced labour as well as the right to join or form a trade union and the compliance with GlaxoSmithKline's anti-bribery requirements. Although these principles are firm and verifiable, they do not contain the main obligations of the contract which are supply and purchase. Due to the range of possible breaches of these terms, it would again be preferable to treat them as innominate terms rather than conditions or warranties.

---

[157]   The word used here in the terms and conditions is the verb 'to warrant', but the contractual term itself does not stipulate that the following are 'warranties'. Moreover, although the parties own classification of the contractual terms is one method of classification, it is not conclusive evidence that the parties intended to use the word in such a way. See *Schuler AG v Wickman Machine Tool Sales Ltd* [1974] AC 235.

As with Rio Tinto, it can be argued that serious breaches of the principle referring to bribery would deprive GlaxoSmithKline of the commercial benefit of the contract due to the potential liability under the Bribery Act. Such breaches could therefore be seen as repudiatory. However, as indicated above, given the flexibility that the courts have, it is likely that less severe cases of bribery will rather be considered to give right to damages only. While breaches of the term prohibiting the use of child or forced labour would entail significant reputational damage, they would not deprive GlaxoSmithKline of the commercial benefit of the contract as the company would not have to fear any liability as the buyer in the supply chain. The company would therefore procure the right to damages in case of a breach of these terms. In any case, GlaxoSmith-Kline might also be able to base a termination right on its terms and conditions which it incorporates into the supply contracts, as a clause in the terms and conditions allows either party to terminate the agreement in the case that the other party is in breach of the agreement and does not remedy the breach within 30 days of notice from the other party.[158]

GlaxoSmithKline's terms and conditions confirm the previous finding that employee rights and anti-bribery clauses tend to be given a particularly strong position by the buyer as they are usually firm and verifiable. Notably, the company even refers to its policies on bribery set out in Annex A of the contract. This reinforces the observation made above that the threat of liability under the Bribery Act seems to have an effect on how seriously English companies treat bribery in their supply chain through due diligence mechanisms. However, none of the express terms referring to CSR in GlaxoSmithKline's terms and conditions establishes a principle about the protection of the environment. The fact that this company does not even refer to its third party code[159] in its terms, but rather requires its suppliers to have their own ethical and human rights policies, makes environmental considerations more or less optional. They are given a much lower standing than employee rights and bribery and appear to be a minor consideration.

Given the traditionally restrictive approach of the courts to granting specific performance, it is difficult to foresee if courts would grant this remedy in the three cases just analysed. It also depends on the buyer if he seeks an order of specific performance since the breach has already

---

[158] GlaxoSmithKline, *Terms and Conditions of Purchase*, section 22.1 'Termination'.

[159] GlaxoSmithKline, *Third Party Code of Conduct*, available at http://www.gsk.com/media/279797/gsk-third-party-code-of-conduct.pdf (accessed 16 November 2014).

occurred by the time a remedy is sought. The buyer's reputation might therefore have already been damaged which could make the buyer prefer a termination of the contract or damages.

The third company analysed here is Unilever. This company, too, refers to its code of conduct in its terms and conditions:

13. Responsible Sourcing Policy

> Each Supplier and the Lead Supplier acknowledges that it has reviewed Unilever's Responsible Sourcing Policy (**'RSP'**) and agrees that all of their activities shall be conducted in accordance with the RSP ... The RSP can be accessed at the internet address: www ...[160]

As with Rio Tinto, the code is not incorporated, it is a reference document. It is therefore a point of reference to determine whether or not the supplier is in breach of its contractual commitment, that is, the term in section 13 of Unilever's terms and conditions. Failure to comply with the principles of Unilever's Responsible Sourcing Policy ('shall be conducted in accordance with the code') may therefore give right to a repudiatory breach depending on the classification of the term. The breach of the code is again a point of reference when determining what remedy the buyer procures. With its reference to the code of conduct the term is again difficult to classify as either a condition or warranty, as Unilever's Responsible Sourcing Policy contains a diverse list of principles ranging from the prohibition of bribery to environmental issues. It is therefore preferable to classify the term here as an innominate term. The principle pertaining to bribery is again strict ('There is a prohibition of any and all forms of bribery, corruption extortion or embezzlement and there are adequate procedures to prevent bribery in all commercial dealings undertaken by the supplier.') as is the principle that prohibits the use of child labour ('There shall be no use of child labour, ...').

It can be argued that the situation is comparable to the assessment of Rio Tinto's code of conduct above. While a breach of the principle not to use child labour would entail a significant reputational damage, Unilever would not be deprived of the economic benefit of the contract with their suppliers per se. In contrast, it can be argued that the situation is different in serious cases of bribery due to the possible fines under the Bribery Act 2010. A breach of this principle could therefore be seen as undermining the purpose of the contract and hence give right to repudiation. However,

---

[160]   Unilever, *General Terms & Conditions of Purchase of Goods of Unilever Supply Chain Company AG ('Conditions')*, section 13.

the court will assess every case of bribery on its facts in order to determine whether or not it is repudiatory. It is therefore probable that less severe cases of bribery will give rise to damages only. Still, it is important to note that Unilever's Responsible Sourcing Policy addresses bribery as the first issue within its mandatory requirements. This prioritisation does indicate the importance attached to it by Unilever.

The situation is again different in terms of the environment as the relevant principle is rather openly phrased ('Operations, sourcing, manufacture, distribution of products and the supply of services, are conducted with the aim to protect and preserve the environment'). As environmental standards in the developing world are often rather weak the reference to the local law does not necessarily entail any duties for the supplier that he must adhere to. The phrase 'aim to protect and preserve the environment' is rather indefinite, which means that the principle is relatively easy to fulfil. This principle is therefore weaker than the mentioned principles on bribery and the use of child labour. Moreover, even if the supplier is found to be in breach with the relevant legislation of the country concerned, it is unlikely that this breach would deprive Unilever of the economic benefit of the contract. Therefore, in terms of breaches of the principle relating to the environment, Unilever would, if at all, only procure a right to damages.

Bringing the analysis of the three companies together, it appears as if there is a hierarchy of CSR issues in the various documents reviewed. It is noticeable that the wording related to bribery is particularly strong. Bribery is therefore at the stronger end of the continuum. This view is supported by the fact that GlaxoSmithKline even has a detailed Annex A about bribery which is referred to in the terms and conditions.[161] It is evident that the company deals in greater detail with bribery than with its other CSR policies. The policies of Rio Tinto and Unilever are similarly strict regarding bribery. Unilever addresses the prohibition as the very first issue within its 'mandatory requirements' imposed on its suppliers. It is likely that the strong stance taken by the companies on bribery is influenced by the Bribery Act 2010 which, inter alia, creates under certain circumstances an offence for commercial organisations.[162] Appropriate due diligence mechanisms can be a defence to the offence of bribery. Moreover, it can be argued that serious cases of bribery are repudiatory as the buyer can incur a fine for the committing of bribery by

---

[161]   GlaxoSmithKline, *Terms and Conditions of Purchase, Annex A GSK Anti Bribery and Corruption Requirements*.
[162]   Section 7 of the UK Bribery Act.

its suppliers. However, the buyer might only procure a right to damages in less severe cases of bribery, but that decision depends on the court. Domestic statutory provisions therefore seem to have an impact on the use of supply chains to promote CSR.

In contrast, breaches of the principles relating to the use of child labour and forced labour are, despite the strict wording of these clauses, unlikely to result in a right to repudiation. The reason for this assessment is that such breaches would not deprive the buyer of the purpose of the contract, regardless of the reputational damage. The buyer would therefore procure a right to damages in case of a breach. Still, although not English law, the recently introduced Californian Transparency in Supply Chains Act of 2010[163] shows how domestic statutory requirements can influence the use of the supply chain to promote CSR, including UK multinational companies, in terms of forced labour. The Californian Act requires retail sellers and manufacturers to disclose their efforts to combat slavery and human trafficking and to eliminate it from their direct supply chains.[164] The Californian Act might have an impact on some UK multinational companies, too, as all retail sellers and manufacturers that do business in California and that have annual worldwide gross receipts that exceed one hundred million dollars fall within the scope of the Act's disclosure requirements.[165] Shell, for instance, has therefore published a note about its compliance with this Act on its website.[166] This Act is another example of how domestic law can influence the use of the supply contracts for promoting CSR by imposing liabilities or duties for the Western buyers. It is therefore noticeable that the CSR issues which are dealt with in the strictest manner in the supply chain contracts are addressed by domestic regulation.[167] In comparison to the issues of bribery and forced labour, however, it is doubtful if the buyer procures a remedy for environmental pollution at all, given that the respective provisions about the environment, for example in Unilever's Responsible Sourcing Policy, are rather openly worded and, in case of GlaxoSmith-Kline, not even included in an express list of CSR obligations in the

---

[163]   The Act is available at http://leginfo.ca.gov/pub/09-10/bill/sen/sb_0651-0700/sb_657_bill_20100930_chaptered.html (accessed 16 November 2014).
[164]   Section 3 of the California Transparency in Supply Chains Act of 2010.
[165]   ibid.
[166]   http://www-static.shell.com/static/products_services/downloads/suppliers/california_transparency_disclosure.pdf (accessed 16 November 2014).
[167]   As regards the Californian Act, it is important to note that it only applies to those companies which do business in California and whose income exceeds the threshold, as in the case of Shell.

company's terms and conditions. The comparison between the issues of bribery, forced and child labour as well as environment matters indicates that there is a difference in the way these aspects of CSR are addressed.

In conclusion, the buyer can procure an appropriate remedy for several violations of its CSR principles due to the classification of the CSR clauses as innominate terms which allows for flexibility based on the particularities of the case. However, the question of whether the buyer can procure a remedy at all depends on the question of how firmly and verifiably the respective CSR principle is phrased. In the examples analysed here the buyers are likely to procure a right to repudiation for the committing of bribery by their suppliers. However, the use of forced or child labour will only give right to damages. The situation is again different for environmental protection, as it will often be difficult to establish a breach of CSR principles referring to the environment in the first place.

VIII. THE BUYER'S AWARENESS OF BREACHES

Finally, the Western companies (the buyers) must be sufficiently aware of breaches of the terms to at least consider using contract law to promote socially responsible behaviour among their suppliers. Entitlements to use contract law to encourage or require compliance with CSR obligations are useless in practice if the buyer is unaware of a lack of compliance. This part of the chapter will therefore analyse how buyers can monitor the supplier's compliance with their CSR obligations.

Monitoring serves two purposes: First, it signals the buyer's commitment to CSR to the public and it adds legitimacy to the buyers' efforts. Secondly, it is an attempt to ensure compliance of the supplier with the CSR provisions.[168] Monitoring systems can be divided into internal and external systems.[169] Internal monitoring is undertaken by internal staff of the buyer or even by the staff of the supplier who conduct self-audits to assess their own performance. External monitoring or third party auditing describes the practice of using consultants external to an organisation to conduct the audits. The process of monitoring the supplier's site through

---

[168]   D Boyed et al., 'Corporate social responsibility in global supply chains: a procedural justice perspective' (2007) 40 *Long Range Planning* 341, 344.

[169]   Mamic (n 6) 95.

a visit can usually be broken down into a physical inspection of the supplier factory, a documentation inspection and interviews with workers.[170]

Self-auditing still seems to be a popular tool in practice, perhaps because of the high number of suppliers which many Western companies have. It facilitates the auditing process for them and reduces the cost of monitoring. Some companies operate a system where existing suppliers must complete an online questionnaire and renew their information annually. The system is then usually operated by a third party administrator. This system is a mixture of self-auditing by the supplier with external review of the data by a third party. Other companies operate a combination of self-audits, third party and their own audits of the supplier to assess supplier performance. A further tool of self-auditing applied by the companies reviewed for this chapter is a system of pre-contractual checks of potential suppliers. The companies that follow this tool operate a qualification process to identify potential risks. The emphasis of the regimes is on the filling in of online questionnaires and the providing of documents by the potential suppliers themselves, so it is questionable how objective the system is and if any supplier is turned away at all.

Third party auditing by global accounting firms and non-profit organisations has increased in recent years, partly because self-auditing was increasingly criticised for not being objective enough as staff from the companies themselves conduct the monitoring.[171] As third-party auditors are independent from the suppliers, these audits can be more objective than self-auditing and can help the buyer to become aware of breaches in his supply chain more quickly. However, accounting firms which conduct such third party audits have been found to exercise their role inadequately due to a lack of training about how to detect instances of non-compliance with CSR codes.[172] They have also often asked the factory manager to select the workers for the interview instead of randomly choosing workers themselves in order to possibly get a wider range and more objective views. As multinational companies tend to develop their own CSR code of conduct, third party auditors have to deal with a variety of different CSR codes of conduct which makes it more

---

[170]   ibid, 96.
[171]   R Locke, F Qin and A Brause, 'Does monitoring improve labor standards? Lessons from NIKE' (2007–2008) 61 *Industrial and Labor Relations Review* 3, 5.
[172]   ibid, 56–7.

difficult for them to attain special knowledge about all different codes.[173] A further criticism is the fact that these firms are instructed by the buyers and are therefore dependent on them as they are on their clients.[174] Non-profit NGOs such as the multi-stakeholder initiative Fair Labour Association[175] are seen as more independent than auditing firms, but they, too, are criticised for commonly lacking the capacity to sufficiently monitor the suppliers, especially given the vast number of suppliers which are used by multinational buyers.[176] These deliberations show that, while self-auditing is likely to be limited in its objectivity and in its reach, third party audits do not necessarily provide the buyer with a comprehensive picture either, as they have their limitations, too.

Some of the firms reviewed for this chapter have contractually stipulated a right to conduct audits such as GlaxoSmithKline:

21.4. GSK reserves the right upon reasonable notice ... to enter upon Supplier's premises to monitor compliance by the Supplier ...[177]

Unilever established a similar right in its terms and conditions:

13. Responsible Sourcing Policy

... Unilever may from time to time carry out an audit ...[178]

These audit clauses provide the Western buyer with a right to conduct an audit when the company wishes to do so.

Although the buyer has the right to audit the supplier, this system faces challenges. First, it is important that, if he uses third party auditors, these are skilled and independent in order to detect breaches of the CSR codes. The strictest CSR policy is essentially ineffective if it is not followed up by an effective system of monitoring. The inconsistent manner in which companies currently monitor the CSR policies of their suppliers has

---

[173]   ibid, 5.

[174]   Wells (n 19) 56–7.

[175]   Multi-stakeholder NGOs are non-profit organisations and they have a certain degree of autonomy from the multinational companies. The Fair Labour Association is the most significant multi-stakeholder NGO outside Europe. It is a coalition of NGOs (human rights, labour rights and consumer rights organisations), transnational companies and universities. For more information see: Wells (n 19) 60.

[176]   ibid, 63.

[177]   GlaxoSmithKline, *Terms and Conditions of Purchase*, para 21.4.

[178]   Unilever, *General Terms and Conditions of Purchase of Goods of Unilever Supply Chain Company AG ('Conditions')* para 13.

consequently been criticised.[179] Secondly, as the supply chain is a private system between companies, there is also the financial factor that must be taken into account. Monitoring increases the transaction costs and the high number of suppliers used by some companies makes it difficult to put an effective and comprehensive monitoring system in place. Unilever, for example, has 160,000 suppliers.[180] Thirdly, a further difficulty is the lack of monitoring beyond first tier suppliers. As discussed above, supply chains usually go much deeper below the buyers and their first-tier suppliers. However, as sub-suppliers are not encompassed by the contract between buyer and their first-tier supplier, the Western buyer usually only monitors the compliance of his direct supplier. Monitoring further down the supply chain is also difficult to implement, given that the buyers already struggle to monitor the high number of their direct suppliers. All in all, despite the different means of monitoring the compliance of the suppliers, the system remains patchy.

Although the buyer has means to monitor the compliance of its suppliers (and often even a contractual right to carry out monitoring), the monitoring system is somewhat restricted. Among other things, it is difficult for the buyer to monitor a high number of suppliers. The Western companies will therefore not always be aware of breaches of their CSR terms. The enforcement of contracts is limited as a regulatory strategy when the buyer does not know about the lack of compliance with the contract.

IX. CONCLUSION

This chapter has shown that CSR has become an important feature of global supply chains in recent years. Due to political and public pressure, multinational companies have increasingly incorporated CSR codes of conduct into the supply chain contracts with their suppliers using three different mechanisms through which CSR becomes part of the contract: First, terms and conditions incorporated into the buyer's purchase order; secondly, expressly negotiated contracts; and thirdly, inclusion of the CSR policy into the tenderer process. The signing up to the buyer's code of conduct by the supplier does not make the code part of the contractual relations of the two parties, however. The prevalent method in practice is

---

[179] Boyed et al. (n 168) 341.
[180] Unilever, Unilever Procurement, available at http://www.unilever.com/aboutus/supplier/unileverprocurement (accessed 16 November 2014).

the incorporation of the buyer's terms and conditions, which contain CSR provisions, into the contract.

While the buyer's CSR policy becomes part of the contracts between buyer and supplier and hence creates enforceable contractual terms, it is important to note that contract law faces severe drawbacks in its ability to promote socially responsible behaviour in suppliers in the developing world. First, this situation is particularly due to the doctrine of privity of contract which in general confines the contractual reach of the supply contract to the buyer and their first-tier supplier and does not allow the contract to reach beyond that. The reach of these supply contracts does not expand to sub-suppliers. Secondly, although third parties such as the supplier's employees can acquire a right to enforce contractual duties against the promisor, for example, the right to join a trade union, due to the Contracts (Rights of Third Parties) Act 1999, this right is regularly excluded by the buyer and supplier. This exclusion significantly limits the ability of contractual law to promote CSR. The situation that the parties can easily exclude liability to third parties reduces the ability of contract law to promote greater socially responsible behaviour of corporations. The intended beneficiaries of the CSR policies are left without a right of action and the enforcement is left to the companies themselves. The purpose of the Contracts (Rights of Third Parties) Act 1999 to promote the position of third parties is therefore effectively contradicted. Thirdly, a further limitation of the use of supply chain contracts for the promotion of CSR is that it is difficult for many companies to monitor all of their suppliers and to always be aware of non-compliance in practice. The reason for this difficulty is that many Western buyers use a high number of suppliers and that the supply chain relationship is based on private arrangements with the intention to derive profits. The effective monitoring of compliance would significantly increase the transaction cost of the supply contract. The challenges posed by monitoring are therefore a practical limitation of the ability of supply chain contracts to promote CSR. Fourthly, the use of supply chain contracts as a means to promote CSR and the enforcement of contractual clauses that refer to CSR principles all depend on the Western buyers. It is their decision how they include, monitor and enforce CSR in their supply chain. The fact that the research for this chapter has not shown a single decided case about the breach of CSR terms reveals the economic reality of CSR. It is often just not considered as being important enough for companies to litigate. The promotion of CSR through supply chain contracts between private parties is therefore patchy as the inclusion of CSR into supply contracts as well as the enforcement of CSR terms is a matter of choice for the Western buyer, although reputational risks are an important factor to consider. The limitations of contract law have to be seen in the context of the theoretical framing of contract law, however. It is often said that it is the primary function of contract law to facilitate exchange.[181] English contract law is said to be embedded in the two principal ideologies of 'market-individualism' and 'consumer-welfarism'.[182] The former of the two ideologies focusses on the holding of contractors to their freely agreed exchanges whereas the latter pursues a fair deal for contractors, in particular consumers.[183] These ideologies of contract law focus on the rights and interests of the contractual parties, but not on the use of contract law to promote the socially responsible conduct of companies for the benefit of the wider public good.

On the other hand, the analysis of the terms and conditions of three multinational companies has shown that the buyer would often be able to procure a remedy for breaches of CSR principles in supply contracts. The contractual terms referring to CSR in the buyer's terms and conditions are classified as innominate terms which allows for flexibility depending on the seriousness of the breach. Among the different CSR principles which are incorporated into supply chain contracts, some are given more prominence than others. Bribery appears to be the strictest, followed by the use of child labour/forced labour. In the middle there are clauses about the conditions at the workplace (e.g. the use of inappropriate language). In contrast, environmental concerns have so far not resulted in binding contractual provisions. It is important to note in this regard that bribery is incidentally subject to the Bribery Act 2010 with its newly created statutory offence for commercial enterprises. It can be argued that severe breaches of the principles prohibiting bribery are repudiatory due to the potential liability that buyers can incur for the conduct of their suppliers. It is therefore argued here that liability in the home states of the buyers can have a positive impact on the promotion of CSR through supply contracts. Breaches of the principles about the use of forced labour and child labour will rather give right to damages. Nevertheless, the fact that buyers can procure a remedy for breaches of CSR principles in supply chain contracts at all demonstrates that, despite its limitations,

---

[181]   Lord Irvine, 'The law: an engine for trade' (2001) 64 *MLR* 333. Brownsword outlines further objectives of contract law: Its protective function (e.g. the protection of consumers) and, in case of disputes, to put in place machinery for the resolution of such disputes. See: R Brownsword, *Contract Law: Themes for the Twenty-first Century* (2nd edn, OUP 2006) 39–41.

[182]   See J Adams and R Brownsword, 'The ideologies of contract' (1987) 7 *LS* 207.

[183]   Brownsword (n 181) 137–8.

contract law could promote CSR by making CSR codes of conduct contractually enforceable. This situation challenges the common understanding of codes of conduct as being purely voluntary. Through contract law, CSR obligations can be imposed on suppliers in different countries of the world, particularly in those countries which are known to have a weak legal system or a weak law enforcement mechanism.

4. Consumer protection law and corporate social responsibility

I. THE LINK BETWEEN CONSUMER PROTECTION LAW AND CSR

Consumers are increasingly a driver of CSR activities of companies.[1] Surveys have shown that up to 90 per cent of consumers consider the social responsibility of companies in their purchase and consumption behaviour.[2] The term 'ethical consumerism' denotes the situation that consumers care about issues of CSR and are positively influenced by a company's CSR engagement in their purchase behaviours.[3] Consumers' perceptions of companies are better if they believe that companies are committed to CSR.[4] This trend provides an incentive for companies to be socially responsible. Companies have responded to ethical consumerism by giving CSR an increasingly important role in their marketing activities.[5] Brands are

---

[1] See N C Smith, 'Consumers as drivers of corporate social responsibility' in A Crane, A McWilliams, D Matten et al. (eds), *The Oxford Handbook of Corporate Social Responsibility* (OUP 2008) 281.

[2] D Vogel, *The Market for Virtue: The Potential and Limits for Corporate Social Responsibility* (Brookings Institute Press 2006).

[3] It is, however, doubtful to what extent CSR plays a role in the actual purchase decision. Studies suggest that stated ethical intentions rarely translate into actual ethical buying behaviour. See: M Carrington, B Neville and G Whitwell, 'Why ethical consumers don't walk their talk: Towards a framework for understanding the gap between the ethical purchase intentions and actual buying behaviour of ethically minded consumers' (2010) 97 *Journal of Business Ethics* 139; G Eckhardt, R Belk and T Devinney, 'Why don't consumers consume ethically?' (2010) 9 *Journal of Consumer Behaviour* 426.

[4] N C Smith (n 1) 291.

[5] J Leigh and S Waddock, 'The emergence of total responsibility management systems: J. Sainsbury's (plc) voluntary responsibility management systems for global food retail supply chains' (2006) 111 (4) *Business and Society Review* 409.

portrayed as being socially responsible.[6] Many companies therefore publicise information about their engagement with CSR, including the codes of conduct to which they have signed up.[7] These codes of conduct account for a significant part of the CSR strategy of companies as they usually contain principles of socially responsible behaviour with which companies pledge to comply.[8] Increasingly, these codes also address the supply chain of the company. A corporate code of conduct is defined as a document which states a number of social and environmental standards and principles that the firm which is a signatory of it is expected to fulfil.[9] Figures show a constant increase of such codes of conduct pertaining to CSR in the past few years.[10] Consumers can view information about the CSR engagement of companies on most corporate websites. These documents often also contain information about the company's adherence to a code of conduct and the method with which it addresses CSR in its supply chain.

It is difficult to define the exact scope of consumer protection. Generally speaking, consumer protection is 'the protection, especially by legal means, of consumers'.[11] The Consumer Protection from Unfair Trading Regulations 2008 which are analysed in this chapter define a consumer as 'any individual who in relation to a commercial practice is acting for purposes which are outside his business'.[12] It is the aim of this

---

[6] M Polonsky and C Jevons, 'Global branding and strategic CSR: an overview of three types of complexity' (2009) 26 *International Marketing Review* 327, 328.

[7] A study published in 2010 shows that 77 out of the 100 constituent FTSE 100 firms had adopted codes of conduct which contain the CSR commitments of the companies. See: L Preuss, 'Codes of conduct in organisational context: from cascade to lattice-work of codes' (2010) 94 *Journal of Business Ethics* 471, 475: Preuss analysed the range of codes that constituent firms of the FTSE 100 index use. His findings show that 77 companies used a general company-wide code of conduct which often also include stipulations for suppliers.

[8] A Sobczak, 'Are codes of conduct in global supply chains really voluntary? From soft law regulation of labour relations to consumer law' (2006) 16 (2) *Business Ethics Quarterly* 167.

[9] I Mamic, 'Managing global supply chains: the sports footwear, apparel and retail sectors' (2005) 59 *Journal of Business Ethics* 81.

[10] M Anderson and T Skjoett-Larsen, 'Corporate social responsibility in global supply chains' (2009) 14 (2) *Supply Chain Management: An International Journal* 75.

[11] J Law (ed.), *Oxford Dictionary of Law* (7th edn, OUP 2009).

[12] This definition is amended by the Consumer Protection (Amendment) Regulations 2014 as follows: '"Consumer" means an individual acting for purposes that are wholly or mainly outside that individual's business'.

chapter to analyse to what extent English consumer law promotes socially responsible behaviour in corporations. Upon the basis of this legal analysis, the chapter also seeks to discuss how English consumer law could better encourage greater corporate social responsibility. The structure of the chapter reflects these two purposes. It will first address the question to what extent English consumer law currently promotes CSR. To that end, the chapter will analyse if breaches of CSR policies by companies are encompassed by English consumer law at all and, if this is the case, then examine whether consumers may procure an appropriate remedy in such a situation. Secondly, the chapter will address the question of how consumer law could better promote CSR. This section will discuss in particular the Consumer Protection (Amendment) Regulations 2014.[13] These are based on recommendations of the Law Commission about consumer redress for misleading and aggressive practices which were published in March 2012.[14] As the amendments to the Consumer Protection from Unfair Trading Regulations 2008 are introduced at the time of writing, this chapter will first analyse the Consumer Protection from Unfair Trading Regulations 2008 and then discuss the amendments to it that are introduced through the 2014 Regulations. That way, it is possible to critically compare if the changes have had a positive impact on the rights of consumers with regard to CSR. In terms of jurisdictional scope, the chapter addresses those situations where English law is applicable.

The rise of ethical consumerism raises the question of how reliable the information is which companies release about their CSR record and which is targeted, inter alia, at their customers. Companies are using CSR as part of their marketing strategy to positively influence their image in the perception of consumers.[15] In return, as there is an indication that consumers are influenced in their purchase decisions by the CSR commitment of companies,[16] it is important that the material which

---

[13]   The Consumer Protection (Amendment) Regulations 2014.

[14]   The Law Commission and the Scottish Law Commission, *Consumer Redress For Misleading And Aggressive Practices*, March 2012 (Law Com No 332; Scot Law Com No 226), available at http://lawcommission.justice.gov.uk/docs/lc332_consumer_redress.pdf (accessed 16 November 2014).

[15]   Y-S Lii and M Lee, 'Doing right leads to doing well: when the type of CSR and reputation interact to affect consumer evaluations of the firm' (2012) 105 *Journal of Business Ethics* 69, 78.

[16]   J Singh, O Iglesias and J Batista-Foguet, 'Does having an ethical brand matter? The influence of consumer perceived ethicality on trust, affect and loyalty' (2011) 111 *Journal of Business Ethics* 541.

companies release about their CSR policies is accurate. Consumers, as the targets of CSR marketing activities, require protection against false information. It is against this background that consumer law could overlap with CSR, as it is the object of consumer law to address the inequality of economic power between consumers and business.[17] Consumer law is not directly linked to CSR, as it is commonly rather associated with issues such as consumers' revocation rights, for example in case of doorstep sales, or with the protection of consumers from the small print in business terms and conditions.[18] However, consumer law and CSR could be linked as consumer law prohibits misleading actions by traders.[19] False information by companies about their CSR practices could constitute such misleading actions. Consumer law could therefore protect consumers in case companies are in breach of their publicly announced CSR commitments, for example, if a company violates the principles of its code of conduct which it has published on its website and to which it pledges to adhere. Consumer law therefore has a potentially important role to play in relation to CSR by protecting consumers against false statements made by companies about their CSR record.

Corporate codes of conduct have often been criticised for being purely voluntary which means that a code could be used by a company to publicly demonstrate its CSR commitment whereas, in reality, the company does not adhere to the principles contained in the code.[20] It is therefore an important question if the publication of the companies' CSR policies, and particularly the corporate codes of conduct, entails any consequences in consumer law if the information is found to be inaccurate.[21]

---

[17] G Howells and S Weatherill, *Consumer Protection Law* (2nd edn, Ashgate 2005) 6.

[18] See G Woodroffe and L Lowe, *Woodroffe and Lowe's Consumer Law and Practice* (8th edn, Sweet & Maxwell 2010) paras 6.24 and 9.01.

[19] Reg 5 (2) or reg 5 (3) Consumer Protection from Unfair Trading Regulations 2008.

[20] See Sobczak (n 8) 167.

[21] See for an introduction into this issue: C Glinski, 'Corporate codes of conduct: Moral or legal obligation?' in D McBarnet, A Voiculescu and T Campbell (eds), *The New Corporate Accountability: Corporate Social Responsibility and the Law* (CUP 2007) 119.

II. THE BREACH OF CSR COMMITMENTS UNDER THE CONSUMER PROTECTION FROM UNFAIR TRADING REGULATIONS 2008

A. The Scope of the Regulations

Breaches of CSR could be covered by the Consumer Protection from Unfair Trading Regulations 2008 (hereafter: CPRs) which implement the EU Unfair Commercial Practices Directive 2005.[22] The CPRs primarily address business-to-consumer transactions.[23] They apply to conduct before, during and after the contract is made.

As this book focusses on private law, it is important to note that the Law Commission classified the CPRs as public law when it discussed whether or not a private remedy should be introduced in English consumer law. The reason for that classification is that the CPRs in their 2008 version only provide for public enforcement. In contrast, the law of misrepresentation was classified as the private law on misleading and aggressive trading practices. However, both the CPRs and the law of misrepresentation will be analysed in this chapter with regard to the promotion of CSR through consumer law. There are two reasons for this approach: First, the CPRs and the law of misrepresentation (which is often also called the 'pre-existing private law' in respect of consumer protection) extensively overlap. Both areas address the protection of consumers from unfair commercial actions by business. It would be difficult to understand the effects of one source without analysing the other. Secondly, and closely related to this point, is the fact that the government has now followed the recommendation of the Law Commission to introduce a private remedy in English consumer law which will provide consumers with a private right of action where they have suffered from an unfair commercial practice under the CPRs. This right of redress is added to the CPRs through the Consumer Protection (Amendment)

---

[22] Directive 2005/29/EC.

[23] This sentence refers to 'primarily', as most commercial practices will occur where a trader deals directly with consumers. However, any commercial practice that has the potential to affect consumers can be encompassed by the CPRs. For example where a trader sells a product to a consumer, acts or omissions which occur further up the supply chain may also constitute commercial practices. See: OFT, *Guidance on the Consumer Protection from Unfair Trading Regulations 2008*, para 4.4., available at http://www.oft.gov.uk/shared_oft/business_leaflets/cpregs/oft1008.pdf (accessed 16 November 2014).

Regulations 2014. It is therefore no longer accurate to classify the CPRs as purely being public law.

The CPRs prohibit the use of 'unfair commercial practices' pursuant to reg 3 (1) CPRs. A 'commercial practice' is defined in reg 2 (1) CPRs as 'any act, omission, course of conduct, representation or commercial communication (including advertising or marketing) by a trader which is directly connected with the promotion, sale or supply of a product to or from consumers, whether occurring before, during or after a commercial transaction (if any) in relation to the product'. A category of unfair commercial practices is misleading actions.[24] Pursuant to reg 5 (3) (b) CPRs a commercial practice is a misleading action if it concerns the failure by a trader to comply with a commitment contained in a code of conduct with which the trader has undertaken to comply. Reg 2 (1) of the CPRs defines 'code of conduct' in the following way: 'an agreement or set of rules (which is not imposed by legal or administrative require- ments), which defines the behaviour of traders who undertake to be bound by it in relation to one or more commercial practices or business sectors'.

In this situation, the following conditions must be satisfied: First, the trader must indicate in a commercial practice that he is bound by that code of conduct. Secondly, it is required that the commitment is firm and capable of being verified and not aspirational. Moreover, the commitment must cause or be likely to cause the average consumer to take a transactional decision he would not have taken otherwise, taking account of its factual context and of all its features and circumstances.

Against this background, it will now be analysed if a breach of the Ethical Trading Initiative (ETI) Base Code could constitute a misleading action pursuant to reg 5 (3) (b) of the CPRs if it were shown that a company that has adopted this code has not followed one or more of its clauses. The ETI is an organisation whose members are companies, trade unions and voluntary organisations.[25] It promotes ethical trading and its aim is to improve working conditions in the supply chains of com- panies.[26] Companies that join the ETI must adopt the ETI Base Code in

---

[24] Reg 5 CPRs.
[25] http://www.ethicaltrade.org/about-eti (accessed 18 October 2014).
[26] See the statement on ETI's website: 'Our vision is a world where all workers are free from exploitation and discrimination, and work in conditions of freedom, security and equity' see: http://www.ethicaltrade.org/about-eti (accessed 18 October 2014).

full.[27] The ETI Base Code is based on the Conventions of the International Labour Organization (ILO).[28] The ETI's members (that have consequently signed up to the ETI Base Code) comprise a range of large English companies in the retail and garment industry such as Tesco, Next, River Island, Sainsbury's and Marks & Spencer.[29] The ETI Base Code was chosen for the case study in this chapter, as it is an important code of conduct in terms of the CSR commitments of English companies due to its membership which consists of firms which account for a significant part of the retail of food and clothes in England. Many consumers will purchase goods from one or more of these companies on a regular basis. Consumers are therefore commonly exposed to advertisement of these companies. The companies usually outline their CSR commitments in a specific section on their website.[30]

The following clauses are examples of the ETI Base Code:

1. **Employment is freely chosen**
   1.1. There is no forced, bonded or involuntary prison labour.

2. **Freedom of association and the right to collective bargaining are respected**
   2.1 Workers, without distinction, have the right to join or form trade unions of their own choosing and to bargain collectively.
   2.2. The employer adopts an open attitude towards the activities of trade unions and their organisational activities.

4. **Child labour shall not be used**
   4.1. There shall be no new recruitment of child labour.

6. **Working hours are not excessive**
   6.2. In any event, workers shall not on a regular basis be required to work in excess of 48 hours per week and shall be provided with at least one day off for every 7 day period on average. Overtime shall be voluntary, shall not exceed 12 hours per week, shall not be demanded on a regular basis and shall always be compensated at a premium rate.

---

[27] http://www.ethicaltrade.org/about-eti/what-companies-sign-up-to (accessed 18 October 2014).
[28] ibid.
[29] For a list of members see: http://www.ethicaltrade.org/about-eti/our-members (accessed 18 October 2014).
[30] See for example the reference to the ETI by Tesco at http://www.tescoplc.com/site/library/policiesandfactsheets/ethical-trading-at-tesco.htm (accessed 18 October 2014).

B. Indication in a Commercial Practice that the Company is Bound by its Code of Conduct

The first condition of reg 5 (3) (b) CPRs is that a company must indicate in a commercial practice that it is bound by this code. This condition consists of two elements: First, there must be a code of conduct in terms of regs 5 (3) (b), 2 (1) CPRs. Secondly, a company must have indicated in a commercial practice that it is bound by this code.

If this route of promoting CSR is to be successful, the ETI Base Code must first be a code of conduct.[31] The CPRs define a code of conduct in the following way:

> 'Code of conduct' means an agreement or set of rules (which is not imposed by legal or administrative requirements), which defines the behaviour of traders who undertake to be bound by it in relation to one or more commercial practices.[32]

This definition requires that it is necessary that there is an agreement or a set of rules which are not imposed by law, regulation or administrative provision. With its clauses pertaining to the working condition, the ETI Base Code contains a set of rules. These rules were developed by the ETI without involvement of the state. The companies that adopt this code must undertake to be bound by it. What is not included in this definition is a clarification of the question of what kinds of codes of conduct are encompassed by this definition, that is, corporate codes of conduct (codes of conduct that companies have produced themselves) or codes of conduct developed by third parties. The guidance on the CPRs, published by the Office of Fair Trading (OFT), does not provide further assistance with the question.[33] The same applies to the guidance issued by the European Commission on the Unfair Commercial Practices Directive,

---

[31] Regs 5 (3) (b), 2 (1) CPRs.
[32] Regs 2 (1).
[33] See OFT, *Guidance on the Consumer Protection from Unfair Trading Regulations 2008*. The Office of Fair Trading was responsible for protecting consumer interests throughout the UK. It closed on 1 April 2014, with its responsibilities passing to a number of different organisations including the Competition and Markets Authority (CMA) and the Financial Conduct Authority, see https://www.gov.uk/government/organisations/office-of-fair-trading (accessed 18 October 2014).

which underlies the CPRs.[34] Moreover, this issue has not yet been decided by a court.

As the guidance does not discuss this issue, one could assume that the CPRs encompass both types of code of conduct. However, on a literal reading of the definition in reg 2 (1) CPRs, it is important to note the following clause: 'which defines the behaviour of traders ...'. The definition therefore refers to codes of conduct that are adopted by traders rather than just one trader which is, most of the time, the case if a company develops and adopts its own code of conduct. Moreover, the example of a breach of a commitment made in a code of conduct used by the OFT in its guidance on the CPRs (which was subsequently also used as an example by the Commission in its guidance on the Unfair Commercial Practices Directive which were published later than the document from the OFT) refers to a trader who has agreed to be bound by a code of practice that promotes the sustainable use of woods and which requires its members not to use hardwood from unsustainable sources. This example also refers to members of the code in the plural. It is therefore assumed here that, in any case, the CPRs encompass third party codes of conduct that are adopted by more than just one company. The ETI Base Code is such a code, as the ETI is an organisation which has several members. The ETI has developed the Base Code that its members must adopt. However, it could also be argued that the interpretation of 'code of conduct' is wider and also encompasses the codes developed by one company only, as the definition of 'code owner' only refers to 'a trader or a body responsible for ...'. It is therefore also possible that a code which is developed by one company satisfies the condition of reg 2 (1) CPRs, as this code of conduct could later on be adopted by other companies, too, hence ensuring that it defines the behaviour of 'traders'. Howells therefore emphasises that the definition makes clear that 'even a trader or group of traders may qualify' as code owner.[35]

While an interpretation that also includes corporate codes of conduct is possible, this chapter uses the ETI Base Code as a third party code in accordance with reg 2 (1) CPRs. Moreover, as already noted, this code is

---

[34] European Commission, 'Commission staff working document, Guidance on the implementation/application of Directive 2005/29/EC on unfair commercial practices', SEC (2009) 1666, available at http://ec.europa.eu/consumers/rights/index_en.htm (accessed 18 October 2014).

[35] G Howells, 'Codes of conduct', in G Howells, H W Micklitz and T Wilhelmsson (eds), *European Fair Trading Law: The Unfair Commercial Practices Directive* (Ashgate Publishing Limited 2006) 206.

also of a significant relevance in commercial practice due to the number of large companies that have adopted it.

Secondly, it is necessary that a company must have indicated in a commercial practice that it is bound by this code.

Pursuant to reg 2 (1) CPRs, commercial practice means

> any act, omission, course of conduct, representation or commercial communication (including advertising and marketing) by a trader, which is directly connected with the promotion, sale or supply of a product to or from consumers, whether occurring before, during or after a commercial transaction (if any) in relation to a product.

It is therefore necessary that the company has declared that it is bound to the ETI Base Code in direct connection with the promotion or sale of a product to consumers. The example used in the OFT Guidance refers to labels and logos used by companies on the product.[36] This condition might limit the actual scope of reg 5 (3) CPRs, as it could be interpreted in a way that the CSR commitments of a company are not automatically directly linked to the promotion or sale of a product unless the company uses its CSR policies in its marketing material. Although membership of the ETI Base Code is not placed upon products by way of a logo or label, it is argued here that information on a company's website about its CSR commitments which is close to the online shopping facilities is closely linked to the promotion and the sale of products. This situation applies, for example, to the website of the fashion retailer River Island in terms of its ETI membership. Upon River Island's website, there is a section on Corporate Social Responsibility and the Ethical Trading Initiative which is very close to the online shop and therefore directly linked to the promotion of its goods. In the sections on CSR and the ETI, the company outlines its commitment to CSR and to 'safeguarding and improving the rights and working conditions of workers in those factories which supply our products'.[37] The information provided on the ETI is linked to the promotion and sale of products, as the website is used both to promote and to sell the clothes currently offered by River Island. As online shoppers do not need to undertake a lengthy search for CSR and ETI, it is argued here that this situation satisfies the condition of being 'directly

---

[36] See OFT, *Guidance on the Consumer Protection from Unfair Trading Regulations 2008*, paras 4.4. and 7.11.

[37] River Island, Ethical Trading Initiative, available at http://www.river island.com/inside-river-island/about-us/ethical-trading-initiatives (accessed 18 October 2014).

connected with the promotion, sale or supply of a product to or from consumers'.

For example, River Island publishes the following statement on its website intended for public relations:

> Code of Practice: River Island is firmly committed to the adoption and integration of the ETI Base Code into our World Wide Ethical Policy, throughout our global supply chain and into our core business activities. We feel that by working with the ETI and its other members we will be able to draw on the wider pool of experience which exists in the collective organisation.[38]

This statement can be understood as a declaration that River Island is bound by the ETI Base Code. The company has indicated its binding to the code in a commercial practice connected with the promotion of a product to consumers pursuant to reg 2 (1) CPRs.

C.   Firm, Verifiable and Non-aspirational Commitments

The second condition of reg 5 (3) (b) CPRs is that the commitment is firm and verifiable and not aspirational. In this respect, it is necessary to distinguish between the different exemplary clauses of the ETI Base Code referred to above. The clauses pertaining to the prohibition of forced labour[39] and the right to join or to form trade unions of their own choosing and to bargain collectively[40] are firm and verifiable. The same applies to the clause that no new child labour will be recruited.[41]

Slightly less firm than these clauses is the provision that workers shall not be required to work in excess of 48 hours per week due to the limitation 'on a regular basis'.[42] This limitation means that it is possible that workers will be required to work overtime as long as this keeps within the obligation that overtime shall not exceed 12 hours. Finally, in

---

[38]   Ibid.

[39]   Clause 1.1 ETI Base Code.

[40]   Clause 2.1 ETI Base Code.

[41]   Clause 4.1 ETI Base Code. Child is defined in the appendices of the ETI Base Code as 'any person less than 15 years of age'. However, where the local minimum age law is set at 14 years of age in accordance with developing country exceptions under ILO Convention No. 138, the lower will apply. With regards to existing child labour, there is a clause in the ETI Base Code that requires companies to provide for the transition of any child found to be performing child labour to enable him or her to attend to remain in quality education until no longer a child.

[42]   Clause 6.2. ETI Base Code.

comparison to these clauses, the obligation on companies to 'adopt an open attitude towards the activities of trade unions and their organisational activities' is rather vague.[43] While employees are allowed to join or to form a trade union, there might still be significant varieties in the ways in which companies undertake their 'open attitude towards the activities of trade unions'. It is not prescribed to what extent they actually respect the right of their employees to bargain collectively. It is still possible that companies formally allow their employees to be members of trade unions, while they practically exercise influence on them not to negotiate for significant improvements of working conditions or pay increases. A company that has adopted the ETI Base Code could therefore still claim to comply with the clauses of the code, even if it restricts the collective bargaining of its employees. This clause is therefore not firm. Hence, breaches of the clause pertaining to the actual enjoyment of the right to collective bargaining are difficult to verify. It is therefore unlikely that a company that has adopted the ETI Base Code will commit an unfair constitutional practice in accordance with the CPRs for a breach of this clause.

D. The Commitment must Cause or be likely to Cause the Average Consumer to take a Transactional Decision

The final condition of reg 5 (3) (b) CPRs is that commitments in the ETI Base Code which satisfy the first two conditions must also cause or be likely to cause the average consumer to take a transactional decision he would otherwise not have taken. The two abstract terms which require interpretation are 'average consumer' and 'transactional decision'. The High Court has recently construed these concepts in *Office of Fair Trading v Purely Creative Ltd*.[44] In this case, the OFT applied for an enforcement order in relation to the CPRs. The High Court held that 'it was common ground' that any decision with an 'economic consequence'

---

[43] Clause 2.2. ETI Base Code. An even clearer example of a purely aspirational clause is the following commitment in Unilever's Responsible Sourcing Policy, clause 12: 'Business is conducted in a manner which embraces sustainability and reduces environmental impact: Operations, sourcing manufacture, distribution of products and the supply of services are conducted with the aim to protect and preserve the environment.'

[44] *Office of Fair Trading v Purely Creative Ltd* [2011] EWHC 106 (Ch). The European Court of Justice (ECJ) has now decided in reference for a preliminary ruling in this case by the Court of Appeal (England and Wales), see: *Purely Creative Ltd and Others v Office of Fair Trading* (Case C-428/11), [2013] 1 C.M.L.R. 35.

was a transactional decision. This broad interpretation is based on reg 2 (1) CPRs which stipulates that a transactional decision means any decision taken by a consumer, whether it is to act or to refrain from acting concerning, inter alia, whether, how and on what terms to purchase. Consequently, the term encompasses any purchase decision of a consumer which is based on the seller's CSR record.

With regard to the concept of an 'average consumer', reg 2 (1) CPRs stipulates that this term shall be construed in accordance with paragraphs (2) to (6) of reg 2 CPRs. Pursuant to s2 (2) CPRs, in determining the effect of a commercial practice on the average consumer, account shall be taken of the material characteristics of such an average consumer including his being reasonably well-informed, reasonably observant and circumspect.[45] The paragraphs (3) to (6) are of little use in the context here, however, as they only further specify the concept of the average consumer in relation to particular groups of consumers. The decision of the High Court, inter alia, concerned the question how an average consumer would understand the mailing of promotions to consumers which suggests that they had won a prize when they had not or would have had to pay to receive the prize.[46] In this respect, the court held that there is a proposition that the CPRs would protect consumers who take reasonable care of themselves rather than ignorant, careless or over-hasty consumers.[47] Notably, it would not necessarily follow from this standard that the average consumer would read the entirety of a promotion.[48] The High Court's approach is said to follow the interpretation adopted by the

---

[45] The concept of the average consumer was developed by the European Court of Justice. The ECJ, when weighing the risk of misleading consumers against the requirements of the free movement of goods, has held that, '... in order to determine whether a particular description, trade mark or promotional description or statement is misleading, it is necessary to take into account the presumed expectations of an average consumer who is reasonably well informed and reasonably observant and circumspect'. See Case C-210/96 *Gut Springenheide GmbH, Rudolf Tusky v Oberkreisdirektor des Kreises Steinfurt-Amt für Lebensmittelüberwachung and Another* [1998] ECR I-4657, para 31.

[46] ibid.

[47] Similarly, the Law Commission states that the 'average consumer' test would be based on a consumer who is critical and rational, see The Law Commission and The Scottish Law Commission (n 14) para 2.32.

[48] ibid.

European Commission.[49] In its guidance on the Unfair Commercial Practices Directive (which underlies the CPRs), the Commission interprets the 'average consumer' as a critical person who is conscious and circumspect in his or her market behaviour.[50] He or she should inform themselves about the quality and price of products and make efficient choices. In its preliminary ruling in this case, the ECJ emphasised that it is for the national courts to establish the typical reaction of the average consumer in a case.[51] So, in summary, the average consumer is one who is informed, observant and able to take care of himself.

Linking the concept back to the final condition of reg 5 (3) (b), the key issue here is if firm and verifiable commitments in the ETI Base Code would cause or are likely to cause the average consumer to purchase or refrain from purchasing goods from a company. Studies have shown that up to 90 per cent of consumers consider CSR in their purchase and consumption behaviour,[52] although it is doubtful to what extent this consideration has an impact on the actual purchase decision of consumers.[53] However, the issue raised by reg 5 (3) (b) CPRs is not to what extent consumers generally make their purchase decision on the basis of the CSR engagement of companies. Rather the issue here is if the breach of a CSR commitment in a code of conduct which the company has publicly declared to adhere to has an effect on the purchase decision of the average consumer. One can assume that a well-informed, observant and circumspect consumer would expect a company to comply with the CSR commitments that it publicly promises. Such a consumer would be likely to make purchase decisions on the basis of this expectation, for example, if the average consumer reads that a company in the garment industry does not employ child labour then an informed and observant consumer would expect the company to comply with this commitment.

Further information about the question whether the breach of a code of conduct 'causes or is likely to cause the average consumer to take a

---

[49] O Bray and M Starmer, 'Office of Fair Trading v Purely Creative Ltd: the net tightens on exponents of sharp commercial practices' (2011) 22 *Entertainment Law Review* 118, 121.

[50] European Commission, 'Guidance on the implementation and application of Directive 2005/29/EC on unfair commercial practices' SEC (2009) 1666, available at http://ec.europa.eu/consumers/rights/docs/Guidance_UCP_Directive_en.pdf (accessed 18 October 2014).

[51] *Purely Creative Ltd and Others v Office of Fair Trading* (Case C-428/11), [2013] 1 C.M.L.R. 35.

[52] Vogel (n 2).

[53] Carrington, Neville and Whitwell (n 3) 139.

transactional decision he would not have taken otherwise' can be found in the guidance on the CPRs, published by the OFT. Until its closure in April 2014, the OFT was the responsible body for the enforcement of the regulations.[54] The CPRs are now enforceable by the Competition and Markets Authority and Local Authority Trading Standards. The OFT's guidance provides an example of the breach of a corporate code of conduct which would constitute a breach of reg 5 (3) (b) CPRs. This example is significant from a CSR point of view. It outlines the scenario of a trader who has agreed to be bound by a code of practice which promotes the sustainable use of wood. The trader consequently displays the logo of this code in advertising campaigns.[55] If this code contains a commitment by signatories of the code that they will not use hardwood from unsustainable sources, but the trader in the example here, in fact, uses hardwood from endangered rainforests he would not comply with the code. Consequently, he would breach reg 5 (3) (b) CPRs as the commitment he has failed to comply with is a firm and verifiable breach. Moreover, the average consumer could expect members of the code to sell products which comply with the code and is deemed likely to make a purchase decision on the basis of this expectation. The breach of the code of conduct would therefore amount to a misleading action which, in turn, constitutes an unfair commercial practice. If one applies this approach in the OFT's guidance to the clauses of the ETI Base Code used in this section, then consumers would expect a company that has adopted the ETI Base Code to comply with the firm and verifiable commitments referring to forced labour and child labour as well as the joining of trade unions. Consumers would be likely to be deemed to have made purchase decisions on the basis of this expectation. Consequently, the condition in reg 5 (3) (b) CPRs that the breach must have caused or be likely to cause a transactional decision of an average consumer would be satisfied if a company such as River Island that has adopted the ETI Base Code were found to be in breach with these commitments.

This analysis shows that breaches of firm and verifiable commitments in the ETI Base Code are likely to constitute an unfair commercial practice under the CPRs as long as the company indicates its membership of the ETI in a way that is directly linked and connected with the promotion, sale or supply of a product. Unfair commercial practices are

---

[54]   Under the Enterprise Act 2002, the enforcement body of the Consumer Protection form Unfair Trading Regulations was the OFT as well as trading standards. For the OFT guidance see: OFT (n 23).
[55]   ibid, 33.

prohibited by reg 3 (1) CPRs. Consumer law, through the CPRs, therefore encompasses breaches of CSR commitments in corporate codes of conduct.

E. Remedies for Unlawful Commercial Practices

However, these regulations only promote CSR in a meaningful way if the consumers procure an appropriate remedy where a company is found to have committed an unlawful commercial practice by breaching a CSR commitment in its code of conduct.

The CPRs make certain unfair commercial practices a criminal offence (see reg 8 and reg 9 CPRs). These entail a penalty.[56] Breaches of corporate codes of conduct pursuant to reg 5 (3) (b) CPRs do not constitute offences pursuant to reg 9 CPRs. On the contrary, all other misleading actions in reg 5 CPRs are encompassed by the scope of reg 9 CPRs. The CPRs therefore give breaches of corporate codes of conduct a lower level of protection than other unfair commercial practices. This situation is a severe limitation of the CPRs' ability to address breaches of codes of conduct, as strict liability would mean that every breach of a code of conduct which satisfies the conditions of reg 5 (3) (b) would automatically be an offence. Breaches of corporate codes of conduct can, however, be enforced through injunctive civil actions.[57] The responsible bodies for the enforcement of the regulations are the Competition and Markets Authority and Local Authority Trading Standards. Notably, consumers were initially not given the right to enforce the CPRs, but the Consumer Protection (Amendment) Regulations 2014 have introduced a private remedy which will be discussed below.

The enforcement bodies have a variety of means to enforce consumer protection legislation. In its statement of the enforcement principles, the OFT emphasised that formal legal action is a last resort.[58] If an

---

[56] Reg 13 CPRs.

[57] See OFT, *Guidance on the Consumer Protection from Unfair Trading Regulations*, para 11.15.

[58] OFT, *Statement of Consumer Protection Enforcement Principles*, (February 2012), para 2.14. Court action will only be taken after undertakings have been sought, wherever possible. The enforcement body will therefore usually first consult with the business in question in order to stop the infringement before taking court action by applying for an enforcement order. Applications for an enforcement order are made pursuant to s215 of the Enterprise Act 2002 if the enforcer thinks that a person has engaged or is engaging in conduct which constitutes a domestic or a Community infringement, or is likely in engage in conduct which constitutes a Community infringement. Pursuant to s215 (5) (a)

enforcement body applies for an enforcement order, the court may make an enforcement order which must indicate the nature of the conduct to which the order applies.[59] Such an order requires the cessation of the infringement. Failure to comply with the enforcement order could be found by a court to be contempt of court, which could lead to a fine or imprisonment.[60]

An important point in this enforcement regime is the position of the consumers who are the intended beneficiaries of the CPRs in particular and of consumer law in general. Part 8 of the Enterprise Act 2002 which provides the enforcement mechanisms for certain consumer laws including the CPRs does not allow consumers to initiate injunctive civil actions themselves. This power is the right of the public enforcement authorities. While the 2014 Regulations, which are analysed below, introduce a right to redress for consumers in the form of rescission or discount/damages, they still do not contain injunctions which are the most effective regime against misleading statements as they would prohibit a company from continuing with a misleading claim. So, although the civil enforcement of the CPRs will now no longer purely be in the competence of public authorities, there is still a significant gap as injunctive civil actions cannot be brought by the consumers themselves as the intended beneficiaries of consumer protection law. Even though public authorities have possibly more resources to enforce the CPRs than private individuals, it is a serious weakness of the CPRs in their 2008 version that the enforcement of the provision in reg 5 (3) (b) CPRs, with its potential to promote CSR, is subject to the decision of public authorities to take action and not down to the consumers.

The reason why prior to the 2014 Regulations the CPRs did not provide for any private remedy was that the legislator did not want to open floodgates. However, the result was that the CPRs were only rarely enforced at all. In its annual report 2011–12, the OFT declares that it obtained 13 undertakings and five court orders through its enforcement of consumer protection laws via its powers in the Enterprise Act 2002. All but one court order concerned the breach of the CPRs.[61] These figures

---

Enterprise Act 2002, the High Court or a county court have jurisdiction to make an enforcement order if the person against whom the order is sought carries on business or has a place of business in England and Wales or Northern Ireland.

[59]   S217 (3), (5) CPRs.

[60]   OFT, *Enforcement of Consumer Protection Legislation, Guidance on Part 8 of the Enterprise Act* (2003) para 3.51.

[61]   See the information provided by the OFT in its annual report: OFT, *Annual Report 2011–12, Annex A.*

are not particularly high. From a CSR point of view, it can be concluded that while the CPRs encompass breaches of CSR through the prohibition of misleading practices, there was no effective enforcement regime in place. The potential of the CPRs to promote the socially responsible behaviour of companies, therefore, remained unused.

The background to the absence of a private remedy in English law in the CPRs was that the Unfair Commercial Practices Directive which was implemented through the CPRs gives member states some choice of appropriate domestic enforcement remedies for non-compliance in Articles 11 to 13 of the Directive.[62] The Directive left it to the member states to decide whether or not to introduce a private remedy.[63] It therefore did not harmonise the enforcement systems. The UK decided against such a private remedy for consumers when it implemented the Directive through the CPRs in 2008.[64] However, this decision did not bring the discussion to an end. The absence of an enforcement right for

---

[62] Article 11 Enforcement: '1. Member States shall ensure that adequate and effective means exist to combat unfair commercial practices in order to enforce compliance with the provisions of this Directive in the interest of consumers. Such means shall include legal provisions under which persons or organisations regarded under national law as having a legitimate interest in combating unfair commercial practices, including competitors, may: (a) take legal action against such unfair commercial practices; and/or (b) bring such unfair commercial practices before an administrative authority competent either to decide on complaints or to initiate appropriate legal proceedings. It shall be for each Member State to decide which of these facilities shall be available and whether to enable the courts or administrative authorities to require prior recourse to other established means of dealing with complaints, including those referred to in Article 10. These facilities shall be available regardless of whether the consumers affected are in the territory of the Member State where the trader is located or in another Member State.'

[63] Directive 2005/29/EEC, The Consumer Protection From Unfair Trading Regulations 2008. The directive does not preclude member states from conferring a private right of redress on consumers.

[64] The government asked the Law Commission to consider the issue of private enforcement of the regulations. The Law Commission concluded that the introduction of a private remedy for consumers could create more problems than it would solve. See: Law Commission, *A Private Right of Redress for Unfair Commercial Practices? Preliminary Advice to the Department of Business, Enterprise and Regulatory Reform* (November 2008), available at http://law commission.justice.gov.uk/docs/rights_of_redress_advice1(2).pdf (accessed 18 October 2014).

consumers was subject to much criticism and debate.[65] For example, the statutory consumer organisation Consumer Focus called for the introduction of a private right of redress in the CPRs for all consumers after the implementation of the Directive.[66] In its report, Consumer Focus highlighted that there were only relatively few prosecutions under the current regime despite a large number of violations of the CPRs.[67] In a study of the extent of unfair commercial practices, 64 per cent of the respondents said that they had fallen victim to an unfair commercial practice within the past 24 months.[68] Consumer Focus therefore argued that there was an enforcement gap in the public enforcement system.[69] This situation would justify providing consumers with a private remedy. The consumer organisation concluded that enforcement would be more effective if public authorities and consumers 'worked in tandem' using both private and public enforcement sanctions against misleading and aggressive trade practices.[70]

In conclusion, the enforcement regime of the CPRs prior to the Consumer Protection (Amendment) Regulations 2014 which lacked a private remedy to prosecute breaches of consumer laws was severely deficient. Although the CPRs encompass breaches of firm and verifiable CSR commitments in codes of conduct, the consumers as the intended beneficiaries of the CPRs were left without a right of redress against companies. They therefore did not procure an appropriate remedy for unlawful commercial practices.

III. LAW OF MISREPRESENTATION

Consumers could also be protected against breaches of CSR commitments by companies through the law of misrepresentation. The law of misrepresentation is sometimes referred to as the 'pre-existing private law'[71] in respect of consumer actions as it predates the implementation of

---

[65] For example: Consumer Focus, *Waiting to be Heard: Giving Consumers the Right of Redress over Unfair Commercial Practices* (August 2009), available at http://www.consumerfocus.org.uk/files/2010/12/Waiting-to-be-heard.pdf (accessed 18 October 2014).

[66] ibid, 3.

[67] ibid.

[68] ibid, 9.

[69] ibid.

[70] ibid, 3.

[71] The law relating to misrepresentation is mainly found in common law with the Misrepresentation Act 1967 providing some further details.

the CPRs.[72] It is a separate body of law which lies on the boundary of contract, tort and restitution.[73] Still, the law of misrepresentation will be addressed in this chapter on consumer law and CSR. The reason for this approach is that the law of misrepresentation is said to cover similar ground to the Unfair Commercial Practices Directive 2005/29 in the consumer context.[74] As the law of misrepresentations covers false statements which have induced the party misled into entering into the contract, it could provide consumers with redress in the context of breaches of publicly announced CSR commitments. In this case the law of misrepresentation would protect consumers and hence serve consumer law ends. As the law of misrepresentation could be utilised to protect consumers, textbooks on consumer law consequently often contain a section on it.[75] This approach is in line with the view that the scope of consumer law is open-ended.[76]

When the Law Commission was consulted upon the issue of the possible introduction of a private remedy for consumers it discussed the scope of the law of misrepresentation as legal actions in private law.[77] The discussion of the law of misrepresentation in these documents remains somewhat general, however. In particular, it does not apply the law of misrepresentation to breaches of commitments in codes of conduct which is the key issue from a CSR point of view. In the discussion about the possible introduction of a private remedy, Consumer Focus criticised the complexity of the law of misrepresentation.[78] It argued that there are gaps in terms of the kinds of statements which constitute misrepresentations, for example, statements which are literally true, but misleading, are not covered by the law of misrepresentation, whereas they are under the

---

[72] Consumer Focus (n 65) 17.

[73] E McKendrick, *Contract Law* (8th edn, Palgrave Macmillan 2009) para 13.1. Art 2 (2) of the Unfair Commercial Practices Directive clarifies that the directive is 'without prejudice to contract law and, in particular, to the rules on the validity, formation or effect of a contract'.

[74] The Law Commission and The Scottish Law Commission (n 14) 23.

[75] See Howells and Weatherill (n 17) para 3.4; Woodroffe and Lowe (n18) paras 7.03–7.11.

[76] Howells and Weatherill (n 17) 5.

[77] The Law Commission and The Scottish Law Commission, *Consumer Redress For Misleading And Aggressive Practices: A Joint Consultation Paper* (Consultation Paper No 199 / Discussion Paper 149, April 2011), 54–79; The Law Commission and The Scottish Law Commission (n 14) 23–40.

[78] Consumer Focus (n 65) 17.

CPRs.[79] The Law Commission is similarly critical of the law of misrepresentation as the private law way of providing redress to consumers for misleading and aggressive practices.[80] In its final report it states that although the law of misrepresentation would, in theory, provide redress for most misleading trade practices where consumers suffer detriment, it would be 'fragmented, complex and unclear'.[81] Moreover, it would be difficult to apply in a consumer context as it primarily evolved to deal with business disputes.[82]

This section will apply the law of misrepresentation to CSR. It will analyse whether the law of misrepresentation encompasses breaches of corporate CSR commitments in codes of conduct and, if it does, if consumers procure an appropriate remedy.

A.   Are Breaches of CSR Commitments by Companies Covered?

Following the case study of the ETI Base Code in the previous section on the CPRs, the law of misrepresentation will be applied here to the same clauses of this code, used as an example of an important code of conduct to which many English companies selling consumer goods are committed.

The clauses from the ETI Base Code used above are:

1. **Employment is freely chosen**
   1.1. There is no forced, bonded or involuntary prison labour.

2. **Freedom of association and the right to collective bargaining are respected**
   2.1. Workers, without distinction, have the right to join or form trade unions of their own choosing and to bargain collectively.
   2.2. The employer adopts an open attitude towards the activities of trade unions and their organisational activities.

4. **Child labour shall not be used**
   4.1. There shall be no new recruitment of child labour.

6. **Working hours are not excessive**
   6.2. In any event, workers shall not on a regular basis be required to work in excess of 48 hours per week and shall be provided with at least one day off for every 7 day period on average. Overtime shall

---

[79]   ibid, 18.
[80]   The Law Commission and The Scottish Law Commission (n 14) x.
[81]   ibid.
[82]   ibid.

be voluntary, shall not exceed 12 hours per week, shall not be demanded on a regular basis and shall always be compensated at a premium rate.

A misrepresentation can be defined as an unambiguous, false statement of fact or law which is addressed to the party misled, which is material and which also induces the contract.[83]

B.   An Unambiguous, False Statement of Fact

The first condition is that there is an unambiguous, false statement of existing fact or law.[84] There is no further definition of 'statement of fact' in cases dealing with alleged misrepresentations other than that these statements are distinguished from the following statements which do not constitute statements of fact: statements of opinion, 'mere puffs' and statements of intention or promises.[85] Companies commonly communicate their CSR policies on their website, in brochures or other public relations material.[86] The CSR communication is easily available by consumers. In these documents companies make statements about how they behave in socially responsible ways. As mentioned above, codes of conduct usually form a core element of the CSR policy of companies.[87] These codes of conduct regularly contain a list of CSR commitments to which companies pledge to comply. It depends on the way the commitments are phrased, if they are to be regarded as statement of facts for the purpose of the law of misrepresentation or if they are rather statements of intention or promises (which, even if untrue, could not qualify as misrepresentations).

In the above examples from the ETI Base Code, the clauses pertaining to the prohibition of forced labour and the recruitment of new child labour as well as the granting of the right to join a trade union are all

---

[83]   McKendrick (n 73) para 13.2.

[84]   Following *Kleinwort Benson Ltd v Lincoln City Council* [1999] 2 AC 349, mistakes of law can also cause an actionable misrepresentation.

[85]   See J Poole, *Textbook on Contract Law* (11th edn, OUP 2012) para 14.2.1.3.

[86]   For example, River Island as an ETI member has published information about its CSR engagement and the ETI on a special section on its website (the website also has an online shop): http://www.riverisland.com/inside-river-island/about-us/ethical-trading-initiatives (accessed 18 October 2014).

[87]   See for example: Vodafone, *The Vodafone Code of Conduct*, available at http://www.vodafone.com/content/dam/vodafone/about/sustainability/2012/pdf/vodafone_code_of_conduct_2012.pdf (accessed 18 October 2014).

firm and verifiable statements and not just statements of intention. They therefore constitute statements of fact. The assessment of the principle referring to the activities of trade unions leads to a different outcome, however. The wording 'open attitude to the activities' is not as definite as the previous examples. A company could claim that it pursues this goal even though it does exercise certain restrictions on these activities in practice in a perhaps more subtle way. In conclusion, breaches of the clause pertaining to the activities of trade unions are hard to verify. It would be difficult to prove that this clause was a false statement. This clause can therefore rather be interpreted to be a promise.

Overall, this analysis mirrors the assessment of the same principles of the ETI Base Code with regard to the CPRs. If a company was found to be in breach of the commitments pertaining to the use of child labour or forced labour or the right to join a trade union, then this breach would constitute an unambiguous, false statement of fact.

C. The Representation must have been Addressed to the Party Misled

The second requirement of misrepresentations is that the representation must have been addressed to the party misled. The statement can be addressed through direct communication of the misrepresentation or alternatively by addressing it to a third party with the intention of it being passed on to the claimant.[88] The CSR policies of the companies are publicly communicated in order to enhance the brand reputation vis-à-vis the companies' (present and potential) customers, for example the section on the ETI on River Island's website. This condition is satisfied whenever information about the companies' CSR policies is directed to consumers.

D. The Representation must have Induced the other Party to Enter into the Contract

The third condition is that the representation must have induced the other party to enter into the contract and possibly it must have also been a material misrepresentation.[89] The misrepresentation does not need to be

---

[88]   McKendrick (n 73) para 13.4.

[89]   ibid, para 13.5. The requirement of the misrepresentation being material is doubted. It seems as if courts now no longer distinguish between materiality and inducement. The situation is now that if the misrepresentation would have induced a reasonable person to enter into the contract, then the courts will presume that it did induce the representee to enter into the contract and the onus of proof is then placed upon the representor to show that the representee did not

the sole inducement; it is sufficient to be an inducement which was actively present to the representee's mind.[90] It must represent a fact which would positively influence a reasonable person who considers entering the contract to decide positively in favour of so doing.[91] The consumer will be unable to show that the representation induced the contract where the consumer was unaware of the existence of the representation, where he knew that the representation was untrue and where he did not allow the representation to affect his judgment. The latter is the case where the claimant regards the representation as being unimportant.[92] A study has shown that up to 90 per cent of consumers consider the CSR record of companies in their purchase and consumption behaviours.[93] Although other studies have revealed that the actual purchase decision is only rarely based on CSR considerations,[94] it is proven that CSR generally influences consumers positively. CSR commitments are therefore facts which would positively influence a reasonable person in favour of entering a contract which the person considers entering into anyway. It is therefore likely that CSR commitments are considered to be representations which have induced the other party into the contract.

In conclusion, the law of misrepresentation encompasses breaches of CSR commitments by companies, if customers can prove that they were influenced in their purchase decision by the CSR commitments of a company. The important condition is that the CSR commitment in question must be a false statement of fact. As shown in the analysis of the ETI Base Code this condition is not satisfied in respect of all CSR principles in this code of conduct. The results in relation to the scope of the law of misrepresentation and the CPRs is similar, as the same CSR commitments were found to be encompassed by the two different legal sources. This finding seems to confirm the contention found in the Law Commission's review that the law of misrepresentation would cover the breaches of CSR commitments in private law which are prohibited by the CPRs.[95]

---

in fact rely on the representation. On the other hand, where the misrepresentation would not have induced a reasonable person to enter into the contract, then the onus of proof is on the representee to show that the misrepresentation did in fact induce him to enter into the contract.

90   *Edgington v Fitzmaurice* (1885) 29 Ch D 459.
91   Poole (n 85) para 14.2.2.1.
92   McKendrick (n 73) para 13.5.
93   Vogel (n 2).
94   Eckhardt, Belk and Devinney (n 3) 426.
95   The Law Commission and The Scottish Law Commission (n 14) 10.

However, it is important to consider that the existence of a misrepresentation depends on whether the consumer has been induced to enter into a contract. Private law claims based on misrepresentation therefore presuppose that a contract was formed in the first place.[96] This situation is a difference to the CPRs which only require that the failure to comply with a commitment in a code of conduct 'causes or is likely to cause the average consumer to take a transactional decision he would not have taken otherwise'. Actions against companies for breach of the CPRs, following the violation of their codes of conduct, are therefore possible without a previously formed contract if the breach was likely to cause the average consumer to make a purchase decision on this basis. In contrast, misrepresentations only exist where a consumer has indeed purchased a good. The law of misrepresentation therefore does not encompass breaches of CSR to the same extent as the CPRs.

E.   Do Consumers Procure an Appropriate Remedy for a Misrepresentation?

The law of misrepresentation only promotes CSR in a meaningful way if consumers procure an appropriate remedy where a company is found to have committed a misrepresentation by violating a CSR principle in its code of conduct. It is necessary to distinguish which type of misrepresentation is at issue in order to determine the remedial consequences of the breach. A distinction is made between fraudulent misrepresentations,[97] negligent misrepresentations in common law, misrepresentations which are liable under section 2 (1) of the Misrepresentation Act 1967 and innocent misrepresentations which are neither fraudulent, nor negligent.[98]

i.   Right to rescind the contract
All types of misrepresentation entitle the representee to rescind the contract (i.e. setting aside the contract which was subject to the misrepresentation), but not all types of misrepresentation give rise to an

---

[96]   The supply chain contracts in the previous chapter also require the formation of a contract in order to give effect to the CSR policies which the buyer imposes on the supplier.

[97]   Fraudulent misrepresentations also constitute the tort of deceit. Following *Derry v Peek* (1889) 14 App Cas 337, in order to be fraudulent the false statement must be made knowingly or without belief in its truth or recklessly careless, whether it be true or false.

[98]   Poole (n 85) para 14.4.

action for damages.[99] A misrepresentation renders the contract void-able.[100] If a contract is voidable, the representee can decide either to rescind or to affirm the contract.[101] The availability of the right to rescind the contract, upon finding a misrepresentation, is a powerful tool for consumers. It enables them to decide whether or not to keep the contract. Consumers have the right to be put back into the position they were in before entering into the contract under the influence of the misrepresentation, that is, the false belief that a company complies with its CSR commitments, although, in fact, it does not adhere to these. The company, on the other hand, faces a severe consequence in case of such a misrepresentation, that is, to lose its contracts with consumers who considered the accuracy of the company's CSR commitments to be an important aspect for their purchase decision. The law of misrepresentation therefore provides an appropriate remedy in case of breaches of CSR commitments through the availability of the right to rescind the contract.[102]

ii. Right to damages

Apart from rescission, the other principal remedy for misrepresentation is damages. A claim for damages cannot be based on contract unless the misrepresentation has been subsequently incorporated into the contract as a term, in which case damages can be claimed for breach of contract. But damages can be recovered in tort where the misrepresentation was made fraudulently or negligently.[103] Fraud will be difficult to prove in respect of breaches of CSR commitments, however, as this would presuppose that the company has made the false statements 'knowingly, or without belief in its truth, or recklessly, careless whether it be true or false'.[104] Negligent misrepresentations are misrepresentations made without due care. They can either be based on common law or on the Misrepresentation Act 1967. Those which are based on common law require the existence of a duty of care.[105] This requirement of a duty of care

---

[99]   McKendrick (n 73) para 13.6.
[100]   ibid.
[101]   ibid.
[102]   However, one needs to take into account that there has not as yet been a single case. The absence of any relevant case law questions the ability of the law of misrepresentation to adequately protect consumers in relation to breaches of CSR commitments by companies. This issue will be discussed below.
[103]   McKendrick (n 73) para 13.9.
[104]   *Derry v Peek* (1889) 14 App Cas 337.
[105]   *Hedley Byrne & Co Ltd v Heller & Partners Ltd* [1964] AC 465.

establishes an extra hurdle which a consumer, who makes a claim for damages, must overcome. Such a special relationship is not necessary for a misrepresentation pursuant to s2 (1) of the Misrepresentation Act 1967 which entitles the representee to damages.[106] Provided that there is no double recovery, the right to damages is additional to the right to rescission.[107]

This Act also reverses the burden of proof to the advantage of the consumer. Once the consumer (the representee) has established the existence of a false statement of fact which induced him into entering into the contract, the defendant (the representor) must prove that he had 'reasonable ground to believe and did believe up to the time the contract was made that the facts represented were true'.[108] This reversal of the burden of proof is a considerable advantage for the representee (consumer) who makes a claim to be awarded damages. The final category is innocent misrepresentations. These are false statements which were neither made fraudulently nor negligently.[109] Victims of innocent misrepresentations are entitled to rescission of the contract, but they have no right to damages.[110] However, the court has discretion under s2 (2) of the Misrepresentation Act 1967 to award damages in lieu of rescission in this instance.

Damages compensate the consumer for the financial loss he has suffered.[111] It is necessary to distinguish between the different types of misrepresentation in order to consider the entitlement of a consumer to damages.[112] With regard to the Misrepresentation Act 1967 as the most likely base for such a claim, the measure of damages is the reliance measure.[113] The claimant is put into the same position he would have

---

[106]   S2 (1) of the Misrepresentation Act 1967 provides: 'Where a person has entered into a contract after a misrepresentation has been made to him by another party thereto and as a result thereof he has suffered loss, then, if the person making the misrepresentation would be liable to damages in respect thereof had the misrepresentation been made fraudulently, that person shall be so liable notwithstanding that the misrepresentation was not made fraudulently, unless he proves that he had reasonable ground to believe and did believe up to the time the contract was made that the facts represented were true.'

[107]   S2 (2) of the Misrepresentation Act 1967.

[108]   S2 (1) of the Misrepresentation Act 1967.

[109]   Poole (n 85) para 14.4.4.

[110]   ibid.

[111]   McKendrick (n 73) para 13.7.

[112]   ibid, para 13.9.

[113]   *Royscot Trust Ltd v Rogerson* [1991] 2 QB 297; *Sharneyford Supplies Ltd v Barrington Black and Co* [1987] Ch 305, 323.

been in had the misrepresentation not been made as he relied upon the truth of the statement. It is, however, doubtful if there are many instances where consumers would need to claim damages in order to be restored to their original position if they have been the victim of a misrepresentation regarding CSR commitments. In most cases where a consumer has purchased a product from a company, he would be able to claim back the money he paid for the good as a consequence of the rescission. The return of the purchase price will commonly put the consumer back into his original position. For instance, where a consumer purchases a product from a fashion retailer such as River Island because of River Island's commitment not to use forced labour, he would be able to claim back the purchase price through rescission if River Island were to be found to be in breach of this commitment. The return of the purchase price would put the consumer back into the position he was in prior to the purchase of the good from River Island.

However, a hypothetical situation where a consumer would not be fully restored to his original position through rescission is where the consumer incurred further expenses when purchasing a good from a company which he believes to have a positive CSR record due to the information released by that company. In this example, further expenses might be incurred if the product from this particular company is not available in the city where the consumer lives, but only further away and if the consumer then travels to that place for making the purchase. This situation might occur in respect of the garment industry in case of expensive high-end clothes which have a smaller customer base and are therefore not sold as widely as cheaper competitors. It is unlikely that this situation would occur in relation to goods produced by a company such as Unilever as these are mainly foods, refreshments, homecare or personal care, hence products used on a daily basis which are usually available in most supermarkets. So, if in this hypothetical example a CSR-conscious consumer who lives in Sheffield deliberately choses to buy clothes from a particular brand which is only sold in London, then this consumer incurs further travel expenses. If the company which has produced the clothes and which proclaims to have a good CSR record is later on found to be in breach of its CSR commitments, then the consumer would have suffered a loss through the extra travel expenses which will not be recoverable by rescission.

The fact that consumers not only procure a right to rescind the contract, but also to damages where they have made a loss as a consequence of the misrepresentation provides the consumers with an appropriate range of remedies. If they have fallen victim to a company which is in breach of CSR commitments that it has undertaken to comply with, then the consumers will be able to be restored into their position prior to the misrepresentation. However, in most cases, consumers will not need to use the right to damages in relation to the breach of CSR commitments as the rescission will put them back into their original position and as double recovery is not permitted.

F.   The Ability of the Law of Misrepresentation to Promote CSR

Although this analysis has shown that the law of misrepresentation covers breaches of CSR commitments by corporations and also provides an appropriate remedy for consumers in such a situation, the ability of the law of misrepresentation to promote consumer protection is limited. Both Consumer Focus and the Law Commission are right in their criticism that the law of misrepresentation is a somewhat complicated way for consumers to procure a remedy for misleading practices such as breaches of CSR commitments by companies. The analysis in this section has shown that the main drawback of the law of misrepresentation is its rather abstract nature. Its sources can mainly be found in the common law with some codification in the Misrepresentation Act 1967. The law of misrepresentation is therefore less accessible than a designated Consumer Act. In comparison, the CPRs are written in a very detailed manner and their sole purpose is to protect consumers. There is also guidance on the application of the CPRs with examples, provided by the OFT, which makes it easier both for laypeople and lawyers to consider their application to business-to-consumer transactions. The law of misrepresentation is therefore a less obvious legal basis for consumer claims. Although consumers can use the law of misrepresentations as a means to procure private redress, the complex nature of this legal area is likely to limit its ability to promote CSR meaningfully. It is therefore noticeable that the research for this chapter has not found a single case where a consumer has made a claim for a misrepresentation based on the breach of a CSR commitment by a company. The absence of applicable case law in respect of violations of CSR commitments is an indication that the law of misrepresentation seems to be difficult to understand and to apply in this area. Moreover, the lack of injunctions as a remedy upon making a misrepresentation is a further limitation in terms of promoting CSR. Consumers are unable to stop companies from continuing with the false claims that they make about their CSR record.

IV. BUSINESS PROTECTION FROM MISLEADING MARKETING REGULATIONS 2008

Advertisement regulation, particularly the Business Protection from Misleading Marketing Regulations 2008,[114] also address misleading advertisement practices in corporate communications. These laws could also encompass the breach of a CSR commitment by a company with which it publicly declares to comply. However, as the Business Protection from Misleading Marketing Regulations 2008 apply only to business-to-business relationships they are not part of consumer law and hence beyond the scope of this chapter.

V. DO THE CONSUMER PROTECTION (AMENDMENT) REGULATIONS 2014 IMPROVE THE PROMOTION OF CSR?

This chapter has shown that English consumer law provides some private law protection for consumers through the law of misrepresentation. However, the law of misrepresentation is less accessible than a designated Act such as the CPRs. The situation that, so far, the CPRs have only protected consumers against breaches of publicly-made CSR commitments by companies through public enforcement is a serious drawback for the ability of English consumer law to promote the socially responsible behaviour of companies. As indicated above, the government has now introduced changes to the Act through the Consumer Protection (Amendment) Regulations 2014 which include a private remedy. This section will analyse the new regime and discuss if, following these amendments, English consumer law is in a better position to promote CSR.

A. Background to the Amendments to the CPRs

Calls for the introduction of a private remedy for consumers for misleading and aggressive practices were not just made domestically by Consumer Focus and the OFT, but also at the European Union level. For example, the European Parliament passed a resolution in January 2009

---

[114] The regulations implement Directive 2006/114/EC concerning misleading and comparative advertising and on unfair commercial practices affecting businesses.

which asked member states 'to consider the necessity of giving consumers a direct right of redress in order to ensure that they are sufficiently protected against unfair commercial practices'.[115] And in July 2010, the European Parliament's Internal Market and Consumer Protection Committee identified a private right of redress as one of the options for improving the enforcement of the Unfair Commercial Practices Directive.[116] The Law Commission published preliminary advice on the issue in November 2008 before the implementation of the Directive into domestic English law.[117] The Law Commission then stated that a private right of redress could be beneficial to consumers, seeing that Ireland had included such a private remedy in its implementation of the Directive.[118]

Nevertheless, the Law Commission was concerned that such an introduction could cause significant problems.[119] It rather suggested improving and simplifying the existing law of misrepresentation. In February 2010, BIS asked the Law Commission and Scottish Law Commission to advise, inter alia, on the possible restatement and simplification of the law of misrepresentation and to reconsider the introduction of a private right of redress where there is clear evidence that consumers have suffered loss as a result of an unfair commercial practice and where no private remedy currently exists.[120] The Law Commission then consulted on the introduction of a private remedy and

---

[115]   European Parliament, 'Resolution on the Transposition, Implementation and Enforcement of Directive 2005/29/EC and Directive 2006/114/EC' (13 January 2009) para 12, available at http://eur-lex.europa.eu/LexUriServ/ LexUriServ.do?uri=OJ:C:2010:046E:0026:0030:EN:PDF (accessed 18 October 2014).

[116]   Internal Market and Consumer Protection Committee, *State of Play of the Implementation of the Provisions on Advertising in the Unfair Commercial Practices Legislation* (July 2010) para 2.6.2., available at http://www.europarl. europa.eu/document/activities/cont/201007/20100713ATT78792/20100713ATT7 8792EN.pdf (accessed 18 October 2014).

[117]   Law Commission, *A Private Right of Redress for Unfair commercial practices? Preliminary Advice to the Department for Business, Enterprise and Regulatory Reform on the Issues Raised* (November 2008).

[118]   Irish Consumer Protection Act 2007, s 74.

[119]   Law Commission (n 117) para 4.19.

[120]   'Law Commissions consult on creating new consumer right', 12 April 2010, available at http://www.out-law.com/page-10911 (accessed 18 October 2014).

published a consultation paper to that effect in April 2011.[121] The respondents overwhelmingly supported the view of the Law Commission that reform was needed and that a private right to redress was missing under the existing law. The Law Commission then published its report in March 2012.[122]

At about the same time, the European Commission reviewed the application of the Unfair Commercial Practices Directive, as stipulated by Article 18 of the Directive. In its communication and the accompanying report, published in March 2013, the Commission concluded that it would be inappropriate to amend the Directive as the enforcement experience in the member states was still too limited.[123] However, while the Commission noted that, generally, member states and stakeholders consider the enforcement of the Directive at national level to be 'appropriate and effective', some would be critical of the 'lack of resources of national enforcers', the 'complexity/length of enforcement procedures' and the 'insufficient deterrent effect of the penalties'.[124]

In its 2012 review, the Law Commission recommended 'targeted reform'.[125] It suggested that consumers should not automatically have a private right of redress because there has been a breach of the Regulations, but only 'where there is a clear problem in the marketplace'.[126] The recommendations propose the introduction of a new statutory right

---

[121] The Law Commission and The Scottish Law Commission, *Consumer Redress For Misleading And Aggressive Practices: A Joint Consultation Paper* (Consultation Paper No 199 / Discussion Paper 149, April 2011).

[122] The Law Commission and The Scottish Law Commission (n 14).

[123] European Commission, 'Communication on the application of the Unfair Commercial Practices Directive: Achieving a high level of consumer protection, Building trust in the Internal Market' COM (2013) 138 final 9, available at http://ec.europa.eu/justice/consumer-marketing/files/ucpd_communication_en.pdf (accessed 18 October 2014).

[124] European Commission, 'First report on the application of Directive 2005/29/EC of the European Parliament and of the Council of 11 May 2005 concerning unfair business-to-consumer commercial practices in the internal market and amending Council Directive 84/450/EEC, Directives 97/7/EC, 98/27/EC and 2002/65/EC of the European Parliament and of the Council and Regulation (EC) No 2006/2004 of the European Parliament and of the Council ("Unfair Commercial Practices Directive")' COM (2013) 139 final 27, available at http://ec.europa.eu/justice/consumer-marketing/files/ucpd_report_en.pdf (accessed 18 October 2014).

[125] The Law Commission and The Scottish Law Commission (n 14) para 4.40.

[126] ibid, para 4.41.

of redress for a consumer against a trader in private law for consumers who have suffered from misleading and aggressive trade practices. The new law should be simple and accessible.[127] Following its review of the recommendations, the government decided to amend the CPRs through the Consumer Protection (Amendment) Regulations 2014. They came into force on 1 October 2014 and will be reviewed in the following section in terms of their ability to promote CSR.

B.   The Promotion of CSR after the Consumer Protection (Amendment) Regulations 2014

From a CSR point of view, the important issues are if the amendments to the CPRs have an impact on the way violations of CSR commitments by companies are encompassed and if the consumers will procure an appropriate private remedy in such a situation (which they do not under the CPRs).

With regard to the first issue, it is important to note that while the 2014 Regulations made amendments to some definitions such as 'consumer' or 'goods', they did not affect the approach to breaches of codes of conduct in any way. Reg 5 (3) (b) which is the relevant provision for violations of CSR commitments in codes of conduct remains in its existing form. There are no changes to 'misleading actions' under the CPRs. Violations of CSR principles are, therefore, encompassed by the CPRs to the same extent as under the CPRs in their 2008 form.

However, the key aspect of the amendments to the CPRs for the analysis here is the introduction of the private right of redress for consumers. This will be inserted as a new part 4A of the CPRs. A consumer now has a right to redress under the CPRs if the following conditions are met: First, the consumer enters into a contract with a trader for the sale or supply of a product by the trader (a 'business to consumer contract'); secondly, the trader engages in a prohibited practice in relation to the product; thirdly, the prohibited practice is a significant factor in the consumer's decision to enter into the contract or make the payment.[128]

A consumer can therefore only acquire a private right of redress against a trader for violations of CSR principles if he has entered into a contract with a trader for the sale of a product in the first place. The purchase of a good is therefore a condition of the private remedy.

---

[127]   ibid, xiii.
[128]   Reg 27A (2) – (6).

Moreover, the trader must have engaged in a 'prohibited practice'. A 'prohibited practice' under the CPRs is, inter alia, a misleading action under regulation 5 (which includes the non-compliance with commitments in codes of conduct discussed above).[129] Finally, it is important that the prohibited practice, that is, the misleading action (e.g. breach of code of conduct) is a significant factor in the sale of the product. It is important to note that the prohibited practice only needs to be 'a' significant factor, but that it does not have to be 'the decisive' factor for the purchase. It therefore does not constitute a much higher threshold than the condition 'must cause or be likely to cause the average consumer to take a transactional decision' which is a condition of 'misleading action' in the first place. The fact that many consumers consider the CSR record/reputation of a company to be an important factor for their purchase decision is, therefore, sufficient to meet the criterion 'significant'. It is necessary that the consumer considered the truth of the company's statements about its compliance with its adopted CSR commitments to be important when making the purchase decision. However, the consumer does not have to prove that the purchase was purely based on the fact that the company pursues a certain CSR strategy.

Additionally, the consumer must meet the specific conditions of the respective private remedies.[130] The remedies that are available to consumers in the business-to-consumer contract situation are the right to unwind the contract (regulation 27F), the right to a discount (regulation 27I) and the right to damages (regulation 27J). The consumer has the right to unwind the contract if he indicates to the trader that he rejects the product and does so within the relevant period and at a time when the product is capable of being rejected.[131] The 'relevant period' means the period of 90 days beginning with the later of the day on which the consumer enters into the contract and the relevant day.[132] The definition of 'relevant day' depends on the circumstances of the respective contract and is, inter alia, the day on which the goods are first delivered.[133] The consequence of the exercise of the right to unwind is that the contract comes to an end so that the consumer and the trader are released from their obligations under it. The trader has then a duty to give the consumer a refund and if the contract was wholly or partly for the sale or supply of goods then the consumer must make the goods available for collection by

---

[129]   Reg 27B.
[130]   Reg 27A (1) (b).
[131]   Reg 27E.
[132]   Reg 27E (3).
[133]   Reg 27E (4).

the trader.[134] Moreover, the right to a discount and the right to damages are available.[135] The right to a discount is an alternative to the right to unwind the contract. The consumer can exercise this right if he has made a payment for the product to the trader and if he has not exercised the right to unwind the contract.[136] The right to damages, on the other hand, is available if the consumer has incurred financial loss which he would not have incurred had the prohibited practice in question not taken place or if he has suffered alarm, distress or physical inconvenience or discomfort which he would not have suffered if the prohibited practice in question had not taken place.[137]

The remedies are therefore comparable to the law of misrepresentation. The primary remedy in case of a company that has violated its CSR commitments is the right to unwind the contract, that is, to rescind it. However, this remedy presupposes the formation of a contract in the first place. It is necessary that a consumer has purchased a good before he can exercise this remedy. The right to damages would, as in the example used above, only apply where a consumer incurs extra cost associated with the purchase of the product. This would be the case in the hypothetical example used above which referred to a customer from Sheffield who travels to London to buy clothes from a manufacturer with a particular CSR record whose goods are only available in London. The regime under the Consumer Protection (Amendment) Regulations 2014 has two key advantages in terms of promoting CSR in comparison to the previous legal situation. First, this remedy is more accessible and clearer than the law of misrepresentation. Secondly, it does provide the consumer with a private right of action where a company does not comply with its publicly declared CSR commitments. The principal right of the consumer to rescind the contract under the CPRs is likely to be a strong instrument as a rescission puts the consumer into the position he would have been in had he not entered into the contract. The right to rescind the contract for consumers would also constitute some form of deterrent for traders not to engage in misleading and aggressive practices.

However, in practice, this situation is still far from ideal for the promotion of CSR. Although consumers can now pursue companies themselves, their right to do so is limited. Where a company has committed an unfair commercial practice through breaching a CSR

---

[134]   Reg 27F.
[135]   Reg 27I and Reg 27J.
[136]   Reg 27I (1).
[137]   Reg 27J.

commitment in a code of conduct which it has adopted, consumers must enter into a contract in the first place and then only have the right to rescind that contract. Only where many consumers group together and do the same will this right be of any practical value. The likely situation is that although the Consumer Protection (Amendment) Regulations 2014 have generally improved the position of consumers, they have achieved very little for the promotion of CSR through consumer law. The private enforcement regime of the CPRs will probably not expose traders who have breached commitments in codes of conduct to meaningful litigation by consumers. The remedy that could achieve meaningful change would be an injunction against the company which would bar it from continuing with its misleading action, that is, that it claims that it complies with its CSR commitments in a code of conduct when, in fact, it breaches these. This remedy is still not available to consumers under the 2014 amendments to the CPRs. Only the public enforcement bodies continue to have the ability to use this remedy. So far, there is no case available where they have used it in this context, however. It is therefore a significant limitation of the amendments to the CPRs that they do not provide civil injunctions for consumers against companies for the breach of commitments in codes of conduct. Consumers would be able to promote CSR much better if they could enforce compliance with CSR commitments through civil injunctions (i.e. stopping companies from making false claims about their compliance with CSR commitments in codes of conduct). The advantage of such a remedy would be that consumers could directly take action against companies for false claims about their CSR record. Due to the publicity that such actions entail, companies could be expected to take CSR commitments more seriously. An example of a successful complaint (although not brought by consumers themselves) against a company for the publication of misleading information about its CSR record can be found in Germany. The European Centre for Constitutional and Human Rights (ECCHR), together with the Clean Clothes Campaign, initiated a complaint against the retailer LIDL for false claims that the company made about its compliance with social and labour standards in its supplying factories. The complaint was supported by the Customer Protection Agency in Hamburg which, under German law, has standing to bring an action. As a consequence of the complaint, LIDL made a declaration to cease and desist that it would withdraw its claims about its compliance with these CSR commitments. The complaint was based on the German laws of unfair competition (UWG) which implements the Unfair Commercial Practices Directive into German law. The action entailed extensive press coverage.[138]

The private remedies that the amendments to the CPRs establish are therefore a step in the right direction, but no more. They are not a meaningful right in terms of promoting CSR.

VI. CONCLUSION

Consumers are increasingly interested in the CSR record of companies. This development is known as ethical consumerism. Many companies have addressed this trend by developing their own CSR policies which they use in their marketing activities to positively influence their image in the perception of consumers. There is an indication that consumers are influenced in their purchase decisions by the CSR commitment of companies. Consumers therefore require protection from false information by companies about their compliance with their CSR commitments. It is against this background that consumer law overlaps with CSR, as it is the object of consumer law to address the inequality of economic power between consumers and business and to protect consumers. The link between consumer law and CSR is that consumer law prohibits misleading actions by traders. False information by companies about their CSR practices could constitute such misleading actions. Hence, there is potential for consumer law to promote the socially responsible behaviour of corporations.

However, this chapter argues that the way in which consumers are protected in private law against false information of companies about their CSR commitments is inadequate. The analysis here has shown that English consumer law currently only promotes CSR to a limited extent. The most obvious way of doing so, the Consumer Protection from Unfair Trading Regulations 2008, were outside the scope of private law until October 2014 as they were only subject to public enforcement by the public enforcement bodies. Due to amendments to the Regulations, consumers now have private remedies. These are the right to unwind the contract, the right to a discount and the right to damages. Consumers are therefore no longer left without a remedy. This is a step in the right direction, but no more. However, the fact that consumers still do not have the right to injunctions is a missed opportunity from a CSR point of view.

---

[138] See for an overview of the action: European Centre for Constitutional and Human Rights, ECCHR-Newsletter 09/2010 – Complaint against Lidl, available at http://www.ecchr.de (accessed 18 October 2014).

Reg 5 (3) (b) CPRs explicitly makes the breach of a commitment in a code of conduct a misleading action, if some further requirements are satisfied, and therefore brings CSR into the scope of the CPRs. Yet, without the right to an injunction it will be difficult for consumers to meaningfully promote CSR through consumer law. They are still dependent on the public enforcement bodies which have this right.

The law of misrepresentation, as private law, encompasses similar situations to the CPRs and therefore provides protection for consumers, too, but it is nevertheless a complex area of the law which is difficult to access. The fact that there has so far not been a single case for a misleading action for a breach of CSR commitments in a code of conduct, based on the law of misrepresentation, shows that this law does not sufficiently promote CSR. Moreover, the law of misrepresentation does not provide consumers with a right to civil injunctions against misleading statements by companies.

Moreover, a final limiting factor to consider is that, as with the supply contracts analysed in the previous chapter, the particular challenge for the promotion of CSR through consumer law is the conduct of sub-suppliers further down the supply chain. CSR commitments made by companies about the conduct of their sub-suppliers are usually worded in a rather aspirational way which will make it difficult for consumers to follow this conduct up through consumer law.

5. Tort law and corporate social responsibility

I. THE LINK BETWEEN TORT LAW AND CSR

The conduct of companies can harm people. For instance, employees might be injured due to poor health and safety standards at their workplace or members of the local community in the vicinity of factories might suffer from pollution of the environment. These examples would constitute violations of CSR. It is possible that actions by companies which violate CSR also constitute torts.[1] CSR and the law of torts overlap where tort law protects the interests that form part of the CSR principles such as the protection of the company's employees, its consumers or the environment.[2] It is difficult to find a comprehensive definition of tort law as writers tend not to agree on an all-embracing definition of the law of tort.[3] The reason is that there are several different forms of torts such as negligence, nuisance, libel, slander, trespass, assault and battery.[4] Therefore, Giliker and Beckwith suggest defining the law of tort as the law of civil wrongs. Tort law is concerned with behaviour which is legally classified as 'wrong' or 'tortious' and which entitles the claimant to a remedy.[5] This chapter will focus on those 'civil wrongs' which could cover violations of CSR, for example, the tort of

---

[1] J Zerk, *Multinationals and Corporate Social Responsibility* (CUP 2006) 200.

[2] Buhmann points out that, for example, cases in the United Kingdom have demonstrated that the impact of companies on CSR issues such as labour rights, human rights and the environment is of legal relevance with regard to torts, compensation and legal practice. She also mentions that human rights are often considered to be part of CSR. See: K Buhmann, 'Integrating human rights in emerging regulation of corporate social responsibility: the EU case' (2011) 7 *International Journal of Law in Context* 139, 148.

[3] V Harpwood, *Modern Tort Law* (6th edn, Cavendish Publishing 2005) para 1.1.

[4] P Giliker and S Beckwith, *Tort* (4th edn, Sweet & Maxwell 2011) para 1-002.

[5] ibid.

negligence where a company fails to have adequate safety measures in its production site in place, resulting in harm to its employees and the local community.

Due to the protection that tort law offers for personal interests such as health and property, tort law has been identified as a possible means of promoting CSR. Private individuals could use civil claims based on tort to promote greater social responsibility of corporations. Consequently, there have been some discussions in the literature on CSR and law about the liabilities of companies in tort for the pollution of the environment or the treatment of employees (particularly, as the protection of human rights is considered to be part of CSR).[6] However, so far, the debate about corporate liabilities in tort for violations of CSR mainly focusses on transnational tort litigation for torts committed abroad and the liability of parent companies for the conduct of their subsidiaries.[7] The reason for this is that questions about the extraterritorial application of English tort law are relevant in a CSR context, as many violations of CSR which involve Western companies (either directly or through their subsidiaries) occur in developing countries. This literature mainly deals with the territorial application of substantive English tort law which is, however, primarily, an issue of private international law and not English private law.[8] In contrast, this chapter focusses on the use of tort law as an instrument for the promotion of CSR by addressing both the ability of tort law to promote greater socially responsible conduct of companies as well as the challenges of using tort law to that end.

II. JURISDICTIONAL SCOPE OF THE CHAPTER

It is likely that tort victims will bring an action for tort at English courts even where the tort was committed abroad. English courts will be a popular choice due to their independence as well as the reputational damage that a proceeding in England entails for the English company that is sued. The court must apply the Brussels I Regulation in order to

---

[6] See, e.g. Zerk (n 1) 94

[7] See, e.g. M Anderson, 'Transnational corporations and environmental damage: Is tort law the answer?' (2002) 41 *Wasburn Law Journal* 399.

[8] S Baughen, 'Multinationals and the export of hazard' (1995) 58 *Modern Law Review* 54; P Muchlinski, 'Corporations in international litigation: Problems of jurisdiction and the United Kingdom asbestos cases' (2001) 50 *International Company and Commercial Law Review* 1.

determine whether it can assume jurisdiction.[9] Pursuant to Article 2 (1) of the Brussels I Regulation No 44/2001 on jurisdiction and recognition of enforcement of judgments in civil and commercial matters ('Brussels I Regulation'), persons domiciled in a member state shall, whatever their nationality, be sued in the courts of that member state. This rule means that English companies could be sued for their own conduct or the conduct of their subsidiaries in other countries before English courts.[10]

It is a different question, however, if English tort law is applicable where the tort was committed abroad. Generally, the law applicable to non-contractual obligations is determined by the Rome II Regulation.[11] Pursuant to Article 4 (1) of the Regulation, the law applicable to a non-contractual obligation arising out of a tort/delict shall be the law of the country in which the damage occurs, irrespective of the country in which the event giving rise to the damage occurred and irrespective of the country or countries in which the indirect consequences of that event occur. The place where the damage occurs is 'narrowly circumscribed'.[12] This means that, when the tort is committed outside England and Wales, the liability is usually determined by the foreign law of the place where the tort occurred, although there are some exceptions, for instance, for environmental damage.[13]

---

[9] Council Regulation (EC) No 44/2001 of 22 December 2000 on jurisdiction and the recognition and enforcement of judgments in civil and commercial matters (or Council Regulation (EC) 44/2001).

[10] The common law doctrine of *forum non conveniens* had for long established a hurdle for claims against companies for torts committed abroad, either directly or by their subsidiaries. The doctrine enables courts to deny jurisdiction if there is another more appropriate forum where the course may be heard. See: A de Jonge, *Transnational Corporations and International Law* (Edward Elgar 2011) 108. It has been argued that the ECJ decision in *Owusu v Jackson and Ors* (Case C-281/02 (2005) 2 WLR 942) has effectively put an end to the application of *forum non conveniens* by English courts. In its interpretation of the Brussels Regulation, the ECJ decided that it was inconsistent with the Brussels Regulation to apply the *forum non conveniens* doctrine to grant a stay in favour of another jurisdiction of a non-contracting state if the defendant is domiciled in a member state. But note that the applicable law may still be the law of the country where the tort occurred.

[11] Regulation (EC) No 864/2007 of the European Parliament and of the Council of 11 July 2007 on the law applicable to non-contractual obligations (Rome II). This regulation is effective since January 2009. It has, by and large, replaced the Private International Law (Miscellaneous Provisions) Act 1995.

[12] C Clarkson and J Hill, *The Conflicts of Law* (4th edn, OUP 2011) 265.

[13] Article 7 of the Regulation. There are exceptions to this general rule, but it would be beyond the scope of this chapter to address these. An example of

III. THE CONTRIBUTION OF TORT LAW TO THE PROMOTION OF CSR

A. Causes of Action in Tort Law for Violations of CSR

At first sight, there is a strong overlap between CSR and several causes of action in tort, as torts protect personal interests such as health and property that are often violated where companies act in an irresponsible way. Health and property are protected by the torts of negligence, breach of a statutory duty, private and public nuisance. Moreover, other causes of action in tort provide redress for interference with the person. These are the torts of trespass to the person, that is, battery, assault and false imprisonment.[14] Examples often referred to in the CSR literature where these torts can be applicable are the use of forced labour and child labour as well as corporal punishment at the workplace.

As companies are an artificial legal entity, they can only commit torts through the acts of their employees or agents.[15] Companies are liable in tort through vicarious liability which is not a tort in its own right, but a rule of responsibility.[16] Vicarious liability denotes the liability of a company for actions of other people.[17] Companies can commit torts through vicarious liability for the wrongful acts of an employee or agent acting during the course of his employment or scope of his authority.[18] Company directors fall under either or both of these categories, so a company can be vicariously liable for their torts.[19] Vicarious liability

---

such an exception is that English law will be applicable where both the tortfeasor and the tort victim have their habitual residence in England or Wales at the time when the damage occurred (Article 4 para 2 Rome II).

[14] The tort of assault covers an intentional act that threatens violence. The tort of battery consists of an intentional, direct act of the defendant resulting in an undesired contact with the person of the claimant. The tort of false imprisonment consists of the complete restriction of the claimant's freedom of movement without lawful excuse or justification. See for an overview of these torts: S Deakin, A Johnston and B Markesinis, *Markesinis and Deakin's Tort Law* (6th edn, OUP 2008) 451–67.

[15] B Hannigan, *Company Law* (3rd edn, OUP 2012) para 3-64.

[16] Giliker and Beckwith (n 4) para 7-022.

[17] D French, S Mayson and C Ryan, *Mayson, French & Ryan on Company Law* (28th edn, OUP 2011–12) para 19.7.2.

[18] Hannigan (n 15) para 3-64.

[19] P Davies and S Worthington, *Gower and Davies' Principles of Modern Company Law* (9th edn, Sweet & Maxwell 2012) para 7-39. See for a discussion

does not mean that the tortfeasor (e.g. company director) is exempt from his personal liability, but it provides the tort victim with a choice as to whom he sues.[20] In such a situation the defendant will often be the employer (the company), as he usually has better financial means than the employee who committed the tort.[21]

Generally, the interests that causes of action in tort protect largely overlap with the interests that CSR aims to enhance, for example, the protection of private individuals from battery, assault, false imprisonment and indeed other causes of harm to their health and/or property. Tort law therefore provides several groups of people, who are, by definition, encompassed by CSR, with a remedy in tort for violation of their interests. Through the provision of remedies, tort law is a means of enforcing CSR principles. Moreover, as tort law develops incrementally, it can be influenced by CSR. If the idea of CSR gains wider public acceptance, for instance, resulting from the UK government's endorsement of the UN Guiding Principles on Business and Human Rights, then it is possible that the criterion 'just, fair and equitable' for the imposition of a duty of care in the tort of negligence, as well as the standard applied to breaches of duty of care, would be further influenced by CSR considerations. The idea of socially responsible conduct of companies could have an impact on the general perception of what duties of care a company has and when it breaches these duties. The overlap between tort law and CSR provides arguments against those who argue that CSR was a purely voluntary concept. Through the causes of action that tort law provides for violations of CSR it already makes an important contribution to the promotion of CSR in a number of ways.

---

of the personal liability of a company director for torts which he committed: Hannigan (n 15) para 3-67 to 3-81.

[20]   Hannigan (n 15) para 3-64.

[21]   Harpwood (n 3) para 16.1. In order to establish vicarious liability, three conditions must be met: First, the employee must have committed a tort, secondly, there must be an employer/employee relationship, and thirdly, when committing the tort, the employee must have acted in the course of his employment. Employers are generally not vicariously liable for the actions of independent contractors. An employee is considered to be acting in the course of employment if his conduct is authorised by the employer, or is considered to be an authorised means of performing the job for which he is employed. See: Giliker and Beckwith (n 4) para 7-027-7-030.

B. Limitations in the Promotion of CSR

Nevertheless, tort law has several limitations in its ability to promote the socially responsible conduct of companies. First of all, where actions are brought in tort (e.g. negligence), the limitation is the two-party relationship between the claimant and the defendant. The action in tort will only resolve the dispute between these two parties, but not comprehensively for the society as a whole.[22] Although the dispute might encompass CSR principles and, consequently, have a wider impact on society by making a company liable for violations of CSR, the limitation of using tort law for promoting CSR is, nevertheless, the case-by-case development which depends on private parties bringing a case to court. Tort law only develops incrementally. In contrast, public law regulation, for example, about the environment, could comprehensively impose and enforce duties on companies in an area of law. In private law, CSR issues such as the protection of the environment are not necessarily comprehensively regulated in such a way.[23]

Secondly, in civil claims the claimant must prove the conditions of his claim which can be difficult, for example, in environmental torts it may be hard to prove that the damage was caused by the defendant (e.g. by the defendant's emission of gases).[24] Other reasons may have caused the damage, too. Thirdly, as torts are based on damage to personal interests, only parties with such interests can bring an action.[25] Tort actions are, by and large, aimed at protecting private interests.[26] On the contrary, there is no action in tort for the pollution of the environment per se.[27] The environment is only protected by tort law to the extent that the tort has violated private interests. The environment does not gain standing itself and will not be covered per se in the damages payable. The remedy will be granted to the claimant and, therefore, not to the environment. There is

---

[22]   The issue of multiparty (i.e. class actions) access to tort litigation will be further developed in the section on 'Access to civil litigation'.

[23]   For instance, it is argued that the 'fragmented, case-by-case' development of environmental tort would 'undermine the rationality of a consistent legal framework', see: Anderson (n 7) 409.

[24]   S Wolf and N Stanley, *Wolf and Stanley on Environmental Law* (5th edn, Routledge 2011) 505.

[25]   See for a discussion of private law actions being based on private interests: D Howarth, 'Muddying the waters: Tort law and the environment from an English perspective' (2001–2002) 41 *Washburn Law Journal* 469, 472.

[26]   P Cane, 'Using tort law to enforce environmental regulations?' (2001–2002) 41 *Washburn Law Journal* 427, 443.

[27]   Wolf and Stanley (n 24) 505.

no remedy that requires the companies which pollute the environment to fully remedy the negative impact their actions had on the environment generally, other than the damage to personal property. Tort law is therefore restricted in its ability to protect the environment. Fourthly, tort law is only a reactive tool that is brought after the tort has occurred in the first place, although it is acknowledged that the danger of having to pay damages in tort might also act as a deterrent.[28]

Finally, the remedies provided in tort for violations of CSR are also limited in their ability to promote the socially responsible conduct of companies. Due to their compensatory nature, damages for violations of CSR will only be awarded where the claimant has suffered a health injury or damage to property in the first place. The claim is therefore reactive rather than preventive although it is acknowledged that the remedy of damages provides deterrence for potential tortfeasors.[29] The aim of the award of damages is to put the claimant into the position in which he would have been had the harm or damage not occurred.[30] There are different kinds of damages which are awarded for torts. Most damages are of a compensatory nature which means that the aim is to compensate the claimant for loss he has suffered. Courts may also award punitive or exemplary damages for torts.[31] If exemplary damages are awarded, then the courts award additional damages on top of the compensatory damages in order to punish the wrongdoer and also in order to deter others from committing similar acts. However, exemplary damages are only awarded in rare circumstances, for example, where the defendant's conduct was intended to profit from the tort.[32] The award of exemplary damages could be a particular deterrent for companies not to engage with irresponsible activities. While the primary aim of tort is to compensate the tort victim for the harm suffered, the promotion of CSR through tort law could be enhanced if companies were more frequently to face the payment of exemplary damages for particularly irresponsible acts such as environmental pollution.

Tort victims can also seek to be granted an injunction against the tortfeasor to prevent him from committing the tort again.[33] However, the

---

[28]   A Kanner, 'Toxic tort litigation in a regulatory world' (2001–2002) 41 *Wasburn Law Journal* 535, 542.

[29]   See for a discussion about the deterrence function of tort law: S Deakin, A Johnston and B Markesinis (n 14) 50–2.

[30]   Wolf and Stanley (n 24) para 11.3.1.

[31]   ibid, para 19.2.5.

[32]   See *Rookes v Barnard* [1964] AC 1129.

[33]   Harpwood (n 3) para 1.1 and para 19.12.

availability of injunctions is limited. Injunctions are an equitable remedy which is subject to the court's discretion even if the claimant proves the case.[34] This remedy cannot be requested as of right.[35] Injunctions will not be awarded where damages are not appropriate or where it would not be equitable to award them.[36] As injunctions are an order on the defendant not to continue with a certain act or to undo the damage, they would be particularly useful for violations of CSR. For example, an injunction to stop an act that causes environmental pollution would serve the needs of the local community that suffers from the pollution as well as better protect the interests of the environment. The injunction could be granted in addition to damages. Injunctions are therefore a potentially powerful tool in response to violations of CSR as they directly affect the behaviour of the tortfeasor.[37] For tort law to be a more effective means of promoting CSR, it would be necessary to further develop and expand the use of injunctions as a remedy, although this remedy is an equitable remedy which is at the discretion of the courts.

It can therefore be concluded that tort law already makes an important contribution to the promotion of CSR due to the strong overlap between causes of action in tort and CSR. However, tort law is restricted in a number of ways in its ability to promote greater socially responsible conduct of companies such as the limited use of injunctions.

IV. THE CHALLENGES OF USING TORT LAW AS A MEANS TO PROMOTE CSR

Apart from the limitations of tort law, there are particular challenges for using tort law as an instrument to promote greater CSR. These challenges are often not found in tort law itself, but rather in the access to using tort law against companies. The following section will discuss the main obstacles for tort victims who want to use tort law against companies that are relevant in the context of CSR.

---

[34] ibid.
[35] Giliker and Beckwith (n 4) para 17-059.
[36] ibid.
[37] See for a discussion of the suitability of injunctions in case of environmental torts: Wolf and Stanley (n 24) 507.

A. The Use of Corporate Group Structures

The promotion of CSR in tort faces a particular challenge through the use of corporate group structures. Many companies create sophisticated group structures consisting of a parent company with several subsidiaries.[38] As the subsidiaries are, in law, separate entities, the parent company is not responsible for their liabilities, unless the corporate veil is pierced, which happens only rarely.[39] Group structures therefore enable parent companies to reduce their liability risk in tort.[40] Consequently, tort victims of a subsidiary company (e.g. the local community suffering from the emission of hazardous substances) might not be able to recover the loss from the subsidiary, particularly as, in practice, the parent company is often in a better financial position to compensate tort victims than some of its (undercapitalised) subsidiaries.[41] So, if an undercapitalised subsidiary is unable to cover the loss of a tort victim, the tort victim (as an involuntary creditor)[42] faces the danger of being left with nothing.[43]

It will now be reviewed to what extent parent companies are liable in tort for violations of CSR principles by their subsidiaries, either directly or vicariously.

---

[38] See J Birds et al. (eds) *Boyle & Birds' Company Law* (8th edn, Jordans 2011) para 3.9. The Companies Act 2006 defines subsidiary and holding company in s1159. S1159 (1) CA: A company is a 'subsidiary of another company, its "holding company", if that other company: (a) holds a majority of the voting rights in it; or (b) is a member of it and has the right to appoint or remove a majority of its board of directors; or (c) is a member of it and controls alone, pursuant to an agreement with other members, a majority of the voting rights in it, or if it is a subsidiary of a company that is itself a subsidiary of that other company. S1159 (2): A company is a "wholly-owned subsidiary" of another company if it has no members except that other and that other's wholly-owned subsidiaries or persons acting on behalf of that other or its wholly-owned subsidiaries.'

[39] The piercing of the corporate veil is discussed below.

[40] Hannigan (n 15) para 3-44.

[41] See P Muchlinski, 'Holding multinationals to account: Recent developments in English litigation and the Company Law Review' (2002) 23 *Company Lawyer* 168.

[42] Tort victims are often referred to as involuntary creditors: P Muchlinski, 'Limited liability and multinational enterprises: a case for reform?' (2010) 34 *Cambridge Journal of Economics* 915, 918.

[43] See for an overview of the discussion pertaining to the consequence of limited liability for involuntary tort creditors: S Lo, 'Liability of directors as joint tortfeasors' (2009) 2 *Journal of Business Law* 109, 120.

i. The primary liability of a parent company to the employees of its subsidiary

Parent companies could be directly liable in tort to the employees of their subsidiaries.[44] Whereas companies are generally vicariously liable in tort to members of the public for the conduct of their employees, the specific question here is whether a parent company can owe a direct (primary) duty of care to the employees of its subsidiaries for their working conditions. If the parent company does owe such a duty of care itself, then it could be directly liable to the employees of its subsidiaries

---

[44] The most successful example of holding companies liable in tort law is the US Alien Tort Claims Act (ATCA) through which parent companies based in the USA can be held accountable for human rights violations by their subsidiaries abroad. Although this Act has been in existence for about two hundred years (1789), it was discovered by NGOs over 20 years ago. The ATCA confers jurisdiction on the US District Court in respect of 'any civil action by an alien for a tort only, committed in violation of the law of nations or a treaty of the United States'. The Act has been regarded to fill an accountability vacuum resulting from the non-existence of international regulation and the territorial reach of domestic laws. The landmark case of *Filartiga v Pena-Irala* (630 F 2d 876 (2d Cir. 1980)) drew attention to the potential of the ATCA as a means of holding individuals accountable for breaches of human rights standards in other countries. In this case, the court decided that non-American citizens could be punished for tortious acts committed outside the United States which were in violation of public international law (the law of nations) or any treaties to which the United States is a party. The decision therefore extends the jurisdiction of United States' courts to tortious acts committed around the world. In *Sosa v Alvarez* (542 US 692 (2004)), the US Supreme Court allowed courts to hear claims by private individuals for breaches of international law committed in other countries. The number of proceedings under this Act against US parent companies has significantly increased in the past years. The fact that lawsuits are privately initiated has added to its popularity as the proceedings are not reliant on the state. There are limitations to the ATCA such as that the courts are reluctant to assume jurisdiction in cases where the claimants are not resident in the United States. Notably, the future of the Act for holding corporations accountable for human right violations is uncertain, following the decision of the Supreme Court in *Kiobel v Royal Dutch Petroleum Co.* 569 US___(2013), decided 17 April 2013. In that case, the Supreme Court held that the Act would only apply to conduct within the United States or on the high seas. The court held that the presumption against extraterritoriality would apply to claims under the Act and that nothing in the Act would rebut that presumption. Prior to these decisions, there had been a lot of lobbying by US corporations to the government to restrict the applicability of the ATCA. After the Supreme Court decision from April 2013 it is unlikely that the ATCA will be used largely in the future for claims against corporations based on human rights abuses committed abroad.

through the tort of negligence. This tort could, for example, provide a cause of action where employees of a subsidiary suffer injuries to their health at the factory of a subsidiary due to a breach of health and safety standards. If the employees could, in such a situation, gain a remedy against the parent company, too, then they would be in a much stronger position to recover their loss. The law would then recognise that parent companies are responsible for the conduct of their subsidiaries. As a consequence of that recognition, CSR could not simply be avoided by setting up (undercapitalised) subsidiaries.

A parent company can only be directly liable in the tort of negligence, if it owes a direct duty of care to the employees of its subsidiaries. There are some cases where English courts have held that it is, in principle, possible to show that a parent company owes a direct duty of care in tort to anybody injured by a subsidiary company in a group.[45] In *Connelly v RTZ*,[46] an English parent company was sued in relation to injuries in a uranium mine operated by its Namibian subsidiary. The action failed as it was time-barred. However, the court held that, in principle, the parent company could have been under a direct duty of care to the employees of its subsidiary as it had taken on responsibility for devising and operating the policy for health and safety.[47] In *Lubbe and Others v Cape plc*,[48] it was mentioned that a parent company can, in principle, owe a direct duty of care to employees of its subsidiaries.[49] However, the case was stayed on the basis of *forum non conveniens* as it was held that South Africa was the more appropriate forum. In a further case, *Ngcobo and Others v Thor Chemicals*,[50] it was again held that it was arguable that a parent company may owe a duty of care to employees of its subsidiaries. This case was, however, ultimately settled.

The question of whether a parent company can owe a primary duty of care in negligence to the employees of its subsidiary was eventually

---

[45]   See *Connelly v RTZ Corporation plc* [1998] AC 854; *Ngcobo and Others v Thor Chemicals Holding Ltd. And Others,* unreported January 1996; *Lubbe and Others v Cape plc* [2000] All ER 268.

[46]   *Connelly v RTZ Corporation plc & Anor* [1999] C.L.C. 533.

[47]   ibid.

[48]   [2000] All ER 268.

[49]   See for an analysis of the case: P Muchlinski (n 8) 1.

[50]   *Ngcobo and Others v Thor Chemicals Holding Ltd. And Others*, unreported January 1996, per Maurice Kay J.

decided in 2012 in the case *Chandler v Cape plc*.[51] Prior to this case that question had never been finally decided by a court as the cases were either settled or struck out for other reasons.[52] *Chandler v Cape plc* concerned the question of whether the parent company (Cape plc) was directly and jointly liable with its subsidiary (which had been dissolved in the meantime) in negligence for asbestos-related injuries inflicted on the subsidiary's previous employee (the claimant). The employee had contracted asbestosis as a result of his exposure to asbestos. Both the parent company and the subsidiary were based in the UK and the conduct in question occurred in the UK.[53] The case is relevant in terms of CSR, as it concerns the health of an employee which is an issue that is addressed by CSR.

In *Chandler v Cape plc*, the Court of Appeal confirmed the High Court's decision that a parent company and a subsidiary could be jointly and severally liable to pay damages for breach of the duty of care which they owed to the subsidiary's employee.[54] The test for a duty of care (foreseeability, proximity and fair, just and reasonableness) was satisfied in the courts' opinion. The duty of care was imposed on the parent company Cape plc on the basis of an assumption of responsibility. The parent company had superior knowledge of the asbestos-related risks in general and it could and did exercise control over the business behaviour of its subsidiaries. Moreover, the parent company Cape plc dictated the overall health and safety policy. While the subsidiary kept some discretion and independence in this respect, the parent company had the ability to intervene in these issues. Cape plc could therefore foresee the dangers related to asbestos and it had due proximity to the employees of its subsidiary in order to establish a duty of care. The imposition of a duty of care on the parent company was also considered to be fair, just and reasonable in this situation. While confirming the High Court's decision, the Court of Appeal further outlined 'appropriate circumstances' in which 'the law may impose on a parent company responsibility for the health and safety of its subsidiary's employees':

---

[51]   [2012] EWCA Civ 525 which affirms [2011] EWHC 951 (QB).

[52]   However, it was already argued in the academic literature that a parent company could owe a primary duty of care to tort victims of its affiliates. See, for example: Zerk (n 1) 216.

[53]   This case therefore raises no questions as to the extraterritorial application of English tort law.

[54]   The High Court's decision clarified that the duty of care does not arise here just because there is a parent–subsidiary relationship, see: *David Brian Chandler v Cape plc* [2011] EWHC 951 (QB), para 66.

In summary, this case demonstrates that in appropriate circumstances the law may impose on a parent company responsibility for the health and safety of its subsidiary's employees. Those circumstances include a situation where, as in the present case, (1) the business of the parent and subsidiary are in a relevant respect the same; (2) the parent has or ought to have superior knowledge on some relevant aspect of health and safety in the particular industry; (3) the subsidiary's system of work is unsafe as the parent company knew, or ought to have known; and (4) it is not necessary to show that the parent is in the practice of intervening in the health and safety policies of the subsidiary. The court will look at the relationship between the companies more widely. The court may find that element (4) is established where the evidence shows that the parent has a practice of intervening in the trading operations of the subsidiary, for example production and funding issues.[55]

The courts emphasised that this issue was distinct from any question of piercing the corporate veil between a parent company and its subsidiaries which are in law separate legal entities.[56] So, following the decision in *Chandler v Cape plc*, parent companies can owe a duty of care to the employees of their subsidiaries. In order to be liable in tort, it is necessary that the parent company has breached this duty of care and that it has caused the harm of the claimant.[57] This decision is significant for the promotion of CSR, as the conduct of the defendant in this case violated the CSR principle to advance the interests of the employees.

The important question for the promotion of CSR in English tort law generally is to what extent this case constitutes a precedent according to which parent companies are now liable in tort to the employees of their subsidiaries.[58] As indicated, previous cases had only mentioned that a parent company could owe a duty of care, but never finally decided this issue.[59] *Chandler v Cape plc* is therefore an important 'incremental step'

---

[55]   *Chandler v Cape plc* [2012] EWCA Civ 525, para 80.

[56]   ibid, para 69.

[57]   In *Chandler v Cape*, Cape plc was found to be in breach of its duty of care to the defendant. It was also found to have caused the harm.

[58]   The implications for multinational companies with a parent company in the UK and subsidiaries abroad such as in the developing world will be addressed later in this chapter.

[59]   *Lubbe v Cape plc* [2000] 1 WLR 1545; [2000] 4 All ER 268 HL; *Connelly v RTZ Corp plc* [1999] C.L.C. 533 QBD. In *Connelly*, there were obiter comments that, in exceptional circumstances, a parent company could owe a duty of care the employees of its subsidiary. The exceptional circumstances included the holding company's control over the health and safety policies of a subsidiary company. The claim failed in *Connelly*, however, as the proceedings had been commenced outside the statutory time limit.

in establishing a duty of care owed by a parent company to an employee of a subsidiary.[60]

First of all, it is clear from the reasoning of the court that parent companies will, in similar situations, not be vicariously liable for the liabilities of their subsidiaries as the case did not constitute a piercing of the corporate veil. This distinction is important, as one might wonder if the parent company was held to be liable for the mistakes of its subsidiaries here. This situation is different from the piercing of the corporate veil, as it is the conduct and the knowledge of the parent company itself which gives rise to a duty of care. The decision does not therefore affect the way courts treat the separate legal status of the parent company and its subsidiaries in corporate groups. Secondly, the Court of Appeal rejected the idea of restricting the situations which can give rise to a duty of care within a group of companies. The court did so by stating that the way in which groups of companies are run differs significantly.[61] This approach did not limit, for future cases, the circumstances in which a parent company can be liable for the actions of its subsidiaries. The kind of relationship necessary for a duty of care to arise between the parent company and an employee of a subsidiary is therefore difficult to predict. The court emphasised that Cape plc as the parent company assumed responsibility by involving itself in issues relevant to health and safety policy at the subsidiary. Moreover, the court referred to Cape's superior knowledge about asbestos-related risks and asbestos management. This situation means that parent companies are potentially exposed to liability depending on their superior knowledge of health and safety issues and their involvement in the operation of the subsidiary (it is not necessary that this engagement consists of an intervention in the health and safety policies of the subsidiary). Upon that basis, an important consequence of the court's reasoning is that a parent company with superior knowledge of health and safety issues cannot avoid liability purely by not engaging with such matters of the subsidiary if it is or ought to be aware of circumstances that could create such a risk (e.g.

---

[60] J Fulbrook, 'Chandler v Cape: Personal injury: liability: negligence' (2012) 3 *Journal of Personal Injury Law* C135.

[61] The Court of Appeal made the following comment in this respect: 'Moreover, the way in which groups of companies operate is very varied. Sometimes, for example, a subsidiary is run purely as a division of the parent company, even though the separate legal personality of the subsidiary is retained and respected. Accordingly, it is simply not possible to say in all cases what is or is not a normal incident of that relationship.' *Chandler v Cape plc* [2012] EWCA Civ 525, para 67.

when the parent and the subsidiary company are doing business in the same area) and when it gets involved in some aspects of the operation of the subsidiary.

Consequently, the precedent set by *Chandler v Cape plc* makes the CSR principle of providing a safe workplace a much more important consideration for parent companies within corporate groups as they are not able to avoid liability in tort purely by setting up several subsidiaries. The possibility that parent companies can be primarily liable in tort for the conduct of their subsidiaries significantly enhances the position of CSR within companies. The decision impacts on the way parent companies must administer risks within their group.[62] Parent companies cannot easily avoid responsibility for the employees of their subsidiaries. The decision provides potential for English tort law to better promote the socially responsible conduct of companies, as tort victims can sue the parent company (which is often more solvent) in the tort of negligence. However, it is unlikely that the precedent set by *Chandler v Cape plc* expands to parent companies that do not get involved in the running of their subsidiaries at all. Moreover, it is not possible to foresee to what extent the decision in *Chandler v Cape plc* has paved the way for an increased liability of parent companies for the violation of CSR principles other than the health and safety at the workplace, for example, where the subsidiary interferes with the physical integrity of its employees. After all, the Court of Appeal did not establish a duty of care owed by the parent company to the employees of its subsidiaries purely on the grounds of it being the parent company. A final point is that the case has potential to expand the liability of English parent companies to the employees of their subsidiaries abroad, if the criteria of the above-mentioned test for the duty of care are met. However, if a court will indeed be prepared to establish a duty of care in such a situation is not foreseeable yet. The case is therefore a first step in the right direction in terms of holding parent companies accountable, but it remains to be seen to what extent it will promote the socially responsible conduct within a corporate group overall.

---

[62] The question if, following *Chandler v Cape*, parent companies are potentially also exposed to liability in negligence towards the employees of their foreign subsidiaries abroad will be addressed below.

ii. The vicarious liability of a parent company for the tort liabilities of its subsidiaries (piercing the corporate veil)

The direct liability of parent companies in tort to the employees of their subsidiaries, discussed in the previous section, needs to be distinguished from the issue of whether a parent company can be vicariously liable for the tort liabilities of its subsidiaries through the mechanism of piercing the corporate veil. If the corporate veil is pierced, then the parent company would be required to cover the liabilities of its subsidiaries. The idea behind such a claim is that parent companies often establish diversified group structures with many wholly-owned subsidiaries in order to reduce their liability risk.[63] The ability to hold parent companies vicariously liable could significantly improve the ability of tort victims to obtain compensation, especially when subsidiary companies are under-capitalised.[64] Such vicarious liability of parent companies could therefore promote CSR, as parent companies would no longer be able to avoid their liability in tort for conduct which violates CSR principles through the setting up of subsidiaries, for example, where their subsidiaries commit human rights abuses.

In law, the subsidiaries are separate legal entities from the parent company following the decision in *Salomon v Salomon & Co Ltd*.[65] The decision in *Salomon v Salomon* established that a company is a legal entity separate and distinct from its shareholders.[66] The members of the company are only liable for the debts of the company in the amount of their non-paid-up share capital.[67] The legitimacy that the courts gave to single-man companies in the *Salomon* decision has been expanded to corporate groups.[68] The legal position is that all companies in a group of companies are separate legal entities, even in the case of wholly-owned subsidiaries with only little paid-up share capital and a board of directors which predominately or solely consists of directors who are also directors

---

[63]   See for the definition of subsidiary and holding companies in s1159 CA 2006 note 38.

[64]   The fact that there is no minimum capital fund required for the founding of a private limited company means that parent companies can create several subsidiaries without providing them with any financial means.

[65]   [1897] AC 22.

[66]   ibid.

[67]   S3 (2) CA 2006. Shares are usually fully-paid up. S74 (1) (d) IA 1986 clarifies that, 'in the case of a company limited by shares, no contribution is required from any member exceeding the amount (if any) unpaid on the shares in respect of which he is liable as a present or past member'.

[68]   *Adams v Cape Industries plc* [1990] BCLC 479, 520.

of the parent company.[69] Parent companies are vicariously liable for the torts committed by their subsidiary companies when the courts are prepared to 'pierce the corporate veil' which means that the separate legal personality of a company is disregarded and the shareholders are liable for the company.[70] The question of the separate legal status of subsidiary companies has undergone a mixed review in the case law. In *DHN Food Distributors Ltd v Tower Hamlets LBC*,[71] the Court of Appeal treated a group of tightly controlled companies as an economic unit and consequently ignored the separate legal personality of the companies. It was held that the share ownership of the parent company and its influence on its subsidiaries provides an argument that, in reality, these companies are 'one economic unit'.[72] This approach was subsequently criticised by the House of Lords in *Woolfson v Strathclyde Regional Council*[73] where the court stated that it had 'some doubt whether in this respect the Court of Appeal had properly applied the principle that it is appropriate to pierce the corporate veil only where special circumstances exist indicating that it is a mere façade concealing the true facts'. The House of Lords did not overrule the DHN case, but distinguished it on the facts.[74] According to the mere façade test it is appropriate to pierce the corporate veil only where special circumstances exist which indicate that the company is a mere façade which conceals the true facts. The liability of parent companies for the conduct of their subsidiaries was then comprehensively reviewed by the Court of Appeal in *Adams v Cape Industries plc*.[75] The defendant, *Cape Industries plc*, operated a network of subsidiaries which were involved in asbestos mining. The Court of Appeal applied a strict approach to the question of piercing the corporate veil and dismissed the idea of a single economic unit between the parent company and its subsidiaries. This concept could not justify any departure from the principle that companies in a group of companies are separate legal entities. The court held that it is appropriate to pierce the corporate veil only where special circumstances exist indicating that the corporate veil is a mere façade concealing the true facts, that is, where the corporate

---

[69]   See Hannigan (n 15) para 3-35.
[70]   Other expressions apart from 'piercing' in this context are: 'setting aside', 'lifting' or 'going behind' the veil. See: French, Mayson and Ryan (n 17) para 5.3.2.2.
[71]   [1976] 1 WLR 852.
[72]   ibid, per Lord Denning, 860.
[73]   (1979) 38 P & CR 521.
[74]   ibid, 526.
[75]   [1990] BCLC 479.

structure is used to evade rights of relief that third parties may in the future acquire. Moreover, the court held that the situations where a subsidiary can be considered to be the agent of a parent company (which would also enable courts to pierce the corporate veil) must be confined to those instances where this was factually justified. The court emphasised that it would be difficult to prove an agency relationship where there was no express agreement.[76]

Slade LJ noted:

> There is no general principle that all companies in a group of companies are to be regarded as one. On the contrary, the fundamental principle is that 'each company in a group of companies (a relatively modern concept) is a separate legal entity possessed of separate legal rights and liabilities': see *The Albazero* [1975] 3 All ER 21, 28.[77]

Moreover, Slade LJ stated that the use of the corporate group by a parent company as a means to ensure that legal liability and the risk of enforcement of that liability in respect of future activities of the group will fall on another member of that group was 'inherent in our corporate law'.[78]

The consequence of accepting that parent companies can use a corporate group structure to ensure that the liability will fall on its subsidiaries as 'inherent' in English law means that tort victims will not be able to hold parent companies vicariously liable for the conduct of their subsidiaries unless the subsidiary is a mere façade or there is an agency relationship. Parent companies can therefore usually avoid liability for violations of CSR by their subsidiaries. Given that the use of corporate group structures is now widespread, the approach by English courts to the issue of group liability puts tort victims as involuntary

---

[76] ibid, 545–9.

[77] ibid, 508.

[78] In this case the court held that: '... we do not accept as a matter of law that the court is entitled to lift the corporate veil as against a defendant company which is the member of a corporate group merely because the corporate structure has been used so as to ensure that the legal liability (if any) in respect of particular future activities of the group (and correspondingly the risk of enforcement of that liability) will fall on another member of the group rather than the defendant company. Whether or not this is desirable, the right to use a corporate structure in this way is inherent in our corporate law', see: [1990] BCLC 479, 520.

creditors at a severe disadvantage.[79] It is difficult to justify that a solvent parent company can easily limit its potential liability by founding several (undercapitalised) subsidiaries. The ability of a tort victim of a company within such a corporate group to fully recover the loss resulting from a tort depends on which company of that group has committed the tort.[80] Villiers therefore notes that:

> The combination of limited liability with separate legal personality makes a lethal cocktail for victims of harmful endeavours in terms of their ability to pursue a company or its shareholders for compensation.[81]

The parent company will be shielded from any liability.[82] Instead, in case of tort victims, the risk is allocated to the poorer risk taker.[83] This situation appears particularly unsatisfactory with regard to closely held companies in a corporate group which are all wholly-owned by the parent company. Limited liability was developed in the nineteenth century in order to promote economic activities, particularly to enable investors to provide assets without the risk of incurring liabilities.[84] It can be argued that the reality of corporate group structures in the twenty-first century which are used to diversify risks has nothing in common with the reasons for granting limited liability in the first place.

---

[79]   Shirley Quo critically reviews the avoidance of tort liability through a corporate group structure with subsidiaries in Australia. She discusses suggestions to reform Australian company law so that the application of the limited liability principle would be restricted in relation to claims for personal injury against the holding companies. See: S Quo, 'Corporate social responsibility and corporate groups: the James Hardie case' (2011) 32 *Company Lawyer* 249, 252.

[80]   It is necessary to distinguish between different kinds of creditors. In contracts, banks and lenders will usually be able to contract out of the limited liability by securing guarantees from the parent company. Moreover, it can be argued that holding companies will often compensate economically powerful creditors, as they might depend on that partner in the long run. See: Birds et al. (n 38) para 3.10.2.

[81]   C Villiers, 'Corporate law, corporate power and corporate social responsibility' in N Boeger, R Murray and C Villiers (eds), *Perspectives on Corporate Social Responsibility* (Edward Elgar 2008) 95.

[82]   Baughen (n 8) 70.

[83]   Muchlinski (n 42) 918, 923.

[84]   Ibid, 917. See for an overview of the development of limited liability in Anglo-American law, particularly with regard to corporate groups: P Blumberg, 'Limited liability and corporate groups' (1985–1986) 11 *J. Corp. L.* 573.

Violations of CSR by subsidiary companies within a group therefore pose a particular challenge for the promotion of CSR through tort law. The corporate group structure can ensure that parent companies, despite close factual relations with their subsidiaries, do not have to cover for their subsidiaries' tort liabilities, for example, where the subsidiary is liable to its employees for assault, battery, false imprisonment or negligence. The denial of the 'single economic unit concept' by the Court of Appeal in *Adams v Cape Industries plc* severely restricts the ability of English tort law to promote CSR. The criticism can be made that this approach is outdated, given that in over twenty years since that decision, the use of corporate groups by parent companies has been significantly expanded. In fact, the widespread use of corporate groups often serves the very function of avoiding liability.[85]

Therefore, a case can be made that, within a group, the parent company should be made responsible to satisfy the tort obligations of its subsidiaries. The introduction of a statutory rule that attributes liability to the parent company for the negligent acts of the subsidiary, on the basis of the enterprise liability principle, has been suggested.[86] This approach would provide tort victims suffering from a tortious act which violates CSR principles, for example, environmental pollution resulting in damage to property, with a much better chance of receiving damages. The parent company could then not simply avoid liabilities by setting up subsidiary companies to carry out the risky activities. This concept would be a move towards the single economic unit concept (also called enterprise-based approach) that takes account of the economic realities within the corporate group.[87] The imposition of liability on parent

---

[85] The current position is further evident in the following comment about the use of subsidiary companies made in *Re Southard Ltd*: 'A parent company may spawn a number of subsidiary companies, all controlled directly or indirectly by the shareholders of the parent company. If one of the subsidiary companies, to change the metaphor, turns out to the runt of the litter and declines into insolvency to the dismay of the creditors, the parent company and other subsidiary companies may prosper to the joy of the shareholders without any liability for the debts of the insolvent subsidiary.' See: *Re Southard Ltd* [1998] 2 BCLC 447, 458.

[86] Muchlinski (n 42) 926. See also: N Mandelson, 'A control-based approach to shareholder liability for corporate torts' (2002) 102 *Columbia Law Review* 1203.

[87] See for the idea that parent companies should be liable for the debts of their subsidiaries: C Schmitthoff, 'The wholly owned and the controlled subsidiary' (1978) *JBL* 218. See for an overview of the 'enterprise entity' doctrine: P Muchlinski, *Multinational Enterprises & The Law* (2nd edn, OUP 2007) 317.

companies to involuntary tort creditors of their subsidiaries can be justified by the argument that parent companies exercise de facto control over their subsidiaries (and thereby benefit from the profits), but currently, do not face any liability for the conduct of their subsidiaries.[88] Moreover, while, at least in theory, contractual creditors can contract out of limited liability by securing personal guarantees, tort creditors do not have the opportunity to choose who their creditors are going to be.[89] This argument further supports the imposition of liability on parent companies for torts committed by their subsidiaries. It is disappointing that the Company Law Review Steering Group, when discussing the Companies Act 2006, opted against a change in the law with respect to the liabilities of the parent company for its subsidiaries. The Steering Group did so, even though it conceded that the arguments in favour of the legal status quo (allowing companies to take advantage of limited liability by forming subsidiaries) were less strong in terms of tort victims than in relation to contracts voluntarily entered into by the contractual partners.[90] Nevertheless, the Steering Group decided not to address the issue of group liability as it did not find evidence that parent companies abuse the corporate status in order to avoid liabilities:

> The under-capitalisation of subsidiaries, and their operation in a way which creates undue risks of insolvency, are matters best dealt with by insolvency law. We do not therefore propose any reforms in this regard.[91]

In the wake of the global economic and financial crisis, it has become apparent that this position taken by the Steering Group was based on a false assumption. The group accounts which a parent company must now prepare pursuant to s399 (2) CA 2006 are a consolidated balance sheet and consolidated profit and loss account for the whole group.[92] They provide for some disclosure, but do not provide any help for the

---

[88]   See for a discussion of the combination of limited liability with control rights: P Ireland, 'Limited liability, shareholder rights and the problem of corporate irresponsibility' (2010) 34 *Cambridge Journal of Economics* 837, 853.

[89]   But it must be taken into account that the bargaining power of contractual partners to contract out of limited liability will significantly vary. That means that banks will usually be in a position to secure a personal guarantee whereas small traders are unlikely to be in such a strong position.

[90]   Company Law Review, *Completing the Structure* (DTI 2000) para 10.58

[91]   ibid, para 10.59. See for a critical assessment of the Steering Group's approach: Muchlinski (n 41) 173.

[92]   S404 CA 2006.

involuntary tort creditor of a subsidiary as he cannot check the accounts of a group of companies before he becomes their tort victim. It is therefore argued here that English law could better promote CSR if it abandoned its current approach to corporate groups, according to which parent companies are only liable for the liabilities of their subsidiaries in rare circumstances (e.g. where the corporate veil is pierced). Instead, the parent company should be liable to compensate the tort creditors of those subsidiaries which are unable to pay the damages. The fact that parent companies must prepare consolidated group accounts under the Companies Act 2006 already recognises the close relationship within the corporate group and further supports this view.

The use of complex corporate group structures in an international context by Western multinational companies further complicates the issue of holding parent companies to account for torts committed by their subsidiaries. However, it is beyond the scope of this chapter to analyse under what circumstances English tort law is applicable for torts committed abroad, particularly in countries of the developing world which often have a lower standard of workplace health and safety.[93] The issue of extraterritorial application of English tort law, particularly for human rights abuses committed either directly or through subsidiaries in the developing world, is a matter of private international law rather than substantive private English law.[94]

---

[93] The territorial reach of English tort law is of particular interest, as there are many reported violations of CSR principles by the subsidiaries of English companies in the developing world, for example, human rights abuses.

[94] Some authors have suggested that the decision in *Chandler v Cape plc* might result in liabilities of English companies to the employees of their foreign subsidiaries. See for example: 'Chandler v Cape plc: Is there a chink in the corporate veil? (Case comment)' (2012) 18 (3) *Health & Safety at Work*, 1, 2. This chapter will not engage with the details of private international law, but it must be stated here that it is doubtful if the opinion voiced by some authors that English parent companies might now be liable for torts committed abroad is a correct interpretation of the law. The law applicable to non-contractual obligations is determined by the Rome II Regulation. Pursuant to Article 4 (1) of the Regulation, the law applicable to a non-contractual obligation arising out of a tort/dclict shall be the law of the country in which the damage occurs irrespective of the country in which the event giving rise to the damage occurred and irrespective of the country or countries in which the indirect consequences of that event occur. Generally speaking, the law applicable to torts is usually the local law of the place where the damage occurs. See: Clarkson and Hill (n 12) 265.

B.   Access to Civil Litigation

The other main challenge of using tort law as a means to promote greater corporate social responsibility is the access to civil litigation for claimants. Two particular issues that restrict the access to civil litigation for tort victims are addressed here: The availability of class actions and the funding of civil litigation.

i.   Mass torts: class actions

Corporate conduct that violates CSR principles may well harm more than just one person. For example, where a company has emitted toxic gases, it could easily harm the health of numerous employees as well as several members of the local community. The number of people who suffer injuries from coming into contact with these toxic gases could easily reach hundreds or more. In such a situation the use of tort law as an instrument of promoting greater CSR would be more effective where those tort victims who have been injured under similar circumstances could bring a class action.

Where there are several claims related to similar issues of fact or law, civil procedure laws provide a system for the management of such cases called Group Litigation Order (GLO).[95] Pursuant to Rule 19.10 Civil Procedure Rules, a GLO means an order made under rule 19.11 to provide for the case management of claims which give rise to common or related issues of fact or law (the 'GLO issues'). The Senior Master and the Law Society maintain a list of GLOs.[96] There are several procedural requirements for GLOs. The main features of GLOs were summarised by Lord Walker in *Autologic Holdings plc v Commissioners of Inland Revenue*.[97] According to this summary, a GLO identifies the common issues which are a condition for participation in a GLO, it provides for

---

[95]   Ministry of Justice, Group Litigation Orders, http://www.justice.gov.uk/ courts/rcj-rolls-building/queens-bench/group-litigation-orders (accessed 21 November 2014). See also: C Hodges, *Multi-party Actions* (OUP 2001). The Civil Procedure Rules also provide representative actions pursuant to Rule 19.6 CPR. These actions may be made by (or against) one or more persons who have the 'same interest' in a claim. One or more of the persons can then be representatives of any other persons who have that same interest, that is, the named claimant or defendant prosecutes or defends an action on both his behalf and on behalf of a class of individuals.

[96]   A list of Group Litigation Orders can be found at http://www.justice. gov.uk/courts/rcj-rolls-building/queens-bench/group-litigation-orders (accessed 21 November 2014).

[97]   [2005] UKHL 54; [2006] 1 AC 118, at [86].

the establishment and maintenance of a register of GLO claims and it gives the managing court wide powers of case management and issuing directions. If the group loses the case, each group member is liable for that member's share of the common costs of the proceedings and for any individual costs specifically incurred with respect to his claim.[98] The GLO system has been criticised particularly for the requirement that claimants need to 'opt in', as it would prevent claimants from being part of the GLO and would reduce the overall number of GLOs.[99] The current system is therefore criticised for restricting access to justice, particularly in light of the few GLOs that have been made since the introduction of this system in the year 2000.[100] Consequently, the Civil Justice Council[101] published a report in 2008 in which it recommended, inter alia, that England and Wales should introduce a generic collective action and adopt an opt-out system of collective action, capable of awarding aggregate damages.[102] In its response to the report, the government did not support the introduction of a generic right of collective action.[103] It rather suggested that such rights should be considered for specific sectors only.[104] Similarly, the government was of the view that the opt-out systems should only be introduced for specific sectors rather than as a full opt-out model.[105] As part of this 'sector-specific' reform, the Department for Business Innovation and Skills (BIS) published a consultation paper in April 2012 which, inter alia, considered the introduction of

---

[98] N Andrews, 'Multi-party actions and complex litigation in England' (2012) 23 *E.B.L. Rev.* 1.

[99] R Mulheron, 'Justice enhanced: Framing an opt-out class action for England' (2007) 70 *MLR* 550, 580.

[100] Mulheron Report, *Reform of Collective Redress in England and Wales* (2008), available at www.civiljusticecouncil.gov.uk/files/collective_redress.pdf (accessed 20 November 2014), Chapter 3; Statistics provided by the Ministry of Justice on its website (last updated 30 October 2014) show that there have been 85 orders since the year 2000.

[101] The Civil Justice Council (CJC) is an independent public body, funded by the Ministry of Justice.

[102] Civil Justice Council, *Improving Access to Justice through Collective Actions: Developing a More Efficient and Effective Procedure for Collective Actions*, Final Report (November 2008).

[103] Ministry of Justice, *The Government's Response to the Civil Justice Council's Report: Improving Access to Justice through Collective Actions* (July 2009).

[104] See for a critical discussion of this approach: R Mulheron, 'Recent milestones in class actions reform in England: A critique and a proposal' (2011) 127 *LQR* 288.

[105] ibid.

wider collective actions and different collective redress models in competition law.[106] Following the consultation, the government decided to introduce a limited opt-out collective actions regime, albeit only for competition law.[107] At the same time, the European Commission is considering the area of collective redress in competition law.[108] All these developments have in common the move towards amending the currently rather restricted system of class action which, so far, only focusses on competition law. Changes to actions in tort by multiple claimants, for example, for physical injury, are not likely to be introduced in the foreseeable future. This situation limits the ability of tort law to effectively promote CSR by providing a means of redress for groups of people who have suffered harm as the consequence of irresponsible corporate conduct.

ii. Funding of actions in tort

With regard to the cost of litigation, civil claims in personal injury cases are often funded by conditional fee agreements.[109] These agreements have become popular since the public funding for personal injury claims had been significantly reduced through the Access to Justice Act 1999.[110] Under these conditional fees arrangements, commonly known as the 'no win-no fee' system, the claimant's lawyer will not charge any fees if his client loses the case, but may charge an uplift of up to 100 per cent of his normal fees from the other party if he wins.[111] This system is important for claimants with limited financial resources due to the restricted

---

[106] BIS Department for Business Innovation & Skills, *Private Actions in Competition Law: A consultation on options for reform* (April 2012), available at https://www.gov.uk/government/uploads/system/uploads/attachment_data/file/315 28/12-742-private-actions-in-competition-law-consultation.pdf (accessed 21 November 2014).

[107] BIS Department for Business Innovation & Skills, *Private Actions in Competition Law: A consultation on options for reform – government response* (January 2013), available at https://whitehall-admin.production.alphagov.co.uk/ government/uploads/system/uploads/attachment_data/file/70185/13-501-private-actions-in-competition-law-a-consultation-on-options-for-reform-government-response 1.pdf (accessed 20 November 2014).

[108] See http://ec.europa.eu/consumers/redress_cons/collective_redress_en.htm (accessed 20 November 2014).

[109] S27 Access to Justice Act 1999.

[110] BBC News, 'Legal aid axed for personal injury claims' (4 March 1998), available at http://news.bbc.co.uk/1/hi/uk/61882.stm (accessed 20 November 2014).

[111] S4 The Conditional Fee Agreements Order 2000.

availability of public funding for civil litigation.[112] While the party that has lost a case generally pays its own costs as well as the costs of the successful party,[113] the main hurdle for claimants is to fund the costs of their claim in the first place. The purpose of this conditional fee agreement is therefore to encourage lawyers to accept greater risks and hence to promote access to justice.[114] However, the government has made significant changes to this system with the enactment of the Conditional Fee Agreements Order 2013. Under the new regulation, solicitors may still enter into a Conditional Fee Agreement with their clients, but the clients, if successful with their claim, are no longer able to recover their solicitor's success fee from the defendant.[115] If their claim is successful, they are forced to pay their solicitor's success fee (on a contingency fee basis).[116] It is to be expected that, as a consequence of this change, solicitors will find it less attractive to accept cases where the claimant cannot afford the initial cost of litigation.[117] The number of claims in personal injury cases for torts is therefore likely to decline. This situation is particularly dissatisfying, given that in personal injury cases that concern irresponsible conduct of companies, there is often the private individual with limited financial means on the one side and the company with far better financial means on the other side.[118]

Consequently, the access to civil litigation for tort victims is limited. The restricted use of class actions for tort victims through GLOs has, so far, only resulted in few orders being made. Moreover, following the changes to the conditional fee agreement system, the number of tort victims who will be able to bring a claim against the tortfeasor is likely to decline. The potential of tort law to promote greater corporate social responsibility is therefore likely not to be fully used because of the

---

[112]   Andrews (n 98) 1.

[113]   Rule 44.3 (2) Civil Procedure Rules 1998.

[114]   R Meeran, 'Multinationals will profit from the government's civil litigation shakeup', *The Guardian* (London, 24 May 2011), http://www.guardian.co.uk/commentisfree/libertycentral/2011/may/24/civil-litigation-multinationals (accessed 20 November 2014).

[115]   The Conditional Fee Agreements Order 2013.

[116]   See for an overview of the changes to the funding of personal injury claims: E Gretton, 'Jackson – an overview' *The Law Society Gazette* (27 March 2013), available at http://www.lawgazette.co.uk/blogs/blogs/in-business-blog/jackson-overview (accessed 20 November 2014).

[117]   Meeran (n 114).

[118]   Particularly multinational companies usually employ highly-specialised legal teams in order to avoid losing the case. Large companies are particularly driven by the fear of reputational damage in case they lose the case.

difficulties with accessing civil litigation for private claimants. In order to better promote CSR it would be necessary to expand the use of class actions by providing an 'opt out' system and to overcome the financial hurdle that the initiation of civil litigation currently establishes.

V. CONCLUSION

This chapter has shown that, despite its limitations, English tort law already makes an important contribution to the promotion of CSR in private law. Tort law and CSR overlap where tort provides causes of action for the violation of CSR principles, for example the health and property of some of the company's stakeholders such as its employees or the local community. Tort law provides several groups that are, by definition, encompassed by CSR, with a remedy in tort for the violation of their interests (which overlap with CSR) such as the employees and the local community. Through the provision of legal remedies, tort law is a means of enforcing CSR principles. Moreover, as tort law develops incrementally, it can be influenced by CSR, as the idea of the socially responsible conduct of companies can increasingly influence the standard of breach of duty and considerations of when it is 'fair, just and equitable' to impose a duty of care. The findings of this chapter further challenge the view that CSR is purely 'voluntary'. As tort law can therefore be used as an instrument to enforce the socially responsible conduct of companies, it appears, at first sight, to be a strong tool for the promotion of CSR.

However, in fact, tort law is restricted in its ability to enhance greater social responsibility of corporations in a number of ways. First, despite its contribution to the promotion of CSR, tort law protects personal interests such as health and property. The right to action is limited to those persons whose property or other personal interests have been harmed. In consequence, the pollution of the environment is only addressed by tort law to the extent that natural or legal persons have suffered harm. This dependence on private interests severely limits the ability of tort law to control the pollution of the environment, which is a key aspect of CSR. Secondly, tort law is primarily reactive and compensatory. The primary objective of tort law remains to provide compensation for the tort victim who suffers from a civil wrong committed by another party.[119] Actions in tort are brought when the tort has already

---

[119]   Harpwood (n 3) para 1.10.

occurred and the main aim of tort is to compensate the tort victim for the injury sustained. Exemplary damages which could deter companies from irresponsible conduct are only rarely awarded. The restricted use of injunctions further limits the ability of tort law to promote CSR, as in many situations an injunction would be an appropriate remedy in order to stop the company from continuing with committing the tort. Due to their direct impact on the behaviour of a company, the more frequent award of injunctions would be a powerful tool for the promotion of CSR.

Thirdly, the ability of private parties to make use of the potential of tort law as an instrument to promote greater CSR is limited due to the difficulty with accessing justice. This situation is down to two issues: The restricted availability of class actions in tort and the recent changes to the funding of civil litigation. Finally, the particular challenge for using tort law in the context of CSR is that many companies operate corporate group structures in order to diversify their risk of incurring liability. The strict adherence to the *Salomon v Salomon* principle within corporate group structures, that is, that each company is a separate legal entity and not liable for the liabilities of the other companies, does not pay sufficient regard to the fact that, in reality, the parent company often controls the subsidiary and uses the subsidiary as a tool to gain profit for the parent without the need to compensate for its losses. This situation is not fair for a tort victim of a subsidiary whose claim cannot be compensated by that subsidiary, particularly where subsidiaries are undercapitalised. The enforcement of CSR standards through tort law is therefore restricted by legal and financial hurdles.

The recent decision in *Chandler v Cape plc* with its imposition of a primary duty of care on the parent company in specific circumstances is a first step in the right direction in terms of holding parent companies accountable. Following this precedent, tort law now has a wider reach in respect of violations of CSR principles. It is, however, unclear to what extent this decision will pave the way for violations of CSR principles other than the breach of health and safety standards at a production site run by a subsidiary. Moreover, the level of engagement that is required by a parent company in the running of the subsidiary is not clarified, thus leaving it open to speculation if this case is, in practice, going to enable many more successful lawsuits against parent companies.

6. The promotion of corporate social responsibility in English private law

I. PRIVATE LAW AND CSR

The analysis of substantive English private law in the previous chapters has shown that law and CSR are, in fact, related in a number of ways. Against this background, the dichotomy about voluntary or mandatory approaches to CSR is not only a superficial and inaccurate account of the relationship between law and CSR, but it has also restricted the developing understanding of CSR in law. The four areas of private law that were analysed in this book have demonstrated that private law plays an important role for CSR in various ways, for example, through director's duties and the strategic report in company law, the incorporation of CSR standards into supply chain contracts, the liability in tort for violations of CSR principles and through the private remedy of consumers in relation to misleading business practices.

While it is accepted that there are limitations to the promotion of CSR in English private law, it is argued here that private law has made and can continue to make an important contribution to the promotion of CSR and that it could make an even better contribution if these limitations were addressed. Given the international dimension of CSR issues such as human rights in global supply chains, it is important to note that English private law can have an effect beyond the national territory. This chapter will follow the structure of this argument: It will first discuss the limitations of private law in the promotion of CSR and then the contribution that private law makes to the promotion of CSR. Finally, the chapter will provide a list of substantive recommendations for changes to English law that result from the analysis. Within the discussion of the limitations and the strengths of private law in the promotion of CSR, this chapter will also address the question to what extent English private law could contribute to the implementation of the UN Guiding Principles on Business and Human Rights into English law.[1]

---

[1] The UN Guiding Principles are intended to be implemented by countries and by companies. The UK government has made a political commitment to the

II. THE LIMITATIONS OF PRIVATE LAW IN THE PROMOTION OF CSR

First of all, it must be recognised that there are deficiencies in the promotion of CSR in English private law. These will be discussed under three headings: First, the continuing dominance of the shareholder value theory; secondly, the patchy coverage of private law; and thirdly the weaknesses of private law remedies.

A. The Continuing Dominance of the Shareholder Value Theory

It is important to recognise that the contribution that private law makes or could make to the promotion of the CSR concept depends, to a large extent, on company law and corporate governance. Company law and corporate governance are the basis for the pursuing of objectives by companies. Within the company law/corporate governance framework, the company's board of directors decides the direction the company takes; the aims that it pursues and how it pursues those aims.

The UN Guiding Principles emphasise the role of domestic corporate laws for the state's duty to protect human rights.[2] With regard to Principle 3 (b), the commentary highlights the importance of corporate laws for enabling business respect for human rights.[3] The link between corporate laws and human rights is said to remain 'poorly understood' and there is a 'lack of clarity in corporate and securities law regarding what companies and their officers are permitted, let alone required, to do regarding human rights'.[4] Corporate law should provide sufficient guidance in this respect and have sufficient regard to the role of existing governance structures such as corporate boards. Guidance should advise

---

Guiding Principles. Private law could therefore be used by the government to implement the Guiding Principles into English law. See United Nations, *Guiding Principles on Business and Human Rights: Implementing the United Nations 'Protect, Respect and Remedy' Framework* (New York and Geneva 2011), available at http://www.ohchr.org/documents/publications/Guidingprinciples Businesshr_en.pdf (accessed 20 November 2014).

[2]   Principle 3 (b) of the Guiding Principles.

[3]   Principle 3 (b) emphasises that states should ensure that 'other laws and policies governing the creation and ongoing operation of business enterprises, such as corporate law, do not constrain but enable business respect for human rights'.

[4]   Commentary to Principle 3, UN Guiding Principles on Business and Human Rights.

on methods such as human rights due diligence.[5] It was further added that communication from business enterprises on how they address their human rights impacts could range from informal engagement with affected stakeholders to formal public reporting.

In fact, the promotion of CSR is restricted by the continuing fixation of English company law and corporate governance with the shareholder value doctrine. The way in which a company internalises CSR depends on the fundamental question in whose interest the company is run and also on the people who make the business decisions (within the framework of the directors' duties).[6] While the enlightened shareholder value doctrine has opened up the decision-making process of directors to consider other factors than purely the maximisation of shareholder value through s172 (1) CA, the doctrine continues to ultimately equate the interest of the company with the maximisation of the financial interests of shareholders.[7] English company law is still firmly embedded in the shareholder value theory. While directors are permitted to take stakeholder interests into account in the decision-making process, they are not yet sufficiently required to do so. Against this background, it can be concluded that the criticism in the Guiding Principles that corporate laws often do not provide sufficient guidance in relation to the duty to protect human rights applies to English company law.

Moreover, the interests of stakeholders are also subordinated under the interests of shareholders in the strategic report in s414C CA.[8] Reporting about CSR matters is a voluntary exercise for directors, as s414C CA makes it optional for companies to include information about environmental matters, the company's employees as well as social and community and human rights issues in the strategic report as long as the company states which of those kinds of information the report does not contain. This situation conflicts with Principle 3 (d) of the Guiding Principles which recommends that states should 'encourage and, *where appropriate require*, companies to communicate how they address their human rights impacts'. The commentary to this principle expressly

---

[5]   ibid.

[6]   B Horrigan, *Corporate Social Responsibility in the 21st Century: Debates, Models and Practices Across Government, Law and Business* (Edward Elgar 2010) 174.

[7]   S Wen, 'The magnitude of shareholder value as the overriding objective in the UK: the post-crisis perspective' (2011) *Journal of International Banking Law and Regulation* 325, 336.

[8]   As shown in the analysis of s172 CA and s414C CA in Chapter 2 'Company law, corporate governance and CSR'.

includes 'formal public reporting'.[9] It is more than questionable if the strategic report (s414A CA), in its current form, sufficiently implements this principle. The commentary on Principle 3 (d) suggests that a requirement for such reporting 'can be particularly appropriate where the nature of business operations or operating contexts pose a significant risk to human rights'. A relevant example of business operations that pose a significant risk to human rights is the use of suppliers in developing countries. There are numerous reports about gross human rights abuses in the factories of such suppliers.[10] In terms of this example, the reporting about the company's human rights due diligence should contain information about the selection and monitoring of suppliers and, if necessary, the enforcement of the CSR commitments in supply contracts. The strategic report falls short of the recommendation insofar as it does not require companies to communicate how they address their human rights impact. It can be concluded that in the regulation of the strategic report, as with the s172 (1) CA duty, the financial interests of shareholders are given preference over the interests of the various stakeholders. Here, English law needs to be further developed, if the Guiding Principles are to be implemented adequately. Although the strategic report has replaced the business review it has not improved things for the better in terms of promoting CSR. The situation might be improved by the EU Directive on disclosure of nonfinancial and diversity information, with its mandatory reporting requirements on environmental, social and employee matters as well as respect for human rights, anti-corruption and bribery issues. It is envisaged that companies will be required to publish their first reports in compliance with the Directive in 2017.[11] The Directive goes beyond the strategic report in terms of CSR reporting as it will increase the amount of CSR reporting. However, it remains to be seen to what extent it will improve the quality of the reporting with its adherence to the 'comply or explain' approach.

---

[9]   Commentary to Principle 3, Guiding Principles.

[10]   For example, see the allegations that suppliers of the fashion brand Zara have used forced labour in Argentina: M Roper, 'Zara probed over slave labour claims in Argentina' *The Daily Telegraph* (London, 4 April 2013), available at   http://fashion.telegraph.co.uk/news-features/TMG9970846/Zara-probed-over-slave-labour-claims-in-Argentina.html (accessed 13 November 2014).

[11]   European Commission, 'Statement: Disclosure of non-financial information: Europe's largest companies to be more transparent on social and environmental issues' (Brussels 29 September 2014), available at http://europa.eu/rapid/press-release_STATEMENT-14-291_en.htm   (accessed   14   November 2014).

Without a redirection of the corporate objective in English law, CSR will not be sufficiently supported through company law and corporate governance.[12] This situation might change if it is agreed that the corporate irresponsibility that has come to light in the recent financial and economic crisis would require a change to a more pluralistic understanding of the company. Consequently, despite significant overlaps of the Companies Act 2006 with CSR, the ability of private law, through company law and corporate governance, to promote CSR is currently limited. These deficiencies also restrict the ability of English law to implement the UN Guiding Principles.

B.   Private Law is Patchy in its Coverage

Private law differs significantly from public law regulation of companies because the undertaking of CSR commitments and the enforcement of CSR principles depends on the relationship between companies and private parties.

With regard to the former, CSR can only be promoted in contract law and consumer law, if companies decide to undertake CSR commitments in the first place, for example, by adopting a CSR code of conduct or by agreeing to the compliance with CSR principles in a supply chain contract. Those companies that do not incorporate CSR policies into their supply contracts cannot procure a remedy against suppliers and those companies that do not choose to sign up to a code of conduct cannot be liable for violation of CSR principles. The coverage of CSR commitments, by private law, is therefore patchy.

Moreover, the enforcement of CSR principles depends on the decision of private parties. The challenge that the enforcement of CSR principles in private law faces is that private parties need to decide whether they want to make a claim if a company has violated CSR principles. In private law, by definition, this function is not exercised by public authorities. Moreover, the enforcement of CSR commitments presupposes that there are enforcement mechanisms in place. In fact, the analysis of substantive English private law in this book has shown that the enforcement of CSR principles in private law is limited in five main ways.

First, in contract law, only the parties to the contractual relationship are able to enforce contractual commitments. A particular weakness of

---

[12]   See for a discussion of the relationship between a shareholder primary conception of the firm and human rights: D Millon, 'Human rights and Delaware corporate law' (2012) 25 *Pac McGeorge Global Bus & Dev LJ* 173, 174.

contract law is that the enforcement of CSR obligations in supply contracts is, almost without exception, limited to the contractual parties due to the doctrine of privity of contract. This doctrine, in general, confines the contractual reach of the supply contract to the buyers and their first-tier suppliers and does not allow the contract to reach beyond that. In the context of global trade patterns, this situation is a significant limitation of the reach of the CSR policies, as many suppliers use sub-suppliers. Moreover, although third parties to the supply contract such as the supplier's employees can in theory acquire a right to enforce contractual duties against the promisor, for example, the right to join a trade union, due to the Contracts (Rights of Third Parties) Act 1999, this right is regularly excluded by the buyer and supplier.[13] The intended beneficiaries of the CSR commitments in supply contracts such as the supplier's employees are, therefore, in practice, often barred from enforcing these commitments. It is a severe weakness in the promotion of CSR that the parties to a contract can exclude the applicability of the Contracts (Rights of Third Parties) Act 1999. In actual fact, this exclusion contradicts the aim of the Act, namely to provide third parties with a right of enforcement. The intended beneficiaries of CSR policies are left without a right of action. The possible exclusion of the rights of third parties limits the enforcement of contractual CSR obligations and hence reduces the ability of contract law to promote more socially responsible behaviour of corporations. This situation also conflicts with Principle 26 of the Guiding Principles which recommends that states should take appropriate steps to reduce legal barriers that could lead to a denial of access to justice in relation to human rights abuses by companies.

Secondly, the ability of consumers to enforce consumer protection rules which make misleading actions by companies unlawful is currently inadequate. The Consumer Protection from Unfair Trading Regulations 2008 (CPRs) were outside the scope of private law until October 2014 as they were only subject to public enforcement by the public enforcement bodies. This situation has changed due to amendments to the CPRs which provide consumers with private remedies, namely the right to unwind the contract, the right to a discount and the right to damages. However, these remedies are no more than a step into the right direction as, in the context of CSR promotion, they are not effective enough. It is a weakness of the enforcement regime that private parties cannot obtain the right to injunctions against companies that make misleading claims about their

---

[13] A Burrows, 'The Contracts (Right of Third Parties) Act 1999 and its implications for commercial contracts' (2000) LMCLQ 540, 545.

CSR record. Such a remedy would be able to stop false statements by companies. The amendments to the CPRs are therefore a missed opportunity from a CSR point of view. Although CSR is brought into the scope of the CPRs due to reg 5 (3) (b) CPRs which explicitly makes the breach of a commitment in a code of conduct a misleading action, the intended beneficiaries of the CPRs, the consumers, are neglected in this respect. Consequently, consumers will be unable to effectively promote the socially responsible conduct of companies through the CPRs. Although the law of misrepresentation encompasses similar situations to the CPRs and therefore provides protection for consumers, it is a complex area of the law which is difficult to access. The fact that there has so far not been a single case for a breach of CSR commitments in a code of conduct, based on the law of misrepresentation, shows that this law does not sufficiently promote CSR either. The use of consumer law as a means to enforce CSR commitments that companies have publicly made is therefore currently limited at best. Again, the current legal situation conflicts with the recommendations made in Principle 26 of the Guiding Principles.

Thirdly, the enforcement of CSR is also limited in company law and corporate governance. Where a director is in breach of one or more of his duties (e.g. the duty to promote the success of the company for the benefit of its members as a whole),[14] it is, first and foremost, down to the board to decide whether to pursue a claim against that particular director. The significant limitation of the enforcement of s172 (1) CA is that the intended beneficiaries, the various stakeholders enlisted in this duty, do not procure a right of action, as they do not have legal standing.[15] The duty in s172 (1) CA has therefore been called 'a right without a remedy'.[16] This situation limits the ability of company law to promote CSR despite the overlap between s172 (1) CA and CSR issues. The ability to enforce the s172 CA duty is even more limited, as the test applied to the section is likely to be a subjective one (as directors must act in a way which they consider in good faith to be in the best interest of the company for the benefit of its members (i.e. the shareholders) as a

---

[14]   S172 (1) CA.

[15]   A Keay, 'Section 172(1) of the Companies Act 2006: an interpretation and assessment' (2007) 28 (4) *Company Lawyer* 106, 109.

[16]   D Fisher, 'The enlightened shareholder value – leaving stakeholders in the dark: will section 172 (1) of the Companies Act 2006 make directors consider the impact of their decisions on third parties?' (2009) 20 *ICCLR* 10, 15.

whole.[17] The fact that the various stakeholders who are enlisted in s172 (1) CA do not procure a remedy also conflicts with the third pillar of the Guiding Principles, which highlights the need for states to provide sufficient access to effective remedies for victims of business-related human rights abuses.

Where the company decides not to pursue a claim against a director who has breached his duty pursuant to s172 (1) CA, a shareholder can bring a derivative action pursuant to s260 CA in respect of a cause of action vested in the company and seeking relief on behalf of the company. However, the members of the company can also decide to ratify the breach of duty, pursuant to s239 CA, in which case no derivative action can be brought. Where shareholders bring a derivative action, they face significant thresholds before they will succeed with a claim as the courts apply several tests before allowing the application for a derivative action to continue. When exercising their discretion whether or not to give the claimant permission to continue with the claim, courts seem to focus on the commercial interests of the company. Moreover, they are traditionally unwilling to second-guess business decisions. In practice, it is therefore unlikely that claimants will succeed with derivative claims based on alleged disregard for stakeholder interests in s172 (1) CA. Similarly, despite the recent emphasis on the role of institutional investors in the ensuring of good corporate governance of companies, one can only expect little in terms of the promotion of CSR. The UK Stewardship Code contains only little recognition of social and environmental matters. It rather focusses on the monitoring of the investee companies than the pursuit of CSR goals. The enforcement of CSR principles in company law is therefore severely limited.

Fourthly, in tort law, although several causes of action overlap with CSR principles and therefore, in principal, apply to all companies, tort victims still need to decide if they want to make a claim for the tort. In particular, the ability of tort law to promote the socially responsible conduct of companies is restricted due to the approach to corporate group liability in English law, which treats all companies in a corporate group as separate legal entities. The use of corporate group structures enables parent companies to reduce or even to avoid liability, as confirmed in

---

[17]   For example, in *Iesini v Westrip Holdings Ltd* [2009] EWHC 2526; [2010] B.C.C. 420 the court held that it was not in the best position to make judgements about the weight of the considerations in s172 CA except in very clear cases as these are commercial issues and the director's subjective judgements would prevail in these circumstances.

Adams v Cape Industries plc.[18] This situation is particularly unfair for involuntary tort creditors of undercapitalised subsidiaries of a parent company, for example, tort creditors who have suffered from an abuse of their human rights. If the UK government seeks to implement the Guiding Principles adequately, that would be an opportunity for the legislator to re-consider the approach towards liability in corporate groups. The current approach towards liability in corporate groups in English law does not provide effective judicial mechanisms, as tort creditors of (undercapitalised) subsidiaries may not be able to be successful with their claim against a subsidiary irrespective of the financial status of the parent company, even where the parent company is the sole shareholder of the subsidiary and where both the parent and the subsidiary company have the same directors. This situation conflicts with the third pillar of the Guiding Principles, which, as we have already seen, emphasises the need to provide effective remedies for victims of business-related human rights abuses. In particular, the commentary to Principle 26 explicitly refers to the example of the avoidance of appropriate accountability due to the way in which legal responsibility is attributed among group members of a corporate group under domestic criminal and civil laws.[19]

Fifthly, as the enforcement of private law depends on private parties, it is important that they have access to effective civil litigation mechanisms. The cost and time involved is often a barrier for private parties to bring civil litigation. The changes to the conditional fee agreement system (the so-called 'no win-no fee' system) by the government through the Conditional Fee Agreements Order 2013 will make it less attractive for solicitors to accept cases where the claimant cannot afford the initial cost of litigation.[20] The likely outcome is that fewer private claimants will bring an action at all. This situation is particularly dissatisfying, given that the company usually has far better means than the private individual bringing the claim. The changes are likely to reduce the number of claims brought in tort against companies.[21] These changes, too, conflict with the above-noted recommendation of Principle 26 of the Guiding

---

[18] *Adams v Cape Industries plc* [1990] BCLC 479, 543.

[19] Commentary, Principle 26, Guiding Principles.

[20] R Meeran, 'Multinationals will profit from the government's civil litigation shakeup', *The Guardian*, 24 May 2011, available at http://www.guardian.co.uk/commentisfree/libertycentral/2011/may/24/civil-litigation-multinationals (accessed 21 November 2014).

[21] ibid.

Principles that states should provide effective remedies against business-related human rights abuses (third pillar). The effectiveness of civil litigation is also limited by the rather restrictive use of multi-party actions in English law.[22] Group litigation orders are the main approach of the English system's treatment of multiparty litigation (they are an 'opt-in' system). Due to the various procedural requirements of group litigation orders and the need for each individual to 'opt-in', the restricted use of group litigation further limits the ability of private law to promote the socially responsible conduct of companies. This situation, too, is a legal barrier and therefore also conflicts with Principle 26 of the Guiding Principles. The commentary to this principle explicitly refers to the example of 'inadequate options for aggregating claims or enabling representative action (such as class action and other collective action proceedings)'.[23]

In conclusion, the promotion of the socially responsible conduct of companies in English private law is patchy in its coverage. Companies need to agree on the incorporation of CSR obligations into contracts or they must decide to adopt CSR principles. Moreover, the enforcement of CSR commitments depends on the decision of private parties. The enforcement mechanisms for CSR policies in the substantive areas of private law analysed in this book are currently limited at best.

C. Weaknesses of Private Law Remedies

Although the strength of private law is that it enables private parties to enforce CSR commitments, the remedies that are awarded in private law claims are, first and foremost, intended to promote the interests of the claimant. Hence, the remedies in contract are repudiation and damages, in tort the remedies are primarily damages with some injunctions and in consumer law the remedies are the right to rescind the contract and the right to a discount/damages. In company law and corporate governance, if a claim for breach of directors' duties is successful, then the remedies are the same civil consequences under the Companies Act 2006 as would apply if the corresponding common law rule or equitable principle applied.[24] Those remedies are claims for losses and claims for profit and they are only awarded to the company.[25] They would therefore not

---

[22]   See for an introduction into the topic: N Andrews, 'Multi-party actions and complex litigation in England' (2012) 23 *E.B.L.Rev.* 1.

[23]   Commentary, Principle 26, Guiding Principle.

[24]   S178 (1) CA 2006.

[25]   B Hannigan, *Company Law* (3rd edn, OUP 2012) para 13-8.

promote the interests of the stakeholders affected by a breach of s172 (1) CA. The prevalent remedy in private law actions is therefore damages which are awarded in order to account for the losses of the claimant. The underlying aim is to put the claimant back into the position, in which he would have been, had the event giving rise to the claim not occurred.

While these remedies might be appropriate for the claimant, they are not necessarily the most effective means for the promotion of CSR. In particular, these remedies do not directly cover the interests of the stakeholders who have suffered from the violation of CSR principles. This situation is particularly evident in tort law which is closely connected to the protection of personal interests such as health and property. The causes of action in tort are bound to personal interests. Consequently, the pollution of the environment is only addressed by tort law to the extent that the claimant has suffered harm to his personal interests such as health or property. The environment is therefore not protected per se, but only indirectly as a proprietary interest of a person. The compensatory nature of remedies in tort law somewhat limits the promotion of CSR. It is a weakness of the current tort system that exemplary damages, which could deter companies from irresponsible conduct, are only rarely awarded. The restricted use of injunctions which are an equitable remedy further limits the ability of tort law to promote CSR, as an injunction would be an appropriate remedy in many situations where what is desired is to stop the company from continuing with the violation of CSR principles. Injunctions would prohibit companies from continuing with acts that violate CSR principles.

Consequently, despite the ability of private law to provide remedies for the enforcement of CSR commitments, the remedies themselves have deficiencies in their ability to promote the socially responsible conduct of companies. In particular, the focus on compensatory damages restricts the ability to promote CSR.

III. THE WAYS IN WHICH PRIVATE LAW PLAYS AN IMPORTANT PART IN THE PROMOTION OF CSR

Notwithstanding its limitations, the analysis has shown that English private law does play a significant role in the promotion of CSR. The following part will first address the overlap between CSR and private law before looking at the mechanisms that private law provides for the incorporation and enforcement of CSR. Finally, it addresses the contribution of private law to hybrid regulatory systems of CSR.

A. CSR is, at Least in Part, Law

First of all, the analysis in the substantive chapters has shown that CSR is, at least in part, law. This finding contradicts the common understanding of CSR as being 'above and beyond the law' which is often the position adopted by business organisations. Buhmann notes that this understanding of CSR 'has led to an idea that CSR and law are distinct'.[26] In fact, this book has shown that there are direct overlaps between CSR and provisions in company law and causes of action in tort law whereas contract law and consumer law rather provide means for the incorporation and enforcement of CSR commitments, for example, in supply chain contracts. This section will therefore address company law and tort law due to their more direct overlap with CSR.

Company law and corporate governance, within the framework of the enlightened shareholder value doctrine, at least in theory have potential to promote the socially responsible conduct of companies. Company law and corporate governance overlap with CSR in terms of the duty to promote the success of the company for the benefit of its members as a whole[27] and the strategic report.[28] There is a strong correlation between the list of factors in the duty for directors to promote the success of the company in s172 (1) CA and CSR, as directors are required to take various factors into account when discharging this duty, for example, the interests of the company's employees, the need to foster the company's business relationships with suppliers, customers and others, as well as the impact of the company's operation on the community and the environment. The stakeholders enlisted in s172 (1) CA are coterminous with the groups encompassed by the CSR definition adopted here.[29] One could therefore argue that CSR is legally embodied through s172 (1) CA. Moreover, CSR is further embedded in the Companies Act through the strategic report in s414C CA which requires directors to report on how

---

[26] K Buhmann, 'Integrating human rights in emerging regulation of corporate social responsibility: the EU case' (2011) 7 *International Journal of Law in Context* 139, 140.

[27] S172 (1) CA.

[28] S414C CA; see also: J Yap, 'Considering the enlightened shareholder value principle' (2010) 31 *Company Lawyer* 35, 37; J Ho, 'Is section 172 of the Companies Act 2006 the guidance for CSR?' (2010) 31 *Company Lawyer* 207, 210.

[29] K Campbell and D Vick, 'Disclosure law and the market for corporate social responsibility' in D McBarnet, A Voiculescu and T Campbell (eds), *The New Corporate Accountability: Corporate Social Responsibility and the Law* (CUP 2007) 242.

they have performed their duty under s172 (1) CA. This reporting duty creates transparency on the discharge of the s172 duty and therefore enables others to inform themselves if and, if so, how the interests of the stakeholders enlisted in s172 (1) CA were taken into account in decisions of the directors.

There is also an overlap between several causes of action in tort law and the concept of CSR, for example, negligence, private nuisance, public nuisance, breach of a statutory duty and breach of strict product liability provisions. Tort law overlaps with CSR where torts encompass violations of CSR principles. Tort law therefore provides a tool to promote the socially responsible conduct of companies.

In summary, CSR and English private law overlap in a number of ways. CSR is, at least in part, law, despite continuing claims of the opposite. Claims that CSR is *purely* voluntary and beyond the law are, consequently, a superficial and an inaccurate account of the legal situation pertaining to CSR.

B. Private Law Provides Mechanisms to Incorporate CSR

Through contract law, private law also provides a mechanism for incorporating CSR commitments into contracts and thus giving legal effect to these commitments. Multinational companies increasingly incorporate CSR codes of conduct into the contracts with their suppliers.[30] They do so by using three different mechanisms through which CSR becomes part of the supply contracts: First, terms and conditions incorporated into the buyer's purchase order; secondly, expressly negotiated contracts; and thirdly, inclusion of the CSR policy into the tenderer process. In practice, the most common form of the three different mechanisms is the incorporation of the buyer's terms and conditions, which contain CSR provisions, into the contract between the buyer and the supplier.[31]

Contract law therefore differs from company law and tort law insofar as there is no contract law rule per se which overlaps with CSR; rather contract law provides a tool for private parties to incorporate CSR commitments into their legal relationship. Contract law rules enable the

---

[30] M Andersen and T Skjoett-Larsen, 'Corporate social responsibility in global supply chains' (2009) 14 *Supply Chain Management: An International Journal* 75, 77.

[31] See Chapter 3 for an analysis of the different ways in which companies incorporate CSR commitments into their supply chain contracts.

buyer to impose duties on the supplier to comply with CSR commitments, such as the obligation not to commit bribery, not to use child or forced labour and to allow its employees to be members of a trade union. Contract law is therefore able to make CSR codes of conduct, which are commonly perceived of as being voluntary, contractually enforceable. Therefore, through the use of contract law, CSR commitments which are voluntarily undertaken by Western-based multinational companies, often due to public pressure, can become contractual terms and are consequently enforceable against the supplier. Contract law thus provides tools to give legal effect to CSR commitments, if parties choose to incorporate these commitments into their contract. Through contract law, CSR obligations can be imposed on suppliers in different countries of the world, particularly in those countries which are known to have a weak legal system or a weak law enforcement mechanism. This extended territorial reach of contractual CSR commitments is a strength of private law.

C. Private Law Provides Means to Enforce CSR Commitments

Private law also provides persons with remedies for breach of their rights.[32] The previous chapters have shown that private law is a tool to enforce CSR commitments. A distinction can be made between the ability of companies to enforce CSR commitments and the ability of private individuals to do so.

First of all, despite the criticisms of the enforcement of s172 (1) CA discussed above, this duty with its significant overlap with CSR can be enforced by the board of directors or, alternatively, by shareholders through a derivative action. English private law, through company law, therefore, provides a tool to enforce this duty which embodies CSR. Directors who have breached this duty are potentially accountable for the loss that the company has suffered as a consequence of the director's conduct. Secondly, the strength of contract law is that it enables the buyer to incorporate CSR obligations into the supply contract, and hence to create enforceable contractual terms. That way, duties of socially responsible behaviour can be imposed on the supplier in private contracts and these duties can be enforced by the buyer. Where the CSR commitments are conditions or, in case of innominate terms, where breaches are repudiatory, the buyer will procure a right to repudiate the contract. This

---

[32] See D Nolan and A Robertson, 'Rights and private law' in D Nolan and A Robertson, *Rights and Private Law* (Hart Publishing 2011) 18.

right is a powerful tool for buyers, as the supplier would then lose the contract as a consequence of his violation of contractual CSR obligation. Thirdly, despite its limitations, the right to rescind the contract and to discount/damages in consumer law, following the 2014 amendments to the CPRs, provide consumers with a private remedy in case companies violate commitments in a code of conduct that they have publicly announced. As companies commonly portray their brands as being socially responsible in order to positively influence the perception that consumers have of them,[33] the right to rescission constitutes a deterrent for companies not to violate the CSR commitments that they have made to the public. Fourthly, tort law provides causes of action for tort victims who suffer from a tort which also violates CSR principles. Tort law therefore provides the stakeholders who are the intended beneficiaries of CSR, such as the company's employees, with a remedy. Tort law is thus a particularly effective means of enforcing the socially responsible conduct of companies.

On the whole, it is a strength of private law that it enables private parties to enforce CSR commitments. In all four substantive areas of private law analysed in this book, private parties procure a remedy where a company has violated CSR commitments. The prevalent remedy in private law actions is damages. Despite its limitations in the promotion of CSR, addressed above, damages are nevertheless a remedy that accounts for the loss that a private party has suffered from a violation of CSR commitments. While the cause of action in company law and contract law is primarily vested in companies, tort law and consumer law provide private individuals, who are the intended beneficiaries of CSR commitments, with means to enforce CSR principles. Private law remedies are therefore an important instrument for the promotion of the socially responsible conduct of companies.

D.   Private Law Contributes to Hybrid Regulatory Approaches to CSR

A further way in which private law plays an important role in the promotion of CSR is its contribution to hybrid regulatory systems.[34]

---

[33]   M Polonsky and C Jevons, 'Global branding and strategic CSR: an overview of three types of complexity' (2009) 26 (3) *International Marketing Review* 327, 328.

[34]   See for a discussion of the term 'hybrid' in relation to regulation: M Vrielink, C van Montfort and M Bokhorst, 'Codes as hybrid regulation' in D

Based on the conclusions in the previous sections (i.e. CSR is, at least in part, law; private law provides means to incorporate and to enforce CSR principles), it can be argued that private law is one part of a regulatory system in which private law, public law, soft law standards developed by private actors as well as international organisations and private regulation by and between companies, all interact with each other, in order to promote CSR.

Within this integrated, hybrid regulatory system, the various areas of private law analysed in this book serve different functions at various levels. First, company law and corporate governance, within the framework of the enlightened shareholder value theory, set the foundation for the company's CSR engagement through directors' duties and expectations in disclosure rules. Secondly, through contract law, private law provides a mechanism for companies to incorporate and to enforce CSR commitments (which can be based on soft law standards developed at the international or national level by international organisations or non-governmental organisations). The wide-spread incorporation of the same international CSR standards into supply contracts could create a level playing field between companies. Thirdly, since the introduction of a private remedy in consumer law, private law provides a further tool of enforcement for consumers. They can ensure that companies comply with their publicly adopted CSR commitments. Fourthly, tort law contributes to this regulatory system by imposing civil liability for conduct of companies that violates CSR principles.

The analysis of supply contracts has shown that the effectiveness of this regulatory system in promoting CSR can be enhanced by regulation through public and criminal law of companies in their home state, in combination with national private law. The substantive chapters have shown that bribery as well as the use of forced labour and child labour are the aspects of the CSR agenda which are worded in the strictest way in the CSR codes of conduct and in CSR commitments included into supply chain contracts. Commitments about the protection of the environment, in contrast, are commonly phrased in a more aspirational and less definite way. While the use of child and forced labour is of particular reputational concern for companies, bribery is now covered in a wide-reaching domestic sanction system in English law since the introduction of the Bribery Act 2010. This Act makes a company potentially liable in criminal law for the failure to prevent bribery by a person associated with

Levi-Faur (ed.), *Handbook On The Politics Of Regulation* (Edward Elgar 2011) para 35.5.2.

the company, including the company's employees, agents or subsidiaries.[35] The existence of appropriate due diligence procedures can serve as a defence against liability.[36] The research for this book has shown that companies tend to have a rather strict due diligence system in place for bribery, but nothing comparable for the other CSR issues discussed here. Although not English law, an example where companies are required to address certain CSR issues in their supply chain is the California Supply Chain Transparency Act which requires disclosure about the way a company deals with slavery and human trafficking in its supply chain.[37] This example also demonstrates that the home state of multinational companies can have an impact on the way companies address CSR issues, as it requires retail sellers and manufacturers to disclose their efforts to combat slavery and human trafficking and to eliminate it from their direct supply chains.[38] It is to be expected that the EU Directive on the disclosure of nonfinancial and diversity information, once introduced, will enhance the disclosure of the policies that companies have on issues such as human rights, the environment and bribery.

The hierarchy that currently exists in the way different aspects of the CSR agenda are addressed in codes of conduct and/or commitments in supply contracts therefore seems to be influenced by both reputational and liability (especially criminal liability) risks. The different treatment of the various CSR aspects by companies is interesting in so far as the signing up to or drafting of CSR codes of conduct, as well as the incorporation of CSR commitments into supply contracts, is voluntary in the first place (notwithstanding their subsequent legal effects once adopted by a company or incorporated into a contract). So, the companies themselves decide how strictly they phrase these commitments. Particularly, the strict manner in which companies deal with bribery in their business relationships seems to be positively influenced by liability risks resulting from the Bribery Act 2010. It is therefore argued here that the way companies deal with CSR issues within their company and vis-à-vis their suppliers can be enhanced where these CSR principles are supported by domestic sanctions, especially in criminal law. The Bribery Act 2010 shows that it is possible to establish liability in the home state of multinational companies for the conduct of their employees, agents or

---

[35] S7, 8 Bribery Act 2010.
[36] S7 (2) Bribery Act 2010. See the commentary in E O'Shea, *The Bribery Act 2010: A Practical Guide* (Jordans Publishing 2011) Chapter 9.
[37] The Act is available at http://leginfo.ca.gov/pub/09-10/bill/sen/sb_0651-0700/sb_657_bill_20100930_chaptered.html (accessed 21 November 2014).
[38] S3 of the California Transparency in Supply Chains Act of 2010.

suppliers. The voluntary use of CSR commitments within a hybrid regulatory system of CSR can therefore be improved, where it is required by domestic law and where violations of CSR commitments are punishable by sanctions at the domestic level. The advantage of regulatory measures such as the Bribery Act 2010 or the California Supply Chain Transparency Act is also that they ensure that all companies need to address bribery and/or the use of forced labour and that, consequently, loopholes are closed. Stronger EU disclosure laws about CSR policies (despite their 'comply or explain' approach) are therefore likely to positively influence the way in which companies engage with CSR through the voluntary adoption of a code of conduct and the incorporation of CSR policies into supply chain contracts. The likely consequence of such domestic requirements and/or sanctions is that they initiate the undertaking of CSR commitments by companies as well as promoting compliance. The interaction between domestic sanctions and private law is therefore likely to enable private law to better promote CSR.

The particular advantage of private law within such a hybrid regulatory system is that it enables CSR commitments to reach beyond the territory of the home state of the company (i.e. England or Wales in this instance). For example, the incorporation of CSR commitments into supply chain contracts can bind contractual partners across the world. English private law can therefore cross national boundaries and expand the reach of CSR commitments beyond the English territory. Supply chain contracts can consequently be used as a tool to bind companies which are based in countries with lower standards of legal protection and/or law enforcement to comply with certain CSR commitments. Contract law can interact with soft law CSR standards, thereby utilising standards developed by private actors or international organisations and providing the means to incorporate and to enforce these. The private remedy in consumer law, too, enables consumers to enforce compliance by companies with their publicly declared CSR commitments in a more accessible way than currently possible under the law of misrepresentation. Depending on the way in which CSR commitments are phrased, their enforcement through consumer law could also affect the conduct of English companies in other countries or the way their agents and suppliers act. This situation would again lead to an interaction between voluntarily adopted CSR commitments with private law, with the latter enforcing the former.

These different regulatory tools together promote the socially responsible conduct of companies. Private law and public law, soft law and hard law are not conflicting tools in the promotion of CSR; they are rather complementing elements in this hybrid system of regulation. The analysis in this book has shown that private law plays a key role in this hybrid regulatory system.

IV. SUBSTANTIVE RECOMMENDATIONS FOR CHANGES TO ENGLISH PRIVATE LAW TO IMPROVE ITS CONTRIBUTION TO THE PROMOTION OF CSR

The analysis has shown that, despite its limitations, English private law already makes an important contribution to the promotion of CSR. However, if it were to make an even better contribution then some changes would be needed to the substantive areas of private law analysed in this book. These changes would help to better unlock the potential that private law has for the promotion of CSR. The recommendations would also help to implement the UN Guiding Principles into English law, particularly taking the role of the home state of multinational companies into account. This chapter will therefore conclude with a list of substantive recommendations for changes to English private law that result from the analysis. As it is not possible to fully develop the recommendations, they will just be listed here.

A. The Substantive Recommendations for Changes to English Private Law

- The fundamental limitation of English private law is the fact that the enlightened shareholder value theory is still firmly embedded in the goal of maximising shareholder value. It is unlikely that the situation will improve much without a redirection of the corporate objective in English law to a more pluralistic understanding of the firm. A change to a more pluralistic understanding of the firm would inevitably have ramifications for the framing of directors' duties in a way that directors have more discretion to recognise the interests of stakeholders.
- The strategic report leaves too much discretion for directors to decide if, and if so, to what extent they report on CSR matters. The EU Directive on the disclosure of non-financial and diversity information is likely to improve the *amount* of reporting on CSR. Its introduction is therefore a positive development. However, the potential that the Directive has for promoting CSR is likely to be restricted by its adherence to a 'comply or explain' approach.

Instead, the reporting duties about the CSR matters contained in the Directive should be made compulsory and a greater focus on *quality* of reporting should be implemented.

- The ability for contractual parties to exclude the applicability of the Contracts (Rights of Third Parties) Act 1999 should be abolished. Third parties who are expressly identified in contractual clauses in supply contracts as the intended beneficiaries of CSR obligations, for example the supplier's employees, should have a right to enforce these CSR obligations, such as the right to join a trade union. If the contractual parties incorporate CSR obligations benefitting third parties, they should expect these duties to be enforced by these third parties.

- In consumer law, the introduction of a private remedy for consumers through the Consumer Protection (Amendment) Regulations 2014 was a step in the right direction. This remedy enables consumers to enforce compliance of companies with their publicly-declared CSR commitments. However, it is still necessary to provide consumers with a right to an injunction in case companies fall short of the CSR commitments in their codes of conduct as this right would promote CSR compliance more effectively. Moreover, the fact that the private right of action requires the formation of a contract in the first place for consumers to gain a remedy is a further aspect that will reduce the number of potential claims. The sole fact that a company does not meet its CSR commitments in codes of conduct should be sufficient for an action in consumer law.

- Tort law could better promote CSR if a more integrated approach to liability within corporate groups were introduced where parent companies could be made liable for tort liabilities of their subsidiaries. This change would ensure that companies can no longer avoid liability by setting up undercapitalised subsidiaries to the detriment of tort creditors.

- Access to civil litigation for tort victims must be facilitated. The changes to the funding of civil litigation and the restricted use of class actions in personal injury claims limit the promotion of CSR in tort law. Therefore, it is necessary that the demise of conditional fee agreements is reversed and that the provision of class action is expanded.

- Finally, the remedies available in private law for violations of CSR are deficient in their ability to promote the socially responsible conduct of companies. The remedies that are awarded for violations of CSR need to take better account of CSR. As mentioned, consumers would be able to promote CSR much more meaning-fully, if they could enforce compliance with CSR commitments through injunctions instead of terminating their contract with the company. The buyers in supply contracts would be able to better enforce CSR if they could more easily procure the remedy of specific performance. This remedy would compel the obligor to perform the agreed obligation. However, the award of this remedy is within the discretion of the courts as it is an equitable remedy. It is therefore only rarely granted. The situation is similar for tort victims. While they are compensated for the damages that they suffered due to the tort, it would be more beneficial for the promotion of CSR if injunctions (to stop the tort or to undo the harm) and exemplary damages (to punish the tortfeasor) were more frequently awarded.

7. The Rana Plaza building collapse – corporate social responsibility, private law and the global supply chain

I. THE RANA PLAZA TRAGEDY

The collapse of the Rana Plaza Building in Bangladesh in April 2013 dramatically reminded the world of the often hazardous working conditions in the developing world at the bottom of many global supply chains. The tragedy in Bangladesh killed more than 1100 people and over 2500 people were injured.[1]

Rana Plaza was an eight-story commercial building that housed several clothing factories which supplied Western fashion companies, apartments, a bank and other shops. The day before the building collapsed cracks were discovered. The banks and the shops on the lower floors immediately closed; however, the workers at the clothing factories were ordered to return to work the following day on which the building then collapsed.[2] Rana Plaza was not the first tragedy at a supplier factory in Bangladesh, a country which has a particularly high share of production in the garment industry. Just a few months earlier over 100 people were killed in a fire at Tazreen Fashions, a factory in Bangladesh that produced clothes for Walmart.[3]

---

[1] See for a comprehensive coverage of the Rana Plaza disaster and subsequent developments a special section in *The Guardian*, available at http://www.theguardian.com/world/rana-plaza (accessed 23 November 2014).

[2] See for a brief description of the chain of events: Bangladesh All Party Parliamentary Group, *After Rana Plaza: A Report into the Readymade Garment Industry in Bangladesh* (2013) 18. The Bangladesh All Party Parliamentary Group commissioned a report on the ready-made garment industry in Bangladesh, available at http://www.annemain.com/pdf/APPG_Bangladesh_Garment_Industry_Report.pdf (accessed 23 November 2014).

[3] *The Guardian*, 'Bangladesh textile factory fire leaves more than 100 dead' (25 November 2012), available at http://www.theguardian.com/world/2012/nov/25/bangladesh-textile-factory-fire (accessed 23 November 2014).

The Rana Plaza disaster was met with shock around the world and again initiated debates about CSR in global supply chains. Politicians, NGOs and consumer groups criticised the poor and unsafe working conditions of employees in the developing world who work for suppliers of Western brands.[4] Following the public debate about supply chains after the Rana Plaza collapse, the fashion industry responded with initiatives to improve the health and safety of buildings in Bangladesh where suppliers operate.[5] Mainly European companies signed an Accord on Factory and Building Safety in Bangladesh in May 2013.[6] In October 2014, this initiative had more than 150 signatory companies and it covered over 1500 factories. The Accord is a five-year agreement between international labour organisations, non-governmental organisations and retailers in the garment industry which aims to secure minimum safety standards in the Bangladesh textile industry. The majority of the American companies who buy ready-made garments in Bangladesh refused to join this scheme. Instead, they launched a different scheme, called the Alliance for Bangladesh Worker Safety which also intends to improve the safety of factories in Bangladesh.[7] It represents a group of over 20 major retailers.

The Rana Plaza disaster raises serious questions about the effectiveness of the existing CSR mechanisms in global supply chains. In this chapter this tragedy will be used as a case study in order to review the limitations and opportunities of using English private law for the promotion of CSR. The fact that English companies such as Primark were among the retailers that sourced from the factories at Rana Plaza adds to its relevance here. This case study will therefore practically complement the doctrinal legal analysis in the previous chapters.

---

[4] For example, see the critical editorial in *The Guardian*, 'Rana Plaza: the price of indifference' (23 April 2014), available at http://www.theguardian.com/commentisfree/2014/apr/23/rana-plaza-price-of-indifference (accessed 23 November 2014) and Bangladesh All Party Parliamentary Group (n 2).

[5] *The Observer*, 'Bangladeshi factory deaths spark action among high-street clothing chains' (23 June 2013), available at http://www.theguardian.com/world/2013/jun/23/rana-plaza-factory-disaster-bangladesh-primark (accessed 23 November 2014).

[6] Accord on Fire and Building Safety in Bangladesh, available at http://bangladeshaccord.org/ (accessed 23 November 2014).

[7] Alliance for Bangladesh Worker Safety, available at http://www.bangladeshworkersafety.org/ (accessed: 26 November 2014).

II. RANA PLAZA AND THE LIMITS OF PRIVATE LAW IN GLOBAL SUPPLY CHAINS

Prior to its collapse Rana Plaza was audited twice by Primark, but the audit did not include a structural survey.[8] This example highlights the failures of the current system of private governance in supply chains. So far, the creation and promotion of socially responsible supply chains has been, by and large, left to the buyers, the Western companies at the head of the supply chain. Companies commonly adopt CSR codes of conduct that address their responsibility in the supply chain. Many companies also incorporate CSR clauses into their supply contracts. However, this 'voluntary' inclusion of CSR standards into the private contracts between buyer and supplier (the seller) and their enforcement solely depends on the Western buyers. They have a choice as to the clauses that they incorporate, how they monitor the compliance with these clauses, how they report about their commitment to responsible supply chains and how they act upon violations of CSR principles by suppliers.

The substantive areas of private law that were analysed in this book play a role in this failure. This section will not repeat the points made in the preceding chapter. It will rather complement these by highlighting how the substantive areas of private law have contributed to the failure of effectively promoting CSR in global supply chains.

A. The Business Model of Global Supply Chains in Company Law and Corporate Governance

First of all, the engagement of the buyers in supply chains, that is, their voluntary adoption, inclusion and enforcement of CSR standards, is severely limited by the underlying corporate doctrine, the shareholder value theory. This model of the company according to which it is the purpose of the corporation to ultimately maximise the revenue of shareholders puts directors under a duty to prioritise the shareholders in their decision making.[9] Global supply chains are a business tool that allows companies to significantly reduce production costs and keep

---

[8]   *Vogue*, 'How the world has changed since Rana Plaza' (1 April 2014), available at http://www.vogue.co.uk/news/2014/04/01/bangladesh-rana-plaza-anniversary-fashion-revolution-day (accessed 21 November 2014).

[9]   H Hansmann and R Kraakman, 'The end of history for corporate law' (2001) 89 *Geo.L.J.* 439, 448.

prices low.[10] This is particularly important in the textile industry which has witnessed price reductions over the years.[11]

Against this background, the CSR engagement of Western companies is driven by concerns about the reputational damage that the company might be exposed to if it does not have a formal CSR policy.[12] Companies therefore pursue CSR on grounds of the so-called business case. The limitation of this CSR regime is clearly visible. Despite the official CSR engagement of Western buyers in their supply chain not much has changed in reality. Issues such as health and safety at the work place, pay, working hours or the ability to form and join trade unions are often still neglected. With its emphasis on maximising profits and raising share prices, the shareholder value model of the company can therefore be seen as the root cause of the failed supply chain responsibility. At present, CSR mainly plays a public relations role in supply chain management. It is against this background that the promotion of CSR in the global supply chain is very much voluntary, patchy and left to the discretion of the individual company. The economics of supply chain management under the shareholder value model of the firm are clearly not conducive towards the promotion of CSR. Of course, tragedies such as Rana Plaza are not a necessary consequence of this, as weak local laws or weak local law enforcement clearly play a key role in this situation. However, the shareholder value model of the company limits the ability of companies to meaningfully promote socially responsible conduct throughout their entire supply chain.

Within this system of shareholder value, the scope that directors have to promote CSR in supply chains is through the duty to promote the success of the company pursuant to s172 (1) CA. In this section, suppliers are part of the list of factors that a director must have regard to in his decision-making process. However, they are mentioned alongside customers and others in terms of the need to 'foster the company's business relationships'. The focus of the regard that directors should have

---

[10]   A Millington, 'Responsibility in the supply chain' in A Crane, A McWilliams, D Matten et al. (eds), *The Oxford Handbook of Corporate Social Responsibility* (OUP 2008) 363.

[11]   Forbes, 'The real cost of fast fashion' (28 April 2014), available at http://www.forbes.com/sites/lauraheller/2014/04/28/the-real-cost-of-fast-fashion/ (accessed 24 November 2014).

[12]   J Leigh and S Waddock, 'The emergence of total responsibility management systems: J. Sainsbury's (plc) voluntary responsibility management systems for global food retail supply chains' (2006) 111 (4) *Business and Society Review* 409.

to suppliers is therefore on the business relationship with the suppliers rather than on the promotion of CSR. Moreover, the ultimate goal of directors under s172 (1) CA is to enhance shareholder value.[13] S172 (1) CA therefore does not change the outlook of English company law towards a more pluralistic model. Still, directors have some discretion as to how they make decisions within the constraints of s172 (1) and it is this discretion that they can use to actively influence their suppliers to adhere to certain CSR minimum standards and to ensure that sub-contractors, if used at all, also comply with these standards. In business practice, this discretion has regularly not been used. Business relations in the textile industry are often characterised by last-minute orders to satisfy consumer demand, the lack of long-term commitments to suppliers and the driving down of production costs.[14] The gross violations of basic CSR principles through suppliers are therefore caused both by the nature of the buyer-supplier business relationship and the disregard to these standards by suppliers' and sub-suppliers. The way s172 (1) CA has been drafted with its reinforcement of shareholder value has not helped to promote CSR throughout the supply chain in a meaningful way.

Similarly, the existing statutory reporting duties in English law under the strategic report do not have regard for the supply chain. In fact, when the government enacted the strategic report in 2013 it missed an opportunity to include supply chains into the list of issues that companies should report on. The reference to 'social, community and human rights issues' is kept vague and does not refer to the company's supply chain. Although many companies voluntarily issue a CSR report which usually also refers to the supply chain there is no duty to do so and the quality of the reporting is often questionable. Companies usually only generally highlight their positive commitment, but do not outline the human rights violations that occur in their supply chain. Moreover, with the reporting under the Companies Act being optional, the kind of information that would have been useful for a true reflection on CSR in the supply chain is often missing.[15]

---

[13] See the analysis of s172 (1) CA in Chapter 2 'Company law, corporate governance and CSR'.

[14] See C Bader, 'The Bangladesh factory collapse: why CSR is more important than ever', *The Guardian* (7 May 2013), available at http://www.theguardian.com/sustainable-business/blog/bangladesh-factory-collapse-csr-important (accessed 24 November 2014).

[15] See also the critical assessment of the supply chain transparency in Bangladesh All Party Parliamentary Group (n 2).

The allocation of roles in the company further limits the role of CSR. While companies often have a CSR manager and a CSR team, they usually separate the roles of the directors who are in charge of purchase and sales and CSR.[16] Rather than understanding CSR as an issue that is important for the company in all that it does, it is allocated to the CSR/PR team. The message that this sends to suppliers such as the factory owners in Bangladesh is clear: The buyers in the supply chain team dictate low prices and short production times whereas the CSR department adds an additional and separate burden through CSR duties such as inspections. Under such a system CSR is a separate issue, a box-ticking activity, with inspections that often lack teeth and can be tricked, contrary to prices and production deadlines which are firm and non-negotiable.

B.   CSR Contractual Clauses are not Effective

Contract law plays an important role for the promotion of CSR in supply chains as it gives legal quality to CSR standards in supply chains. Nevertheless, it has not prevented the poor and hazardous working conditions of many employees of suppliers. Disasters such as the Rana Plaza building collapse or the violation of workers' rights happen despite the common incorporation of CSR clauses into supply contracts.

There are several reasons why contractual CSR clauses have failed to prevent the violation of CSR principles in the supply chain: Primarily, this is due to the fact that the privity of contract doctrine restricts the reach of the contractual CSR clauses to the parties of the contract. Third parties such as the supplier's employees who are the beneficiaries of the contractual CSR clauses usually do not gain a right to enforcement. As the contracts are bilateral, the only parties with a right to enforcement are the Western buyer and its direct contractual partner, the first-tier supplier. Sub-contractors, though, are not encompassed by these contracts. However, in business practice, supply chains usually go down much further below first-tier suppliers. Moreover, the question if the contractual CSR clauses are enforceable depends on the exact wording. Aspirational, indefinite and vague terms are not enforceable. Finally, inadequate monitoring systems further contribute to the present failure of supply contracts to meaningfully promote CSR. At present, contract law is often of more theoretical than practical relevance for the promotion of CSR in supply chains. The only area where contract law appears to be used

---

[16]   See Bader (n 14).

effectively is bribery, due to the liability risks that are established by the UK Bribery Act 2010. The issues that the Rana Plaza building collapse raises have, so far, clearly not been effectively improved through CSR clauses in supply chain contracts.

C. The Limits of Consumer Law and the Indifference of Many Consumers

Prior to the Consumer Protection (Amendment) Regulations 2014, consumer law did not enable consumers to prevent companies from making false claims about their CSR record. Although consumers could have used the law of misrepresentation, there is no case about this issue so far. It remains to be seen what the new private remedy in consumer law will achieve, but it is likely to be limited with regard to the breach of CSR commitments in codes of conduct. The reason is that a contract is needed in the first place and, moreover, that consumers will not have a right to an injunction. With such a claim they would be able to prevent companies from continuing to making false statements about their supply chain responsibility. The status quo in English law can be contrasted with the German LIDL case which illustrates how companies can be legally pursued for false CSR claims.[17]

At the moment, NGOs and consumer activists can publicly highlight violations of CSR principles in the supply chain of Western companies, but they do not have a cause of action to prevent companies from continuing to gloss over the realities. Moreover, in addition to the weaknesses of consumer law, a key issue in business practice is that too many consumers do not transfer their social conscience into their purchase decisions. Ethical consumerism is still more theory than practice.[18] The purchase behaviour of many customers who buy cheap clothes without asking questions has contributed to the widespread ignorance of human rights by suppliers in the developing world.

---

[17] European Center for Constitutional and Human Rights, 'Swift legal victory in the complaint against LIDL' (ECCHR–Newsletter 9).
[18] M Carrington, B Neville and G Whitwell, 'Why ethical consumers don't walk their talk: Towards a framework for understanding the gap between the ethical purchase intentions and actual buying behaviour of ethically-minded consumers' (2010) 97 (1) *Journal of Business Ethics* 139-58.

D. The Territorial Limit of Tort Law

The fact that private law is largely a national concept leads to a further significant weakness: There is little possibility for extraterritorial claims based on tortious actions that occur outside England and Wales in countries that have weak laws and/or weak law enforcement mechanisms.[19] Moreover, even if claims in tort could be brought for wrongs committed outside England and Wales the further problem is that suppliers are independent companies. It is already only in very rare circumstances possible to hold the parent company liable to the employees of their subsidiaries.[20] However, suppliers pose an almost insurmountable obstacle to hold the Western buyers liable in tort.

E. The Weaknesses of Private Law in Promoting CSR in Global Supply Chains

The largely private governance regime that characterises CSR in supply chains so far, has clearly failed to prevent tragedies such as the Rana Plaza building collapse or the Tazreem Fire.[21] For several years, business leaders have insisted on CSR as being voluntary and companies have adopted CSR codes of conduct and implemented these codes into their supply chain. However, the reality is that not much seems to have changed. As Rana Plaza cost so many lives it brought important questions about supply chain responsibility into the public discussion. The largely business-driven CSR agenda, based on reputational concerns, has not prevented the widespread violation of CSR principles in global supply chains. Although private law has in several ways helped to promote CSR, it has significant weaknesses that were shown in this section. The current CSR system which is business-led, mainly voluntary and bilateral between a particular Western buyer and overseas supplier has not enough teeth to meaningfully promote CSR in global supply chains.

---

[19]   See the analysis in Chapter 5 'Tort law and corporate social responsibility'.

[20]   See *Chandler v Cape plc* [2012] EWCA Civ 525 which affirms [2011] EWHC 951 (QB).

[21]   See also the analysis of the Bangladesh All Party Parliamentary Group (n 2) Part 1: An anatomy of industrial disaster: Tazreen Fashions and Rana Plaza.

III. THE ACCORD AND THE ALLIANCE: A CRITICAL ASSESSMENT

A. Overview of the Two Initiatives

Due to the public outcry that followed the collapse of Rana Plaza, the Western companies that bought ready-made garments from Bangladesh felt under pressure to act.[22] These businesses came up with different initiatives to improve the situation. This section will critically assess the two most widely-known initiatives, the Accord on Fire and Building Safety in Bangladesh and the Alliance for Bangladesh Worker Safety.

The Accord is intended to improve the safety of garment factories in Bangladesh[23] and was established in May 2013. About one and a half years after the agreement was developed, in October 2014, it was signed by over 150 apparel corporations from 20 countries, most of which are from Europe. The Accord, which is a five-year legally binding agreement, stipulates that independent safety inspections must take place at the factories. The results of the inspections are subsequently publicly reported and, in particular, the agreement is signed not only by the companies, but also by two global trade unions (IndustriALL and UNI) as well as several unions from Bangladesh. Moreover, there are some NGO witnesses to the Accord such as the Clean Clothes Campaign and The International Labour Organization (ILO) acts as the independent chair of the Accord.[24] This initiative covers all suppliers of the companies that have signed the Accord.[25] The buyers must require their suppliers to accept inspections and implement remediation measures in their factories. To that end the factories are divided into three groups: 'Tier 1 factories' which are facilities that represent in total not less than 30 per cent of the company's annual production in Bangladesh by volume; 'Tier 2 factories' which are any remaining major or long-term supplier to a company (the Tier 1 and Tier 2 factories shall jointly represent not less than 65 per cent of each signatory company's production in Bangladesh by volume); and 'tier 3 factories' which are facilities with occasional orders, one-time orders or facilities which account for less than 10 per cent of the

---

[22] BBC News, 'Dhaka Rana Plaza collapse: Pressure tells on retailers and government' (14 May 2013), available at http://www.bbc.co.uk/news/world-asia-22525431 (accessed 21 November 2014).

[23] Accord on Fire and Building Safety in Bangladesh.

[24] See the introduction into the Accord at http://bangladeshaccord.org/faqs/ (accessed 21 October 2014).

[25] Accord on Fire and Building Safety in Bangladesh, Scope.

company's production in Bangladesh by volume.[26] The companies that are members of the Accord make a commitment to maintaining their sourcing relationships with Bangladesh. In particular, they undertake to continue their order volumes with their Tier 1 and Tier 2 suppliers for at least two years at levels comparable to or greater than in the year prior to the Accord, taking effect as long as such business is commercially viable for the company and as long as the supplier factories continue to meet the buyer's terms and requirements under the Accord.[27] Funding is secured through a yearly fee that the signatory companies must pay – the amount that they have to pay depends on the yearly volume of sourcing from Bangladesh.[28]

The Accord is governed by a Steering Committee. The Steering Committee consists of equal representation chosen by the trade union members and company members of the agreement (maximum three seats each) and a representation from and chosen by the International Labour Organization (ILO) as a neutral chair.[29] The Steering Committee is responsible for the selection of a Safety Inspector and a Training Coordinator. The committee should reach decisions by consensus. The agreement regulates disputes resulting from the Accord in the following way: Disputes are, in the first instance, decided by the Steering Committee by majority vote within a maximum of 21 days of a petition being filed. Notably, if either party requests this then the decision of the Steering Committee may be appealed to a final and binding arbitration process. The arbitration award is enforceable in a court of law of the domicile of the signatory against whom enforcement is sought and is subject to The Convention on the Recognition and Enforcement of Foreign Arbitral Awards (The New York Convention) where applicable.[30]

The personnel that carries out the inspection of the Tier 1, 2 and 3 factories is selected by and acts under the direction of the Safety Inspector.[31] In the event of flaws being identified in a factory during a safety inspection, the signatory company that has designated the factory as a Tier 1, 2 or 3 supplier must require the factory to implement the corrective actions that were identified.[32] The signatory companies also pledge to support workers who lose their job as a consequence of

---

[26] ibid.
[27] ibid, Supplier Incentives, 23.
[28] ibid, Financial Support, 24.
[29] ibid, Governance, 4.
[30] ibid, Governance, 5.
[31] ibid, Credible Inspection, 8.
[32] ibid, Credible Inspection, 9.

working for a factory that is unsafe. They therefore commit to make reasonable efforts to ensure that those workers are offered employment with safe suppliers.[33] Effectively, this procedure means that where safety issues are identified, retailers commit to ensuring that repairs are carried out, that sufficient funds are made available to do so, and that workers at these factories continue to be paid a salary. The Western buyers agree to require their suppliers to respect the right of a worker(s) to refuse to work should they have reasonable justification to believe conditions are unsafe, without suffering discrimination or loss of pay.[34] The Steering Committee regularly publishes the list of all suppliers in Bangladesh used by the signatory companies, written inspection reports for all factories inspected under the Accord and quarterly aggregate reports that summarise both aggregate industry compliance data.[35]

The second major initiative is the Alliance for Bangladesh Worker Safety[36] which was founded by a group of North American garment companies and retailers. In October 2014, it had twenty-six members upon whom the terms of the five-year agreement are legally binding. The Alliance states that its aim is to be 'transparent, results-oriented, measurable and verifiable',[37] while its members commit to providing safety inspections and safety and empowerment training for all factories in the members' respective supply chains. The members also aim to empower workers to take an active role in their own safety so that they can report fire and building safety risks without risk of retaliation.[38] To that end, they have a commitment to establish a process that ensures that Worker Participation Committees are established in all Alliance Member Factories.[39]

The signatory companies create a fund, the Worker Safety Fund, to underwrite factory-based fire and building safety initiatives in supplier

---

[33] ibid, Remediation, 14.

[34] ibid, Remediation, 15.

[35] ibid, Transparency and Reporting, 19. The reports can be found at http://accord.fairfactories.org/ffcweb/Web/ManageSuppliers/InspectionReportsEnglish.aspx (accessed 30 October 2014).

[36] Alliance for Bangladesh Worker Safety, available at http://www.bangladeshworkersafety.org/.

[37] The Alliance for Bangladesh Worker Safety, 'About the Alliance for Bangladesh Worker Safety', available at http://www.bangladeshworkersafety.org/about/about-the-alliance (accessed 30 October 2014).

[38] Alliance for Bangladesh Worker Safety, Members Agreement, Art 1.1. Purpose.

[39] ibid, Art 3.2. Program.

factories.[40] The fee is based on the volume of sourcing of the respective member. The members also commit to establish a uniform fire and building safety curriculum and training programme.[41] This programme requires training of the workers and the management at supplier factories. Moreover, the members agree that fire and building safety inspections are a critical element of factory safety and that they will conduct fire and building safety inspections of factories using independent qualified inspectors.[42] Should a member resign or terminate its membership early it must pay the Alliance termination fees.[43] A further important aspect of the agreement is that the members stipulate that no rights are created in any third parties by virtue of the undertakings to which the members have committed to in the agreement.[44] Alleged breaches of the commitments can only be enforced through the process prescribed by the bylaws to the agreement.

B. Critical Assessment of the Accord and the Alliance

The Accord and the Alliance will now be critically compared and evaluated in terms of their scope, operation, certainty and remedies.

i. The two agreements are single-issue initiatives

First, while it is positive that both agreements are five-year plans which address the gross health and safety issues in Bangladesh textile factories, these agreements do not cover any other relevant issues such as working hours, pay, child and forced labour as well as trade union membership. The agreements are therefore single-issue initiatives. Both schemes were direct responses to the Rana Plaza building collapse which was the climax of a number of deadly incidents at garment factories, the companies therefore acted due to negative publicity and political pressure. However, they did not use this opportunity to address the range of problematic issues in supply chain factories in the developing world. The companies continued to keep their existing CSR policies that address those concerns. This business-as-usual approach is the same that the companies followed in relation to health and safety at factories prior to

---

[40] ibid, Art 2.2. Worker Safety Fund (WSF).

[41] ibid, Art 4. Train and Educate Factory Workers, Supervisors, and Management on Fire and Building Safety.

[42] Ibid, Art 6.1. Principles.

[43] ibid, Art 9. Termination Fees in the Event of a Resignation Prior to Two Years of Membership.

[44] ibid, Art 10.4. No Third Party Beneficiaries Created.

Rana Plaza after previous incidents at other factories. The fact that the two agreements are single-issue initiatives therefore demonstrates that the companies only acted in an area where action was unavoidable due to public and political concerns, but that they did not change their approach to other CSR issues which affect the same workers.

ii. Membership and structure

A distinctive difference is the membership and structure of the agreements. The Accord follows a multi-stakeholder approach, members of the agreement are companies and trade unions. NGOs act as witnesses and, moreover, the ILO is given a prominent role as it chooses the chair of the Steering Committee. The inclusion of the different actors involved in the production in factories in Bangladesh is a move away from the traditional bilateral approach to CSR in supply chains between Western companies and their overseas suppliers. Under the bilateral regime, the buyer incorporates CSR clauses into its contracts. Through the contractual relationship, the buyer obliges the supplier to comply with certain requirements, however, the inclusion, monitoring and enforcement of CSR requirements is down to the Western buyer. Disasters such as Rana Plaza have clearly demonstrated that these CSR regimes in supply chains have failed as the buyers have tended to take a light-touch approach to them.

In light of the failures of the bilateral approaches, the advantage of the multi-stakeholder structure of the Accord is the power that it gives to parties other than the companies involved. Whereas previously the Western buyer was more or less solely responsible for promoting CSR in supply chains, the power has now shifted towards equal governance between trade unions and companies. The involvement of trade unions in the running of the Accord is significant, as they are also given oversight of the compliance with the commitments made in the Accord. The trade unions can ensure that companies are held responsible for their CSR commitments and that the principles of the agreement are put into practice. The Alliance, on the contrary, lacks the cooperative power-sharing approach that underlies the Accord. The development and government of the Alliance are only in the hands of the Western buyers with no role to be played by worker representatives and NGOs. Therefore, the Alliance misses an important step towards greater CSR promotion by continuing to follow an approach that purely focusses on the Western companies.

iii.   Enforcement regime

While both initiatives claim that they are legally binding, it is important to look more closely at their provisions and their enforcement regime. The Accord provides for a transparent enforcement procedure for both companies and worker representatives due to the composition of the Steering Committee that hears disputes in the first instance and due to the right to an appeal to a final and binding arbitration process. Moreover, the fact that any arbitration award is enforceable in the country where the company is domiciled against whom enforcement is sought gives power to the commitments of the Accord. This system means that the worker representatives can enforce the provisions of the Accord. The lack of such an enforcement regime is one of the main disadvantages and criticisms of most of the business-driven CSR initiatives. It is therefore a flaw of the Alliance that it relies on the companies themselves for its enforcement. Worker representatives have no power of enforcement. Effectively, this is a continuation of the governance and enforcement approach taken prior to the Rana Plaza building collapse. The Alliance is therefore a commitment that lacks teeth. The express provision in Article 10.4 of the members' agreement according to which no rights are created for the benefit of third parties through the undertakings of this initiative is further evidence of this light touch approach. The Accord and the Alliance therefore strongly differ in terms of the rights of enforcement. Although the Alliance talks about empowering workers in the supply chain, it does not put this rhetoric into practice. A further example of the stronger position that the Accord provides to workers is their right to refuse work that they have 'reasonable justification to believe is unsafe', including the right to refuse to enter or to remain in a building that they have 'reasonable justification to believe is unsafe for occupation'.[45] This right is a direct response to the events that led to the deadly Rana Plaza disaster which saw employees being ordered to return to work despite cracks in the building that were detected on the previous day.[46]

iv.   Further differences

There are further points of distinction between the two regimes which are worth noting. Under the Accord, safety inspections are fully independent whereas under the Alliance the companies retain control over the inspection process by running it under their oversight. That is essentially

---

[45]   Accord on Fire and Building Safety in Bangladesh, Remediation, 15.

[46]   See *Vogue,* 'Questions as Bangladesh fund still not full' (20 August 2014), available at http://www.vogue.co.uk/news/2014/08/20/bangladesh-factory-collapse-rana-plaze-fund-still-empty (accessed 30 October 2014).

the status quo that existed prior to Rana Plaza. The cost of repair that is necessary to ensure the safety of factories is handled in different ways, too. While the members of the Accord are obliged to ensure that sufficient funds are available to pay for all necessary safety renovations, the members of the Alliance do this voluntarily. Again, the difference between the two regimes here is the level of bindingness.

v. Two different regimes?

In summary, the Alliance is by and large a continuation of the previous business-driven approach to CSR without the involvement of stakeholders and without means of enforcement. While it addresses the building and fire safety at supplier factories in Bangladesh, much of it is voluntary. It was created in response to the public concern about a deadly catastrophe, but it does not constitute a ground-breaking change for the companies that have signed up to it. In comparison, the Accord is stronger and shows some positive features in terms of promoting CSR with its multi-stakeholder approach, backed up by remedies for worker representatives which could ultimately be enforced in the home courts of each company. However, despite its advantages, the Accord is not the solution to all CSR issues in global supply chains. It is only a step in the right direction. Both the Alliance and the Accord purely focus on one particular issue that has come into the spotlight: Building and fire safety. This matter is of crucial importance for the health and safety of the workers in the textile factories of Bangladesh, but it is not the only CSR issue that urgently needs addressing by Western companies. Topics such as the working hours, fair pay and employee representation continue to be subject to the existing unilateral/bilateral CSR policies of the Western companies sourcing from Bangladesh.

It will take some time to be able to evaluate how effective the Accord and the Alliance are in practice. A first study of the effectiveness of the Accord and the Alliance reveals some critical findings.[47] The authors of the study point out the important role of subcontracting in the sourcing process.[48] They therefore conclude that the two initiatives 'fail to address the greatest risks of this system'.[49] The two schemes would encompass less than 2000 factories whereas the total base of factories in Bangladesh

---

[47] S Labowitz and D Baumann-Pauly, *Business as Usual is Not an Option* (NYU Stern Centre for Business and Human Rights, April 2014), available at http://www.stern.nyu.edu/sites/default/files/assets/documents/con_047408.pdf (accessed 20 November 2014).

[48] ibid, 6.

[49] ibid.

which produce for the export of textiles in global supply chains are between 5000 and 6000. The authors emphasise that the worst conditions are often in the factories that are outside the scope of the Accord and the Alliance, that is, further down the supply chain. These critical observations demonstrate that despite some positive features of the Accord in terms of its structure and enforcement regime it is not a mechanism that has revolutionised the promotion of CSR in supply chains. It still fails to take account of the problem that is caused by subcontracting. Moreover, it is hoped that the commitment of the companies involved does not come to an end after the five-year agreements. There is a real danger that, upon completion of the plan, companies will again return to business as usual. Meaningful change requires long-term commitment.

IV. PRIVATE LAW, GLOBAL SUPPLY CHAINS AND CSR: THE ROLE OF LAW? A ROLE FOR LAW!

Rana Plaza is an example of how the existing business-driven CSR initiatives have particularly failed in global supply chains. It also highlights that a different approach to promoting CSR is needed. So what are the lessons to be learnt from this disaster for the future promotion of CSR in global supply chains?

This section will move beyond the critical analysis of the Accord and the Alliance. It will outline how a more effective CSR regime for global supply chains could be established and what the role of private law should be within such a system. By doing that, this section will also discuss how the Accord could fit into this regime. To that end, the analysis will address the question of how private law could better promote such multi-stakeholder initiatives. It is argued that although private law has contributed to the failures of the promotion of CSR so far, it does have potential to better contribute to more socially responsible business conduct in the future. The previous chapter concluded with a list of substantive recommendations for changes to English private law to improve its contribution to the promotion of CSR. This section will not repeat why these recommendations were made, but will rather show how they would contribute to a more effective regime of CSR promotion in global supply chains.

A. The Contribution of Company Law and Corporate Governance

Unsurprisingly, in light of the above, the root cause for many violations of CSR and the pure lip-service that is taking place can be found in the shareholder-centricity in English company law. The aim to maximize shareholders' profits leads to a culture of reducing costs by all means in order to increase revenues and, consequently, dividends. As long as CSR remains purely a reputational issue rather than a matter that underlies the business practice, not much will change. Companies are aware of the lack of local laws and/or law enforcement in developing countries such as Bangladesh where their suppliers are located. They even exacerbate the situation by making short-term orders which can only be completed by working overtime, by requiring compliance with CSR clauses without providing financial support to achieve these, by turning a blind eye on flaws in the auditing process and by not committing to suppliers long term.[50] As the Accord rightly demonstrates, CSR promotion is a joint enterprise that requires commitment, assurance, trust and financial support. Against this background, it will be difficult to achieve fundamental change in global supply chains without a fundamental re-direction of the purpose of the company towards a more pluralistic understanding. CSR needs to overcome its position as a box-ticking activity towards a genuine business concern in order to achieve socially responsible supply chains.

Company law could have an important positive impact on more socially responsible supply chains through the establishment of a compulsory reporting system that would require companies to report on CSR issues in their supply chain without the option of 'comply or explain'. The mandatory reporting should explicitly require companies to report on their CSR policy and provide information about the selection of suppliers and independent audits that have taken place. The system of 'comply or explain' is too weak. Compulsory reporting will make it harder, albeit not impossible, to gloss over clear violations of CSR in supply chains. Such a reporting regime would make private initiatives by companies less voluntary and patchy. Companies would have a stronger incentive to put their rhetoric into practice and to take the implementation, monitoring and enforcement of CSR clauses in their business relations with their suppliers more seriously than at present. The discussion about the Accord on Fire and Building Safety in Bangladesh has emphasised the importance of independent audits to achieve credible change. The reporting duties in company law should therefore also establish a requirement to report on audits conducted by independent institutions. However, it is admitted that, in practice, there is still much work to be done to improve the quality of independent auditing.

---

[50] See the discussion by Bader (n 14).

B. Enforcement within Multi-stakeholder Initiatives

Another key feature of the Accord that links with the recommendations made in this book is the enforcement of CSR clauses. The chapter on contract law has shown that in the current system of supply chain contracts only the Western buyer can enforce their contractual CSR clauses with their suppliers.[51] This is a significant legal limitation of the present system of CSR promotion. Enabling the beneficiaries of those contractual CSR clauses, the workers in supplier factories, to enforce the promises that companies make would overcome the bilateral, business-driven nature of the existing supply chain contracts. Companies should expect to be held accountable to their 'commitment' to CSR for the benefit of third parties that they currently publicly display. Where they have to fear that third parties such as employees of their suppliers will have standing to enforce contractual clauses that benefit them they will take these issues more seriously rather than paying only lip-service to them, even if such an enforcement is, in reality, in most instances rather of a theoretical nature.

With its multi-stakeholder composition and enforcement regime, the Accord has developed a powerful instrument that can help making the private system of CSR promotion, work more effectively. However, so far it is limited to fire and building safety in Bangladesh only. It is therefore necessary that similar multi-stakeholder regimes are developed for other CSR issues and other countries and industries. Such regimes should be the model rather than the exception. They could be an instrument that would hold companies more accountable. In addition to such regimes, consumers need to be empowered. The private remedy in consumer law is a positive development, but it is limited to the formation of a contract in the first place and rescission and discount/damages only. It is important that consumers are empowered to file an injunction against a company that does not comply with its publicly declared CSR commitments. Such a right would positively contribute to the enforcement of CSR commitments as it would be likely to make more companies put their CSR rhetoric into practice. The consumers would then add a further enforcement dimension to a multi-stakeholder approach towards CSR.

---

[51] See Chapter 3 'Contract law, global supply chains and corporate social responsibility'.

C. Extraterritorial Liability

The final step towards creating more responsible supply chains is the creation of extraterritorial liability for violations of CSR principles in supply chains. While it is already very difficult to hold parent companies liable for the conduct of their subsidiaries, this is almost impossible in a world of networks of suppliers. The idea of extraterritorial liability that includes liability for the conduct of business partners has much potential to make CSR more of a real concern for Western companies. The analysis of contractual CSR documents has revealed that companies treat bribery prevention in their supply chain particularly seriously, largely due to the fear of liability as a consequence of the extraterritorial reach of the UK Bribery Act.[52] Only where companies can demonstrate that they have conducted sufficient due diligence are they able to avoid liability by having a defence. A similar regime for other pressing issues in supply chains would be likely to make an important impact as to how seriously companies take certain issues such as forced and child labour in their supply chain. A detailed examination of this idea is beyond the scope of this book as this recommendation refers to criminal law (and not private law). However, it is argued here that the ability to promote Corporate Social Responsibility through corporate criminal responsibility needs to be further explored. This idea was discussed in the context of establishing supply chain slavery liability during the preparatory stages of the Modern Slavery Bill, but it was eventually dismissed.[53] This dismissal is a missed opportunity for English law to genuinely address CSR issues within global supply chains.

D. The Role of Law? The Role for Law!

The discussions so far have shown that the future of CSR promotion in supply chains requires a multi-dimensional approach. The existing reliance on voluntary, business-driven CSR has failed, not just in supply chains. The biggest challenge is to guarantee that local governments

---

[52] S7 of the UK Bribery Act. See also Transparency International UK, '2010 Bribery Act: How are supply chains affected?' (Briefing Note, December 2010).

[53] Draft Modern Slavery Bill Joint Committee, Report (8 April 2014), available at http://www.publications.parliament.uk/pa/jt201314/jtselect/jtslavery/166/16602.htm. See also: Government Response to the Joint Committee on the draft Modern Slavery Bill (10 June 2014), available at https://www.gov.uk/government/uploads/system/uploads/attachment_data/file/318771/CM8889Draft ModernSlaveryBill.pdf (accessed 30 October 2014).

ensure that fundamental rights are adhered to in supplier factories in their countries and that workers have a right to enforce these rights. In the absence of this situation or indeed any binding international CSR regulation it is important to move on from the purely private system of CSR towards a hybrid regulatory approach. This idea, proposed in the previous chapter, means that different regulatory techniques such as public and private law, soft and hard law would interact and together promote CSR in global supply chains. The recommendations for changes to substantive English law discussed in this section constitute an important element of such a hybrid approach as they would enable private law to play a more effective role than it does at the moment. While private law alone will not be the solution to corporate irresponsibility in global supply chains, it can make an important contribution towards the better promotion of CSR. Such a hybrid approach recognises that there is an important role to play for the state and state laws in the promotion of CSR. The multi-stakeholder concept of the Bangladesh Accord on Fire and Building Safety has much potential in the development of such systems of promoting CSR in global supply chains. Private law could in different ways contribute to making such multi-stakeholder initiatives more effective, such as through empowering consumers to hold companies accountable for their public CSR promises or through more restrictive disclosure laws. Therefore, law has got a role to play in the future promotion of CSR in supply chains.

There is no guarantee that this hybrid system will prevent further disasters in supply chains, but the more effective use of (private) law would ensure that the current CSR rhetoric, of many companies which lacks genuine commitment, will have to change. The UN Guiding Principles have started a process that recognised the importance of supply chains and the role of the home state. It is now time that this role of the home state is filled and that the various regulatory techniques available for the promotion of CSR in English law are used more effectively, such as, requiring, facilitation and enforcement.

V. CONCLUSION

The Rana Plaza disaster led to an international outcry. Companies and politics cannot just return to 'business as usual' and continue to rely on a largely business-driven voluntary CSR agenda. The existing CSR regime has clearly failed despite public commitment by Western companies. At present, too much is left at the discretion of business to voluntarily promote CSR. The Rana Plaza building collapse has reminded the world that this approach has failed. This book has demonstrated how (private) law already plays a role in the promotion of CSR despite ongoing claims by business representatives that it would not. Moreover, this book has further demonstrated that specific legislative reform is needed in order to better promote CSR in English private law. It was outlined how private law already does and could play a better role in the promotion of CSR inside and outside global supply chains. With supply chains the particular limitations are the absence of an international law framework, the territorial limits of law and the fact that many developing countries have not sufficiently addressed CSR violations in supplier factories located within their borders. English private law can contribute to filling these regulatory gaps by regulating the behaviour of (multinational) companies based in the UK within their supply chain. Companies can, for example, be required to pursue CSR policies, to have these adequately monitored and to effectively report on these. Consumers, for example, could make a powerful contribution to the effectiveness of such CSR regimes by ensuring that companies comply with their CSR rhetoric. Private law can be an important element in hybrid regulatory approaches to CSR. However, through enforcement and disclosure instruments private law would make future initiatives more effective.

The Rana Plaza factory collapse is a tragedy that shows not only the limits of the law, but also the ignorance of politicians, businesses and consumers alike. It also highlights the missed opportunities in law to adequately address irresponsible corporate conduct. While the Accord on Building and Fire Safety in Bangladesh is a promising attempt at ensuring a safer workplace in the future, it does not address all the other pressing issues in global supply chains such as working hours, pay and worker representation. More comprehensive multi-stakeholder initiatives, based on the positive features of the Accord such as its governance and enforcement structure, are needed in order to address the CSR issues in other industries and other parts of the world. Violations of CSR are a daily concern, not only in the Bangladesh garment industry. However, companies will only be willing to promote CSR more effectively if there is a combination of public and political pressure as well as a genuine fear of liability in the home state of the parent company such as in case of the UK Bribery Act. The fact that the Modern Slavery Bill, despite suggestions to do so, did not include extraterritorial liability for UK companies, is therefore a missed opportunity for the promotion of CSR in global supply chains.

Bibliography

BOOKS AND BOOK CHAPTERS

Abbott K W and D Snidal, 'Governance triangle' in W Mattli and N Woods (eds), *The Politics of Global Regulation* (Princeton University Press 2009) 50

Abrahams D, *Regulations for Corporations: A historical account of TNC regulation* (UNRISD 2005)

Amao O, *Corporate Social Responsibility, Human Rights and the Law: Multinational corporations in developing countries* (Routledge 2011)

Armstrong D (ed.), *Routledge Handbook of International Law* (Routledge 2009)

Austen-Baker R, *Implied Terms in English Contract Law* (Edward Elgar 2011)

Baldwin R and M Cave, *Understanding Regulation: Theory, strategy and practice* (OUP 1999)

Beatson J and D Friedmann (eds), *Good Faith and Fault in Contract Law* (Oxford 1995)

Berle A and G Means, *The Modern Corporation and Private Property* (Transaction Publishers 1991, originally published in 1932)

Birds J et al. (eds), *Boyle & Birds' Company Law* (8th edn, Jordans 2011)

Birks P, 'Editor's Preface' in P Birks (ed.), *What are Law Schools For?* (OUP 1996)

Black J, 'Law and regulation: The case of finance' in C Parker, C Scott, N Lacey and J Braithwaite (eds), *Regulating Law* (OUP 2004) 33

Blowfield M and A Murray, *Corporate Responsibility: A critical introduction* (OUP 2008)

Boeger N, R Murray and C Villiers 'Introduction' in N Boeger, R Murray and C Villiers (eds), *Perspectives on Corporate Social Responsibility* (Edward Elgar 2008) 1

Boeger N, R Murray and C Villiers (eds), *Perspectives on Corporate Social Responsibility* (Edward Elgar 2008)

Bomhoff J and A Meuwese, 'The Meta-regulation of transnational private regulation', in C Scott, F Cafaggi and L Senden (eds), *The Challenges of Transnational Private Regulation: Conceptual and constitutional debates* (Wiley-Blackwell 2011) 138

Bouckaert B and G De Geest (eds), *The Encyclopaedia of Law and Economics vol III* (Edward Elgar 2000)

Bradgate R, *Commercial Law* (3rd edn, OUP 2005)

Bradgate R, 'Formation of contracts' in A Grubb (ed), *The Law of Contract* (3rd edn, LexisNexis Butterworths 2007)

Bradgate R and F White, *Commercial Law – Legal Practice Course Guides* (OUP 2009)

Brownsword R, *Contract Law: Themes for the twenty-first century* (2nd edn, OUP 2006)

Cafaggi F 'New foundations of transnational private regulation' in C Scott, F Cafaggi and L Senden (eds), *The Challenge of Transnational Private Regulation – Conceptual and Constitutional Debates* (Wiley-Blackwell 2011) 31

Cafaggi F and H Muir-Watt, 'Introduction' in F Cafaggi and H Muir-Watt, *Making European Private Law Governance Design* (Edward Elgar 2008) 2

Campbell D and P Vincent-Jones (eds), *Contract and Economic Organisation, Socio-Legal Initiatives* (Aldershot 1996)

Campbell D and H Collins and J Wightman (eds), *Implicit Dimensions of Contract* (Hart Publishing 2003)

Campbell K and D Vick, 'Disclosure law and the market for corporate social responsibility', in D McBarnet, A Voiculescu and T Campbell (eds), *The New Corporate Accountability: Corporate social responsibility and the law* (CUP 2007) 241

Cane P, *Administrative Law* (OUP 2011)

Clarkson C and J Hill, *The Conflict of Laws* (4th edn, OUP 2011)

Collins H, *Regulating Contracts* (OUP 1999)

Collins H, 'Governance implications for the European Union of the changing character of private law' in F Cafaggi and H Muir-Watt (eds), *Making European Private Law Governance Design* (Edward Elgar 2008) 278

Crane A, A McWilliams, D Matten et al. (eds), *The Oxford Handbook of Corporate Social Responsibility* (OUP 2008)

Davies P and S Worthington, *Gower and Davies' Principles of Modern Company Law* (9th edn, Sweet & Maxwell 2012)

Davis M, *A Crisis of Professional Self-Regulation – the Example of the Solicitors' Profession* (Cardiff Centre for Law and Ethics 2005)

Deakin S, A Johnston and B Markesinis, *Markesinis and Deakin's Tort Law* (6th edn, OUP 2008)

De Jong A, *Transnational Corporations and International Law: Accountability in the global business environment* (Edward Elgar 2011)

Dine J, *Companies, International Trade and Human Rights* (CUP 2005)

Dobler D and D Burt, *Purchasing and Supply Management, Text and Cases* (6th edn, McGraw-Hill 1996)

Easterbrook F and D Fischel, *The Economic Structure of Corporate Law* (Harvard University Press 1991)

Eisenberg M 'Relational contracts', in J Beatson and D Friedmann (eds), *Good Faith and Fault in Contract Law* (Oxford 1995)

Fawcett J and J Carruthers, *Cheshire, North & Fawcett: Private international law* (14th edn, OUP 2008)

Freeman R, *Strategic Management: A stakeholder approach* (Pitman/Ballinger 1984)

French D, S Mayson and C Ryan, *Mayson, French & Ryan on Company Law* (28th edn, OUP 2011–12)

Friedman M, *Capitalism and Freedom* (University of Chicago Press 1962)

Giliker P and S Beckwith, *Tort* (4th edn, Sweet & Maxwell 2011)

Glinski C, 'Corporate codes of conduct: Moral or legal obligation' in D McBarnet, A Voiculescu and T Campbell (eds), *The New Corporate Accountability: Corporate social responsibility and the law* (CUP 2007) 147

Grubb A, *The Law of Contract* (3rd edn, LexisNexis Butterworths 2007)

Hannigan B, *Company Law* (3rd edn, OUP 2012)

Harpwood, V, *Modern Tort Law* (6th edn, Cavendish Publishing 2005)

Hedley S, 'Looking outward or looking inward? Obligations scholarship in the early 21st century' in A Robertson and T H Wu (eds), *The Goals of Private Law* (Hart Publishing 2009) 193

Hodges C, *Multi-party Actions* (OUP 2001)

Horrigan B, *Corporate Social Responsibility in the 21st Century: Debates, models and practices across government, law and business* (Edward Elgar 2010)

Howells G and S Weatherill, *Consumer Protection Law* (2nd edn, Ashgate 2005)

Howells G, 'Codes of conduct', in G Howells, H W Micklitz and T Wilhelmsson (eds), *European Fair Trading Law: The unfair commercial practices directive* (Ashgate Publishing Limited 2006) 206

Howells G, H W Micklitz and T Wilhelmsson (eds), *European Fair Trading Law: The unfair commercial practices directive* (Ashgate Publishing Limited 2006)

Hviid M, 'Long-term contracts and relational contracts', in B Bouckaert and G De Geest (eds), *The Encyclopaedia of Law and Economics, vol III* (Edward Elgar 2000) 46

Johnston A, *EC Regulation of Corporate Governance* (CUP 2009)

Jordana J and D Levi-Faur (eds), *The Politics Of Regulation: Institutions and regulatory reforms for the age of governance* (Edward Elgar 2004) 145

Kakabadse A and N Kakabadse (eds), *CSR in Practice* (Palgrave Macmillan 2007)

Kakabadse A and N Kakabadse, 'CSR in the boardroom: Myth or mindfulness' in A Kakabadse and N Kakabadse (eds), *CSR in Practice* (Palgrave Macmillan 2007)

Keay A, *The Corporate Objective* (Edward Elgar 2011)

Keay A, 'The duty to promote the success of the company: Is it fit for purpose in a post-financial crisis world?' in J Loughrey (ed.), *Directors' Duties and Shareholder Litigation in the Wake of the Financial Crisis* (Edward Elgar 2013) 50

Keay A, *The Enlightened Shareholder Value Principle and Corporate Governance* (Routledge 2013)

Kinley D, J Nolan and N Zerial, 'The norms are dead! Long live the norms! The politics behind the UN human rights norms for corporations' in D McBarnet, A Voiculescu and T Campbell (eds), *The New Corporate Accountability: Corporate social responsibility and the law* (CUP 2007) 459

Kurucz E, B Colbert and D Wheeler, 'The business case for corporate social responsibility' in A Crane and others (eds), *The Oxford Handbook of Corporate Social Responsibility* (OUP 2008) 83

Lawson R and S Singleton, *Commercial Contracts: A practical guide to standard terms* (Tottel Publishing 2006)

Levi-Faur D (ed.), *Handbook on the Politics of Regulation* (Edward Elgar 2011)

Lord Collins of Mapesbury, C G J Morse, D McClean et al. (eds), *Dicey, Morris & Collins on the Conflict of Laws* (15th edn, Vol. 2, Sweet & Maxwell 2012)

Loughlin M, *Public Law and Political Theory* (Clarendon Press 1992)

Macneil I, 'Reflections on relational contract theory after a neo-classical seminar' in D Campbell, H Collins and J Wightman (eds), *Implicit Dimensions of Contract* (Hart Publishing 2003) 207

Mattli W and N Woods (eds), *The Politics of Global Regulation* (Princeton University Press 2009) 156

McBarnet D and M Kurkchiyan, 'Corporate social responsibility through contractual control? Global supply chains and "other-regulation"' in D McBarnet, A Voiculescu and T Campbell (eds), *The New Corporate Accountability: Corporate social responsibility and the law* (CUP 2007) 59

McBarnet D and P Schmidt, 'Corporate accountability through creative enforcement: human rights, the Alien Torts Claims Act and the limits of legal impunity' in D McBarnet, A Voiculescu and T Campbell (eds), *The New Corporate Accountability* (CUP 2007) 148

McBarnet D, A Voiculescu and T Campbell (eds), *The New Corporate Accountability: Corporate social responsibility and the law* (CUP 2007)

McKendrick E, *Contract Law* (8th edn, Palgrave Macmillan 2009)

McKendrick E, *Contract Law: Text, cases and materials* (4th edn, OUP 2010)

Melé D, 'Corporate social responsibility theories' in A Crane and others (eds), *The Oxford Handbook of Corporate Social Responsibility* (OUP 2008) 68

Millington A, 'Responsibility in the supply chain' in A Crane, A McWilliams, D Matten et al. (eds), *The Oxford Handbook of Corporate Social Responsibility* (OUP 2008) 363

Millon D, 'Enlightened shareholder value, social responsibility and the redefinition of corporate purpose without law' in P M Vasudev and S Watson (eds), *Corporate Governance after the Financial Crisis* (Edward Elgar 2012) 68

Milman D, *National Corporate Law in a Globalised Market: The UK experience in perspective* (Edward Elgar 2009)

Mitchell L, 'The board as a path towards corporate social responsibility' in D McBarnet, A Voiculescu and T Campbell (eds), *The New Corporate Accountability: Corporate social responsibility and the law* (CUP 2007) 280

Muchlinski P, 'Corporate social responsibility and international law: The case of human right and multinational enterprises' in D McBarnet, A Voiculescu and T Campbell (eds), *The New Corporate Accountability: Corporate social responsibility and the law* (CUP 2007) 456

Muchlinski P, 'Human rights and multinational enterprises' in D McBarnet, A Voiculescu and T Campbell (eds), *The New Corporate Accountability: Corporate social responsibility and the law* (CUP 2007) 433

Muchlinski P, *Multinational Enterprises and the Law* (2nd ed, OUP 2007)

Murray C, D Holloway and D Timson-Hunt, *Schmitthoff's Export Trade: The law and practice of international trade* (11th edn, Sweet & Maxwell 2007)

Nolan D and A Robertson, 'Rights and private law' in D Nolan and A Robertson, *Rights and Private Law* (Hart Publishing 2011) 1

Oliver D, *Common Values and the Public-Private Divide* (Butterworths 1999)

Owen D and B O'Dwyer, 'Corporate social responsibility – the reporting and assurance dimension' in A Crane and others (eds), *The Oxford Handbook of Corporate Social Responsibility* (OUP 2008) 401

Parker C, 'Meta-regulation: Legal accountability for corporate social responsibility' in D McBarnet, A Voiculescu and T Campbell (eds), *The New Corporate Accountability: Corporate social responsibility and the law* (CUP 2007) 207

Parker C et al. (eds), *Regulating Law* (OUP 2004)

Parkinson J E, *Corporate Power and Responsibility* (OUP 1993)

Poole J, *Textbook on Contract Law* (11th edn, OUP 2012)

Queinnec Y, *The OECD Guidelines for Multinational Enterprises: An evolving legal status* (Sherpa 2007)

Robertson A and T H Wu (eds), *The Goals of Private Law* (Hart Publishing 2009)

Rogowski R and T Wilthagen, *Reflexive Labour Law* (Kluwer Law and Taxation Publishers 1994)

Scott C, 'Regulation in the age of governance: The rise of the post-regulatory state', in J Jordana and D Levi-Faur (eds), *The Politics Of Regulation: Institutions and regulatory reforms for the age of governance* (Edward Elgar 2004) 145

Scott C, 'Reflexive governance, meta-regulation and corporate social responsibility: The "Heineken effect"' in N Boeger, R Murray and C Villiers (eds), *Perspectives on Corporate Social Responsibility* (Edward Elgar 2008) 173

Scott C, F Cafaggi and L Senden (eds), *The Challenge of Transnational Private Regulation: Conceptual and constitutional debates* (Wiley-Blackwell 2011)

Sheikh S, *Corporate Social Responsibilities: Law and practice* (Cavendish 1995)

Sheikh S and W Rees (eds), *Corporate Governance & Corporate Control* (Cavendish 1995)

Shelton D L 'Soft law' in D Armstrong (ed.), *Routledge Handbook of International Law* (Routledge 2009) 68

Sinden, A, 'Power and responsibility: Why human rights should address corporate environmental wrongs' in D McBarnet, A Voiculescu and T Campbell (eds), *The New Corporate Accountability: Corporate social responsibility and the law* (CUP 2007) 519

Smerdon R, *A Practical Guide to Corporate Governance* (4th edn, Sweet & Maxwell 2007)

Smith N C, 'Consumers as drivers of corporate social responsibility' in A Crane, A McWilliams, D Matten et al. (eds), *The Oxford Handbook of Corporate Social Responsibility* (OUP 2008) 281

Solomon J and A Solomon, *Corporate Governance and Accountability* (John Wiley & Sons Ltd. 2003)

Taylor S and A Emir, *Employment Law: An Introduction* (OUP 2006)

Teubner G (ed.), *Global Law Without a State* (Brookfield 1997)

240 *CSR, private law and global supply chains*

Tomasic R and F Akinbami, 'Shareholder activism and litigation against
UK banks – the limits of company law and the desperate resort to
human rights claims?' in J Loughrey, *Directors' Duties and Shareholder Litigation in the Wake of the Financial Crisis* (Edward Elgar
2013) 151
van Hoecke M 'Legal doctrine: Which method(s) for what kind of
discipline?' in M van Hoecke (ed.), *Methodologies of Legal Research:
Which kind of method for what kind of discipline?* (Hart Publishing
2011) 4
van Hoecke M (ed.), *Methodologies of Legal Research: Which kind of
method for what kind of discipline?* (Hart Publishing 2011)
van Opijnen M and J Oldenziel, *Responsible Supply Chain Management,
potential success factors and challenges for addressing prevailing human
rights and other CSR issues in supply chains of EU-based companies*
(commissioned under the European Union's Programme for Employment and Social Solidarity – PROGRESS (2007-2013) (2010), available
at   http://ec.europa.eu/enterprise/policies/sustainable-business/files/
business-human-rights/final_rscm_report-11-04-12_en.pdf (accessed 07
November 2014)
Vasudev P M and S Watson (eds), *Corporate Governance after the
Financial Crisis* (Edward Elgar 2012)
Villiers C, *Corporate Reporting and Company Law* (CUP 2006)
Villiers C, 'Corporate law, corporate power and corporate social respons-
ibility' in N Boeger, R Murray and C Villiers (eds), *Perspectives on
Corporate Social Responsibility* (Edward Elgar 2008) 91
Villiers C, 'Narrative reporting and enlightened shareholder value under
the Companies Act 2006' in J Loughrey (ed.), *Directors' Duties and
Shareholder Litigation in the Wake of the Financial Crisis* (Edward
Elgar 2013) 108
Vogel D, *The Market for Virtue: The potential and limits for corporate
social responsibility* (Brookings Institute Press 2006)
Vogel D, 'The private regulation of global corporate conduct' in W Mattli
and N Woods (eds), *The Politics of Global Regulation* (Princeton
University Press 2009) 156
Voiculescu A, 'Changing paradigms of corporate criminal responsibility:
Lessons for corporate social responsibility' in D McBarnet, A
Voiculescu and T Campbell, *The New Corporate Accountability: Cor-
porate social responsibility and the law* (CUP 2007) 399
Voiculescu A, 'The other European framework for corporate social
responsibility: From the Green Paper to new uses of human rights
instruments' in D Mc Barnet, A Voiculescu and T Campbell (eds), *The
New Corporate Accountability: Corporate social responsibility and the
law* (CUP 2007) 379

Vranken J, 'Methodology of legal doctrinal research: A comment on Westerman' in M van Hoecke (ed.), *Methodologies of Legal Research: Which kind of method for what kind of discipline?* (Hart Publishing 2011) 116

Vrielink M, C van Montfort and M Bokhorst, 'Codes as hybrid regulation' in D Levi-Faur (ed.), *Handbook on the Politics of Regulation* (Edward Elgar 2011) 486

Wolf S and N Stanley, *Wolf and Stanley on Environmental Law* (5th edn, Routledge 2011) 510

Woodroffe G and L Lowe, *Woodroffe and Lowe's Consumer Law and Practice* (8th edn, Sweet & Maxwell 2010)

Zerk J, *Multinationals and Corporate Social Responsibility: Limitations and opportunities in international law* (CUP 2006)

ARTICLES

Adams J, 'The battle of forms' (1983) *JBL* 297

Adams J and R Brownsword, 'The ideologies of contract' (1987) 7 *LS* 207

Adeyeye A, 'The limitations of corporate governance in the CSR agenda' (2010) 31 *Company Lawyer* 114

Agrawal A, A de Meyer and L van Wassenhovez, 'Managing value in supply chain – case studies on the sourcing hub concept' 1, available at http://papers.ssrn.com/sol3/papers.cfm?abstract_id=1888756& (accessed 24 November 2014)

Alcock A, 'An accidental change to directors' duties' (2009) 30 *Company Lawyer* 362

Allen W, 'Contracts and communities in corporation law' (1993) 50 *Wash. & Lee L. Rev* 1395

Amaeshi K, O Osuji and P Nnodim, 'Corporate social responsibility in supply chains of global brands: A boundaryless responsibility? Clarifications, exceptions and implications' (2008) 81 *Journal of Business Ethics* 223

Amao O, 'The foundation for a global company law for multinational corporations' (2010) 21 *ICCLR* 275

Ames J, 'Taking responsibility' (2011) 103 *European Lawyer* 15

Andersen M and T Skjoett-Larsen, 'Corporate social responsibility in global supply chains' (2009) 14 *Supply Chain Management: An International Journal* 75

Anderson M, 'Transnational corporations and environmental damage: Is tort law the answer?' (2002) 41 *Washburn Law Journal* 399

Andrews N, 'Strangers to justice no longer: The reversal of the privity rule under the Contracts (Rights of third parties) Act 1999' (2001) 60 *Cambridge Law Journal* 353

Andrews N, 'Multi-party actions and complex litigation in England' (2012) 23 *E.B.L.Rev.* 1

Arora A, 'The corporate governance failings in financial institutions and directors' legal liability' (2011) 32 *Company Lawyer* 3

Bantekas I, 'Corporate social responsibility in international law' (2004) 22 *Boston University International Law Journal* 309

Baughen S, 'Multinationals and the export of hazard' (1995) 58 *Modern Law Review* 54

Berle A, 'Corporate powers as powers in trust' (1931) 44 *Harvard Law Review* 1049

Bernstein S and E Hannah, 'Non-state global standard setting and the WTO: Legitimacy and the need for regulatory space' (2008) 11 *Journal of International Economic Law* 575

Black J, 'Decentring regulation: Understanding the role of regulation and self-regulation in a post-regulatory world' (2001) 54 *Current Legal Problems* 103

Blair M and L Stout, 'A team production theory of corporate law' (1999) 85 *Virginia Law Review* 247

Blumberg P, 'Limited liability and corporate groups' (1985–1986) 11 *J. Corp. L.* 573

Bondy K, D Matten and J Moon, 'The adoption of voluntary codes of conduct in MNCs: A three-country comparative study' (2004) 109 (4) *Business and Society Review* 449

Boyed D et al., 'Corporate social responsibility in global supply chains: A procedural justice perspective' (2007) 40 *Long Range Planning* 341

Boyle M, 'Employers' liability at common law: Two competing paradigms' (2008) 12 (2) *Edinburgh Law Review* 231

Bray O and M Starmer, 'Office of Fair Trading v Purely Creative Ltd: The net tightens on exponents of sharp commercial practices' (2011) 22 (4) *Entertainment Law Review* 118

Buhmann K, 'Integrating human rights in emerging regulation of corporate social responsibility: The EU case' (2011) 7 (2) *International Journal of Law in Context* 139

Burrows A, 'The Contracts (Rights of third parties) Act 1999 and its implications for commercial contracts' (2000) *LMCLQ* 540

Cane P 'Using tort law to enforce environmental regulations?' (2001–2002) 41 *Washburn Law Journal* 427

Carrington M, B Neville and G Whitwell, 'Why ethical consumers don't walk their talk: Towards a framework for understanding the gap between the ethical purchase intentions and actual buying behaviour of ethically-minded consumers' (2010) 97 *Journal of Business Ethics* 139

Carroll A, 'Social issues in management research' (1994) 33 *Business and Society* 5

Chaterji A and S Listokin, 'Corporate social responsibility' (2007) 3 *Democracy: A Journal of Ideas* 52

Colliver S et al., 'Holding human rights violators accountable by using international law in US courts: Advocacy efforts and complementary strategies' (2005) 19 *Emory International Law Review* 169

Coppy S, 'S172 of the Companies Act 2006 fails people and planet?' (2010) 31 *Company Lawyer* 406

Cragg B, 'Home is where the halt is: Mandating corporate social responsibility through home state regulation and social disclosure' (2010) 24 *Emory International Law Review* 735

Dahlsrud, A, 'How corporate social responsibility is defined: An analysis of 37 definitions' (2008) 15 *Corporate Social Responsibility and Environmental Management* 1

Dawkins J, 'Corporate responsibility: The communication challenge' (2005) 9 *Journal of Communication Management*, 108

Dean J, 'Stakeholding and company law' (2001) 22 *Company Lawyer* 66

Delbruck J, 'Prospects for a "world" (internal) law?: Legal developments in a changing international system' (2002) 9 (2) *Indiana Journal of Global Legal Studies* 401

Dodd E, 'For whom are corporate managers trustees?' (1932) 45 *Harvard Law Review* 1145

Du Plessis J 'Corporate law and corporate governance lessons from the past: Ebbs and flows, but far from "the end of history": Part 1' (2009) 30 (2) *Company Lawyer* 43

Eccles R, I Ioannou and G Serafeim, 'The Impact of Corporate Sustainability on Organizational Processes and Performance' (2011) Harvard Business School Working Paper, 12-035, available at http://papers. ssrn.com/sol3/papers.cfm?abstract_id=1964011 (accessed 21 November 2014)

Eckhardt G, R Belk and T Devinney, 'Why don't consumers consume ethically?' (2010) 9 *Journal of Consumer Behaviour* 426

Eltantawy, R, G Fox and L Giunipero, 'Supply management ethical responsibility: Reputation and performance impacts' (2009) 14 (2) *Supply Chain Management: An International Journal* 99

Emesehe E et al., 'Corporations, CSR and self-regulation: What lessons from the global financial crisis?' (2010) 11 *German Law Journal* 230

Fama E, 'Agency problems and the theory of the firm' (1980) 88 *Journal of Political Economy* 288

Fisher D, 'The enlightened shareholder value – leaving stakeholders in the dark: Will section 172 (1) of the Companies Act 2006 make directors consider the impact of their decisions on third parties?' (2009) *ICCLR* 10

Friedman M, 'The social responsibility of business is to increase its profits', *The New York Times Magazine* (New York, 13 September 1970)

Fulbrook J 'Chandler v Cape: Personal injury: Liability: Negligence' (2012) 3 *Journal of Personal Injury Law* C135

Gamble A and G Kelly, 'Shareholder value and the stakeholder debate in the UK' (2001) 9 *Corporate Governance* 110

Garriga E and D Melé, 'Corporate social responsibility theories: Mapping the territory' (2004) 53 *Journal of Business Ethics* 51

Gibbs D, 'Has the statutory derivative claim fulfilled its objectives? The hypothetical director and CSR: Part 2' (2011) 32 *Company Lawyer* 76

Gretton E, 'Jackson – an overview' *The Law Society Gazette* (27 March 2013)

Hannigan B, 'Board failures in the financial crisis: Tinkering with codes and the need for wider corporate governance reforms: Part 2' (2012) 33 (2) *Company Lawyer* 35

Hansmann H 'Ownership of the firm' (1988) 4 *Journal of Law, Economics and Organisation* 267

Hansmann H and R Kraakman, 'The end of history for corporate law' (2001) 89 *Geo.L.J.* 439

Hedley S, 'Is private law meaningless?' (2011) 64 *Current Legal Problems* 89

Ho J K S, 'Is section 172 of the Companies Act 2006 the guidance for CSR?' (2010) 31 *Company Lawyer* 207, 209

Hoang D and B Jones, 'Why do corporate codes of conduct fail? Women workers and clothing supply chains in Vietnam' (2012) 12 *Global Social Policy* 67

Hopt K J, 'Comparative Corporate Governance: The state of the art and international regulation' (2011) European Corporate Governance Institute, Law Working Paper 170/2011, 6, available at http://ssrn.com/abstract_id=1713750 (accessed 3 November 2014)

Howarth D, 'Muddying the waters: Tort law and the environment from an English perspective' (2001–2002) 41 *Washburn Law Journal* 469

Ireland P, 'Company law and the myth of shareholder ownership' (1999) 62 *MLR* 32

Ireland P, 'Limited liability, shareholder rights and the problem of corporate irresponsibility' (2010) 34 *Cambridge Journal of Economics* 837

Jenkinson T and C Mayer, 'The Assessment: Contracts and competition' (1996) 12 (4) O*xford Review of Economic Policy* 3

Jiang B, 'Implementing supplier codes of conduct in global supply chains: Process explanations from theoretic and empirical perspectives' (2009) 85 *Journal of Business Ethics* 77, 78.

Johnston A, 'After the OFR: Can UK shareholder value still be enlightened?' (2006) 7 (4) *EBOLR* 817

Johnston A, 'Constructing Sustainability Through CSR: A critical appraisal of ISO 26000' (University of Oslo Faculty of Law Research Paper No. 2011-33), available at http://papers.ssrn.com/sol3/papers. cfm?abstract_id=1928397 (accessed 12 November 2014)

Kaleck W and M Saage-Maass, 'Corporate accountability for human rights violations amounting to international crimes: The status quo and its challenges' (2010) 8 (3) *Journal of International Criminal Justice* 699

Kanner A, 'Toxic tort litigation in a regulatory world' (2001–2002) 41 *Wasburn Law Journal* 535

Kay J and A Silberston, 'Corporate governance', available at: http://www. johnkay.com

Keay A, 'Enlightened shareholder value' (2006) *LMCLQ* 335

Keay A, 'Section 172(1) of the Companies Act 2006: An interpretation and assessment' (2007) 28 *Company Lawyer* 106

Keay A, 'Tackling the issue of the corporate objective: An analysis of the United Kingdom's "Enlightened shareholder value approach"' (2007) 29 (4) *SydLawRw* 23

Keay A, 'Good faith and directors' duty to promote the success of their company' (2011) 32 *Company Lawyer* 138

Kelly G and J Parkinson, 'The conceptual foundations of the company: A pluralist approach' (1998) 2 *CfiLR* 174

Kolk A and R van Tulder, 'The effectiveness of self-regulation: Corporate codes of conduct and child labour' (2002) 20 (3) *European Management Journal* 260

Labowitz S and D Baumann-Pauly, 'Business as usual is not an option' (NYU Stern Centre for Business and Human Rights, April 2014), available at http://www.stern.nyu.edu/sites/default/files/assets/docu ments/con_047408.pdf (accessed 20 November 2014)

Lazonick W and M O'Sullivan, 'Maximizing shareholder value: A new ideology for corporate governance' (2000) 29 *Economy and Society* 13

Leigh J and S Waddock, 'The emergence of total responsibility management systems: J. Sainsbury's (plc) voluntary responsibility management systems for global food retail supply chains (2006) 111 (4) *Business and Society Review* 409

Lii Y-S and M Lee, 'Doing right leads to doing well: When the type of CSR and reputation interact to affect consumer evaluations of the firm' (2012) 105 *Journal of Business Ethics* 69

Lo S, 'Liability of directors as joint tortfeasors' (2009) 2 *Journal of Business Law* 109

Locke R, et al., 'Beyond corporate codes of conduct: Work organization and labour standards at NIKE's suppliers' (2007) 146 *International Labour Review* 21

Locke R, F Qin and A Brause, 'Does monitoring improve labor standards? Lessons from NIKE' (2007–2008) 61 *Industrial and Labor Relations Review* 3

Lord Irvine 'The law: An engine for trade' (2001) 64 *MLR* 333

Lord Woolf, 'Droit public – English style' (1995) *PL* 57

Loughrey J, A Keay and L Cerioni, 'Legal practitioners, enlightened shareholder value and the shaping of corporate governance' (2008) 8 (1) *JCLS* 79

Lumsden A and S Fridman, 'Corporate Social Responsibility: The case for a self-regulatory model' (The University of Sydney Law School, Legal Research Studies Paper No. 07/34, 2007)

MacLeod S 'Reconciling regulatory approaches to corporate social responsibility: The European Union, OECD and United Nations compare' (2007) 13 *European Public Law* 671

Maloni M and M Brown, 'Corporate social responsibility in the supply chain: An application in the food industry' (2006) 68 *Journal of Business Ethics*, 35

Mamic I, 'Managing global supply chain: The sports footwear, apparel and retail sectors' (2005) 59 *Journal of Business Ethics* 81

Mandelson N, 'A control-based approach to shareholder liability for corporate torts' (2002) 102 *Columbia Law Review* 1203

Mares R, 'The limits of supply chain responsibility: A critical analysis of corporate social responsibility instruments' (2010) 79 *Nordic Journal of International Law* 193

Marx A 'Global governance and private regulation of supply chains – types, trends and challenges' (Antwerp Management School, Working Papers, 2010) 2

McGaughey E, 'Donoghue v Salomon in the High Court (case comment)' (2011) 4 *Journal of Personal Injury Law* 249

Meeran R, 'Tort litigation against multinational corporations for violations of human rights: An overview of the position outside the United States' (2011) 3 (1) *City University of Hong Kong Law Review* 1

Millon D, 'Theories of the corporation' (1990) *Duke Law Journal* 201

Millon D, 'Communitarians, contractarians, and the crisis in corporate law' (1993) 50 *Wash. & Lee L.Rev.* 1373

Millon D, 'Two models of corporate social responsibility' (2011) 46 *Wake Forest Law Review* 523

Millon D, 'Human rights and Delaware corporate law' (2012) 25 *Pac McGeorge Global Bus & Dev LJ* 173

Millon D, 'Shareholder social responsibility' (2013) 36 *Seattle University Law Review* 912

Muchlinski P, 'Corporations in international litigation: Problems of jurisdiction and the United Kingdom asbestos case' (2001) 50 *ICCLR* 1

Muchlinski P, 'Holding multinationals to account: Recent developments in English litigation and the Company Law Review' (2002) 23 *Company Lawyer* 168

Muchlinski P, 'Limited liability and multinational enterprises: A case for reform?' (2010) 34 *Cambridge Journal of Economics* 915

Muchlinski P, 'Implementing the new UN corporate human rights framework: Implications for corporate law, governance, and regulation' (2012) 22 (1) *Business Ethics Quarterly* 145

Mujih E C, 'The new statutory derivative claim: A paradox of minority shareholder protection: Part 2' (2012) 33 *Company Lawyer* 99

Mulheron R, 'Justice enhanced: Framing an opt-out class action for England' (2007) 70 *MLR* 550

Mulheron R, 'Recent milestones in class actions reform in England: A critique and a proposal' (2011) 127 *LQR* 2

Muller C, W Vermeulen and P Glasbergen, 'Pushing or sharing as value-driven strategies for societal change in global supply chains: Two case studies in the British-South African fresh fruit supply chain' (2012) 21 *Business Strategy and the Environment* 127

Mushkat R, 'Corporate social responsibility, international law, and business economics: Convergences and divergencies' (2010) 12 *Oregon Review of International Law* 55

Nakajima C, 'The importance of legally embedding corporate social responsibility' (2011) 32 *Company Lawyer* 257

Nattier F, 'Regulation of transnational corporations: Latin American actions in international fora' (1984) 19 *Texas International Law Journal* 265

Nygh P, 'The liability of multi-national corporations for the torts of their subsidiaries' (2002) 3 *EBOLR* 51

Okoye N, 'The BIS review and section 172 of the Companies Act 2006: What manner of clarity is needed?' (2012) 33 (1) *Company Lawyer* 15

Omran M, P Atrill and J Pointon, 'Shareholders versus stakeholders: Corporate mission statements and investor returns' (2002) 11 *Business Ethics: A European Review* 318

Pearson R and G Seyfang, 'New hope or false dawn?: Voluntary codes of conduct, labour regulation and social policy in a globalising world' (2001) 1 *Global Social Policy* 48

Pedamon C, 'Corporate social responsibility: A new approach to promoting integrity and responsibility' (2010) 31 *Company Lawyer* 172

Pedersen E and M Andersen, 'Safeguarding corporate social responsibility (CSR) in global supply chains: How codes of conduct are managed in buyer-supplier relationships' (2006) 6 *Journal of Public Affairs* 228

Perry B and L Gregory, 'The European panorama: Directors' economic and social responsibilities' (2009) 20 *ICCLR* 25

Pieters K, 'More efforts needed to improve gender equality in corporate governance in the EU' (2012) 13 *EBOLR* 475

Polonsky M and C Jevons, 'Global branding and strategic CSR: An overview of three types of complexity' (2009) 26 *International Marketing Review* 327

Preuss L, 'Codes of conduct in organisational context: From cascade to lattice-work of codes' (2010) 94 *Journal of Business Ethics* 471

Quo S, 'Corporate social responsibility and corporate groups: The James Hardie case' (2011) 32 *Company Lawyer* 249

Rasche A and D Gilbert, 'Institutionalizing global governance: The role of the United Nation's global compact' (2012) 21 (1) *Business Ethics: A European Review* 100

Reisberg A, 'The notion of stewardship from a company law perspective: Re-defined and re-assessed in light of the recent financial crisis?' (2011) 18 *Journal of Financial Crime* 126

Roach L, 'The paradox of the traditional justifications for exclusive shareholder governance protection: Expanding the pluralist approach' (2001) 22 *Company Lawyer* 9

Roach L, 'The legal model of the company and the company law review' (2005) 26 *Company Lawyer* 98

Robinson P, 'Do voluntary labour initiatives make a difference for the conditions of workers in global supply chains? (2010) 52 *Journal of Industrial Relations* 561

Roe T, 'Contractual intention under section 1(1)(b) and 1(2) of the Contracts (Rights of Third Parties) Act 1999' (2000) 63 *MLR* 887

Ruggie J, 'The construction of the UN "protect, respect and remedy" framework for business and human rights: The true confessions of a principled pragmatist' (2011) *EHRLR* 127

Salacuse J W, 'Corporate governance in the new century' (2004) 25 *Company Lawyer* 69

Schiek D, 'Private rule-making and European governance – issues of legitimacy' (2007) 32 *European Law Review* 443

Schmitthoff C, 'The wholly owned and the controlled subsidiary' (1978) *JBL* 218

Schwarz F, 'The German co-determination system: A model for introducing corporate social responsibility requirements into Australian law? Part 1' (2008), 23 *JIBLR* 125

Schwarz F, 'The German co-determination system: A model for introducing corporate social responsibility requirements into Australian law? Part 2' (2008) 23 *JIBLR* 190

Sheikh S, 'Promoting corporate social responsibilities within the European Union' (2002) 13 *ICCLR* 143

Siems M and D Sithigh, 'Mapping legal research' (2012) 71 *CLJ* 651

Singh J, O Iglesias and J Batista-Foguet, 'Does having an ethical brand matter? The influence of consumer perceived ethicality on trust, affect and loyalty' (2011) 111 *Journal of Business Ethics* 541

Sobczak A, 'Are codes of conduct in global supply chains really voluntary? From soft law regulation of labour relations to consumer law' (2006) 16 (2) *Business Ethics Quarterly* 167

Soosay C, A Fearne and B Dent, 'Sustainable value chain analysis – a case study of Oxford Landing from "vine to dine"' (2012) 17 *Supply Chain Management: An International Journal* 68

Sullivan G, 'Legislative comment: The Bribery Act 2010: Part 1: An overview' (2011) *Criminal Law Review* 87

Tencati A, A Russo and V Quaglia, 'Unintended consequences of CSR: Protectionism and collateral damage in global supply chains: The case of Vietnam' (2008) 8 (4) *Corporate Governance* 518

Tomasic R, 'Towards a new corporate governance after the global financial crisis' (2011) 8 *ICCLR* 237

Utting P, 'Rethinking Business Regulation: From self-regulation to social control' (United Nations Research Institute for Social Development, Technology, Business and Society Programme Paper Number 15 September 2005) 8

Valor C, 'Can consumers buy responsibly? Analysis and solutions for market failures' (2008) 31 *Journal of Consumer Policy* 315

van Gestel R and H-W. Micklitz, 'Revitalizing Doctrinal Legal Research in Europe: What about methodology?' EUI Working Papers (LAW2011/05, Department of Law) 26

Villiers C, 'Achieving gender balance in the boardroom: Is it time for legislative action in the UK?' (2010) 30 *Legal Studies* 533

Villiers C and O Aiyegbayo, 'The enhanced business review: Has it made corporate governance more effective?' (2011) *JBL* 699

Vogel D, 'Is there a market for virtue: The business case for corporate social responsibility' (2005) 47 *California Management Review* 19

Ward C, 'Legal issues in corporate citizenship' (2003) *Swedish Partnership for Global Responsibility*, available at http://www.regeringen.se/content/1/c6/02/18/54/46e90176.pdf (accessed 3 November 2014)

Weiß N, 'Transnationale unternehmen – weltweite standards? Eine Zwischenbilanz des Global Compact' (2002) 2 *MenschenRechtsMagazin* 82

Wells D, 'Too weak for the job: Corporate codes of conduct, non-governmental organisations and the regulation of international labour standards' (2007) 7 *Global Social Policy* 51

Wen S, 'The magnitude of shareholder value as the overriding objective in the UK: The post-crisis perspective' (2011) 26 (7) *Journal of International Banking Law and Regulation* 325

Yap J L, 'Considering the enlightened shareholder value principle' (2010) 31 *Company Lawyer* 35

Zhao J and J Tribe, 'Corporate social responsibility in an insolvent environment: Directors' continuing obligations in English law' (2010) 21 *ICCLR* 305

NEWS AND PRESS RELEASES

Bader C, 'The Bangladesh factory collapse: Why CSR is more important than ever' *The Guardian* (7 May 2013), available at: http://www.theguardian.com/sustainable-business/blog/bangladesh-factory-collapse-csr-important (accessed 24 November 2014)

BBC News, 'Legal aid axed for personal injury claims' (4 March 1998), available at http://news.bbc.co.uk/1/hi/uk/61882.stm (accessed 20 November 2014)

BBC News, 'Dhaka Rana Plaza collapse: Pressure tells on retailers and government' (14 May 2013), available at http://www.bbc.co.uk/news/world-asia-22525431 (accessed 21 November 2014)

European Commission, 'Commission moves to enhance business transparency on social and environmental matters' (Press Release, 16 April 2013), available at http://europa.eu/rapid/press-release_IP-13-330_en.htm (accessed 22 November 2014)

European Commission, 'Statement: Disclosure of non-financial information: Europe's largest companies to be more transparent on social and environmental issues' (Brussels 29 September 2014), available at http://europa.eu/rapid/press-release_STATEMENT-14-291_en.htm (accessed 14 November 2014)

Forbes, 'The real cost of fast fashion' (28 April 2014), available at http://www.forbes.com/sites/lauraheller/2014/04/28/the-real-cost-of-fast-fashion/ (accessed 24 November 2014)

Meeran R, 'Multinationals will profit from the government's civil litigation shakeup', *The Guardian* (London, 24 May 2011), http://www.guardian.co.uk/commentisfree/libertycentral/2011/may/24/civil-litigation-multinationals (last accessed 20 November 2014)

The Daily Telegraph, 'Zara probed over slave labour claims in Argentina' *The Daily Telegraph* (London, 4 April 2013), available at http://fashion.telegraph.co.uk/news-features/TMG9970846/Zara-probed-over-slave-labour-claims-in-Argentina.html (accessed 13 November 2014)

The Guardian, 'Rana Plaza', available at http://www.theguardian.com/world/rana-plaza (accessed 23 November 2014)

The Guardian, 'Bangladesh textile factory fire leaves more than 100 dead' (25 November 2012), available at http://www.theguardian.com/world/2012/nov/25/bangladesh-textile-factory-fire (accessed 23 November 2014)

The Guardian, 'Rana Plaza: The price of indifference' (23 April 2014), available at http://www.theguardian.com/commentisfree/2014/apr/23/rana-plaza-price-of-indifference (accessed 23 November 2014)

The Observer, 'Bangladeshi factory deaths spark action among high-street clothing chains' (23 June 2013), available at http://www.theguardian.com/world/2013/jun/23/rana-plaza-factory-disaster-bangladesh-primark (accessed 23 November 2014)

United Nations, UN Secretary-General, 'Secretary-General appoints John Ruggie of United States Special Representative on issue of human rights, transnational corporations, other business enterprises' (New York, 28 July 2005), UN Doc SGA/A/934, available at: http://www.un.org/News/Press/docs/2005/sga934.doc.htm (last accessed 9 April 2013)

Vogue, 'How the world has changed since Rana Plaza' (1 April 2014), available at http://www.vogue.co.uk/news/2014/04/01/bangladesh-rana-plaza-anniversary-fashion-revolution-day (accessed 21 November 2014)

Vogue, 'Questions as Bangladesh fund still not full' (20 August 2014), available at http://www.vogue.co.uk/news/2014/08/20/bangladesh-factory-collapse-rana-plaze-fund-still-empty (accessed 30 October 2014)

Index

tort law, territorial limit 220
Berle, A 33
Birds, J 29, 50, 54, 172, 182
Blair, M 34, 36
boards *see* directors
Bradgate, R 85, 88, 89, 90, 91, 92, 93
breaches of CSR terms
  breaches of CSR terms, remedies for
    English private law 198–9,
    205–6
  consumer protection law *see*
    consumer protection law and
    corporate social responsibility
  contract law *see* contract law, global
    supply chains and corporate
    social responsibility
bribery
  EU Directive on the Disclosure of
    Non-financial and Diversity
    Information, reporting on
    anti-corruption and bribery 60
  prevention and due diligence
    procedures, English private law
    207–9
  principles, contract law 111–12, 113,
    114, 115, 116–18
Bribery Act 23–4, 111, 113, 115, 117,
    208–9, 231
Brownsword, R 124
Brussels I regulation 83–4, 165–6
business model of global supply chains
  in company law 215–18
business review *see* strategic report
buyers
  contract law, awareness of breaches
    119–22
  contract law, 'battle of forms' 92–3
  contract law, code of conduct
    reference 87–8, 95–6
  supply chain buyers, Bangladesh,
    Rana Plaza Building collapse
    215–16, 217
  terms and conditions, incorporation
    through contract law 89–94

Cafaggi, F 24
Californian Transparency in Supply
  Chains Act 118, 208, 209

Campbell, D 97
Chandler v Cape 175–7, 178, 185, 220
child labour *see* forced labour
civil litigation access, tort law 186–90,
    211
class actions
  and mass torts 186–8, 189–90
*Cobden Investments Ltd v RWM
    Langport Ltd* 42–3, 46
codes of conduct
  consumer protection law 127, 128–9
  consumer protection law, indication
    in commercial practice that
    company is bound by 133–6
  contract law, buyer's code of conduct
    87–8, 95–6
  contract law, supply chains 81–3
  definition, consumer protection law
    133–4
  Ethical Trading Initiative (ETI) Base
    Code 83, 131–2, 133, 134–7,
    139, 140–41, 146–8, 149
Companies Act 21–2, 29, 196
  and corporate governance *see*
    company law, corporate
    governance and corporate social
    responsibility, English company
    law and Companies Act
    headings
company law
  business model of global supply
    chains, Bangladesh, Rana Plaza
    Building collapse 215–18
  Company Law Reform Bill 44
  and English private law, promotion of
    corporate social responsibility,
    limitations 198–9, 201–2
company law, corporate governance and
  corporate social responsibility
    27–78
  board composition 73–7
  EU and transparency on board
    diversity 76–7
  non-executive directors 73–6
  UN Guiding Principles on Business
    and Human Rights 28